The Central Asian Economies
Since Independence

The Central Asian Economies Since Independence

Richard Pomfret

Princeton University Press

Princeton and Oxford

Copyright © 2006 by Princeton University Press

Published by Princeton University Press,
41 William Street, Princeton, New Jersey 08540

In the United Kingdom: Princeton University Press,
3 Market Place, Woodstock, Oxfordshire OX20 1SY

ISBN-13: 978-0-691-12465-5 (alk. paper)
ISBN-10: 0-691-12465-5 (alk. paper)

Library of Congress Control Number: 2006921907

A catalogue record for this book is available from the British Library

This book has been composed in Times and typeset by T&T Productions Ltd, London
Printed on acid-free paper ∞
www.pup.princeton.edu

Printed in the United States of America

10 9 8 7 6 5 4 3 2 1

Contents

Preface

This book is intended as a counterpart to my 1995 book *The Economies of Central Asia*. Whereas that book, written in 1993–94, analyzed the historical background of Soviet Central Asia, economic conditions at the time of the dissolution of the USSR, and the creation of national economies in 1992–93, this book analyzes the economic experience of the five Central Asian countries since they became independent at the end of 1991. Its focus is on the diversity of policies and of types of market economy created in the five countries (Part I), and on relating these national variations to economic performance and prospects (Part II). The reduced emphasis on background conditions is a choice based on the fact that they have been dealt with in my earlier book (and by others), and does not imply that they are unimportant. Indeed, in Part III, there is acknowledgment that geography and resource endowments matter, and that for the newly independent nations the global economy (and their role in it) has assumed an importance that was absent in the Soviet era.

The political, economic, and social changes in Central Asia during the period covered by this book brought with them a greater role for the national languages and many changes in names or in transliteration of the names of towns, provinces, and people. My general rule is to use forms familiar to English speakers (e.g., Bukhara, Samarkand, Tashkent), to avoid unnecessary use of local terms, and where there have been substantive changes to use the name in force at the time of the reference. Regional divisions are referred to as oblasts, because the Russian term remains understood even though it has been replaced by differing national terms.

Several parts of the book draw upon previously published work or papers presented at conferences. Parts of Chapter 1 draw on a paper coauthored with Kathryn Anderson (Pomfret and Anderson 2001), and Chapter 8 is also based on our joint research. Chapter 2 draws on Pomfret (2000c), Chapter 3 draws on Pomfret (2005f), and Chapter 6 draws on Pomfret (2001). Chapter 7 is based on Pomfret (2003c). Chapter 10 contains material from Pomfret (2005b) and from a background paper which I prepared for UNDP (2005). I am grateful to the editors of the journals that printed these papers for permission to reuse copyright material. I have also drawn on the Central Asian country papers in the GDN project reported in Ofer and Pomfret (2004).

The Asian Development Bank funded fieldwork in Central Asia in 2000 and 2001. The Organisation for Economic Co-operation and Development (OECD) supported desk research on the region (circulated as Pomfret (2003b)), as did the World Bank (Pomfret 2004). During 2004 and 2005 the ADB and the UNDP supported travel to conferences in Central Asia related to a UNDP Regional Human Development

Report and an ADB report on trade, transport and transit in Central Asia. I am grateful to all of these organizations for their support and for facilitating participation in conferences and meetings with Central Asian policymakers. Of course, none of the views expressed in this book reflect those of any of the above organizations.

The book has mainly been written at the University of Adelaide, which has provided financial support and a congenial workplace. Christine Kalogeras cheerfully and competently prepared the final typescript. As a Fellow of the Centre for Euro-Asian Studies at the University of Reading, I have benefited from intellectual support and steak dinners from the Centre's Director Yelena Kalyuzhnova, who also provided helpfully detailed comments on a draft manuscript. I am also Associate Fellow of ROSES-CNRS, Université Paris I (Sorbonne), which has provided me with facilities in Paris, for which I am grateful to Gerard Duchene and Boris Najman. Saulesh Yessenova from the Max Planck Institute for Social Anthropology in Halle graciously allowed use of her photograph from Tengiz for the book's cover. For the accuracy and appearance of the final text, I am grateful to the editor, Richard Baggaley, and to Sam Clark, of T&T Productions Ltd, who was a suitably obsessive copy-editor.

The manuscript was completed in 2005, as the president of the Kyrgyz Republic was being ousted by a popular revolt. The book makes no explicit attempt to predict the future, but 2005 seems likely to be a political turning point for the region, and an appropriate stopping point for the book.

List of Abbreviations

ADB	Asian Development Bank
ADF	Agricultural Development Fund (of Turkmenistan)
AIDS	acquired immune deficiency syndrome
ATC	Agreement on Textiles and Clothing (from the WTO's Uruguay Round—to phase out the Multifibre Arrangement)
BEEPS	Business Environment and Enterprise Survey (surveys conducted under the aegis of the EBRD in 1999 and 2002)
BOP	balance of payments
BTC	Baku–Tbilsi–Ceyhan pipeline
CACO	Central Asian Cooperation Organization
CAREC	Central Asia Regional Economic Cooperation
CIS	Commonwealth of Independent States
CMEA	Council for Mutual Economic Assistance (Comecon)
CPC	Caspian Pipeline Consortium
CST	Collective Security Treaty
DFI	direct foreign investment
EBRD	European Bank for Reconstruction and Development
ECE	United Nations Economic Commission for Europe
ECO	Economic Cooperation Organization
ESCAP	United Nations Economic and Social Commission for Asia and the Pacific
GBAO	Gorno Badakhshan autonomous oblast (eastern Tajikistan)
GDN	Global Development Network
GDP	gross domestic product
GNE	gross national expenditure
GNP	gross national product
GUAM	Georgia, Ukraine, Azerbaijan, and Moldova
GUUAM	GUAM during Uzbekistan's participation (1999 until Uzbekistan's effective withdrawal in 2002, and *de jure* in May 2005)
GWh	gigawatt hours
HBS	Household Budget Survey (as inherited from the USSR)
HIV	human immunodeficiency virus
ICOR	incremental capital–output ratio
ICWC	Interstate Commission for Water Coordination
IFAS	Interstate Fund for Saving the Aral Sea
IMF	International Monetary Fund
IMU	Islamic Movement of Uzbekistan
IRP	Islamic Renaissance Party (of Tajikistan)
ISI	import-substituting industrialization
LSMS	Living Standards Measurement Study
MFN	most-favored nation
NATO	North Atlantic Treaty Organization
OECD	Organisation for Economic Cooperation and Development
PPP	purchasing power parity
RRS	Regions of Republican Subordination (central oblast in Tajikistan)
SCO	Shanghai Cooperation Organization
SES	Single Economic Space (Russia, Belarus, Ukraine, and Kazakhstan)

SPECA	Special Programme for the Economies of Central Asia
SPS	sanitary and phytosanitary measures
TBT	technical barriers to trade
TRIPS	trade-related intellectual property rights
UES	Unified Energy System
UNDP	United Nations Development Programme
UNEP	United Nations Environment Programme
UNHCR	Office of the United Nations High Commission for Refugees
UNODC	United Nations Office on Drugs and Crime
UPS	United Power System of Central Asia
USSR	Union of Soviet Socialist Republics
UTO	United Tajik Opposition
VAT	value-added tax
WTO	World Trade Organization
$	all references to dollars are to U.S. dollars

Since the end of the ruble zone, the national currencies have been as follows.

Kazakhstan	tenge (since November 1993)
Kyrgyz Republic	som (since May 1993)
Tajikistan	Tajik ruble (May 1995–October 2000), somoni (since October 2000)
Turkmenistan	manat (since November 1993)
Uzbekistan	sum coupon (November 1993–June 1994), sum (since July 1994)

Map of Central Asia.

1
Introduction

In late 1991, with the sudden collapse of the Soviet Union, the five Central Asian republics of the USSR became independent countries. Kazakhstan, the Kyrgyz Republic, Tajikistan, Turkmenistan, and Uzbekistan had no experience of nationhood before they were incorporated into the Russian empire during the eighteenth and nineteenth centuries. The completely unexpected challenges of nation building were superimposed on the transition from a centrally planned to a market-based economy, which had begun in the late 1980s but had little influence on Central Asia before the Soviet economic system began to unravel in 1991. The indigenous capacity for economic management was limited, because during the Soviet era development strategies were determined in Moscow. The region had been planned as a single unit, or perhaps more accurately as part of the single unit that had been the Soviet economy, and all five countries suffered serious disruption from the replacement of the USSR with fifteen independent countries. Attempts to maintain economic links by retaining the ruble as a common currency in 1992–93 exacerbated the problem of hyperinflation and had been abandoned by the end of 1993. Under these multiple adverse conditions, even the ability of the countries to survive was uncertain.[1]

By the early twenty-first century all five countries had essentially completed the transition from central planning. Within the common bounds of resource-based economies and autocratic regimes, the five countries gradually became more differentiated as their governments introduced national strategies for transition to a market-based economy. The aim of this book is to describe the different economic polices and to analyze the outcomes.

The inherited political structures were identical and in four of the countries First Secretaries appointed by Mikhail Gorbachev remained in power as presidents, but the national leaders adopted surprisingly diverse economic strategies. The Kyrgyz Republic embraced the advice from Western institutions and advocates of rapid

---

[1] The situation before independence and the immediate post-independence period (1992–93) are analyzed in Pomfret (1995). Gleason (1997) and Luong (2002) analyze political development in these years. Islamov (2001) and Gleason (2003a) provide alternative accounts of the region's economic development during the 1990s. Roy (2000) reviews the post-independence political development. Collins (forthcoming) provides an insightful treatment of the wider political and social background, including analysis of the shift from strong support for continuation of the Union in the March 1991 Soviet referendum to the five countries' independence before the year's end.

change and, within limits, its president fostered the emergence of the most liberal regime in the region. Turkmenistan is the polar opposite, where the president has established a personality cult and has minimized economic change. Kazakhstan in the early 1990s appeared to be accompanying the Kyrgyz Republic on a liberal path, but the president became more autocratic as the decade progressed and the economy became dominated by a small group of people who controlled the media and the banks. Uzbekistan retained a tightly controlled political system, but without the personality cult of Turkmenistan, and its economic reforms have been gradual and modest. Tajikistan has been in a different category, because it was the only one of the five countries not to evolve peacefully from Soviet republic to independent state under unchanged leadership. The bloody civil war of 1992–93, which reignited in 1996–97, dominated political developments and delayed implementation of a serious and consistent economic strategy.

The five countries' economic performance has differed, to some extent reflecting policy choices, but since 2000 the comparative situation has been dominated by the global boom in oil prices. During the 1990s Kazakhstan's output performance was inferior to Uzbekistan's, but since the turn of the century Kazakhstan, as a significant oil and gas producer which has also had major new discoveries coming on line, has experienced an economic boom. Turkmenistan, despite its abundant natural-gas reserves, has suffered from dependence on Soviet-era pipelines, but since 1999 the energy boom appears to have alleviated pressures to change the country's poor economic policies. Both gradual-reforming Uzbekistan and rapid-reforming Kyrgyz Republic have enjoyed less spectacular growth, and have clearly lower living standards than Kazakhstan. Tajikistan is even worse placed; the economy has recovered from a very deep trough, but slowly, and Tajikistan now ranks among the world's poorest nations.

The remainder of this chapter provides further background on the initial conditions and choice of development strategies, and provides preliminary assessments of comparative economic performance and a snapshot of social and economic conditions a decade after independence. Chapters 2–6 examine each national economy in greater detail, and Chapter 7 reviews the relative economic performance of the five countries. Patterns of which households gained and which lost from the transition to a market economy are analyzed in Chapter 8. A key issue in explaining international differences in performance is the individual countries' natural-resource endowment, the consequences of which are analyzed in Chapter 9. The importance of natural-resource exports served as a catalyst for integration into a wider economic circle, and Chapter 10 analyzes alternative strategies, multilateral and regional, pursued by the Central Asian countries. Chapter 11 draws some conclusions.

1.1   Initial Conditions and Choice of Economic Policies

Comparing the economic development strategies and the performance of the new independent countries of Central Asia is intellectually exciting because they started from fairly similar initial conditions. Before independence they were all republics of the Soviet Union, and had the same economic system. Although during the Gorbachev era some local economic experiments had taken place in the Baltic republics, parts of the Russian republic, and elsewhere in the USSR, such experiments had been absent from Central Asia, which was generally viewed as the most conservative area in the USSR.

Together with Azerbaijan, the other majority Islamic republic, the Central Asian republics were the poorest Soviet republics. Although inequality, as measured by Gini coefficients, did not differ much from the Soviet norm, they had the largest proportion of households living below the poverty line (Table 1.1). Human-capital measures, such as life expectancy or the almost universal literacy, were, however, high for the income level.

Per capita output in 1990 has been estimated at between $1,130 and $1,690 for the four southernmost republics and $2,600 for the Kazakh republic. Although the relative values in Table 1.1 are a reasonable guide to the ranking of Soviet republics by living standards, the absolute dollar values must be treated with caution due to the insoluble problems of the Soviet Union's artificial relative prices. The World Bank estimates in Table 1.1 place the Kazakh republic's 1990 per capita GNP of $2,600 on a par with that of Hungary ($2,590) and somewhat lower than Iran's ($3,200), while the other four republics had per capita GNP comparable to that of Turkey ($1,370) or Thailand ($1,220); post-1991 experience suggests that the Central Asian republics were behind these comparators.[2]

The Central Asian republics' economic role in the USSR had been as suppliers of primary products—mainly cotton, oil, and natural gas—and minerals, although the specific resource endowment varied from country to country. The Kazakh republic's higher living standards reflect a more diversified economy with grain exports and a variety of mineral and energy resources. Central Asia was the most heavily rural part of the USSR, and Kazakhstan was the only one of the five Central Asian republics with over half of its population living in urban areas (see Wegren 1998, p. 164).[3] The Uzbek republic's economy was dominated by cotton, as were neighboring parts of the other republics. Turkmenistan had experienced a boom in natural-gas production during the final decade of the USSR, while the mainly mountainous Kyrgyz and Tajik republics had fewer exploitable resources.

The terms of trade calculations in Table 1.1 reflect the underpricing of energy and overpricing of manufactured goods in the Soviet economy. Kazakhstan and Turkmenistan as major exporters of oil and natural gas would benefit substantially from replacing the artificial Soviet prices by world prices, while the other Central Asian successor states would gain sufficiently from improved prices for cotton and minerals and lower prices for manufactured goods to more or less offset the higher

---

[2] Figures for Iran, Hungary, Turkey, and Thailand are from the World Bank, *World Development Report 1991*, pp. 204–5. Issues raised by such comparisons are discussed in Chapter 7.

[3] This was still true in 2002 (Table 1.7).

Table 1.1. Initial conditions: republics of the USSR 1989–90.

	Population (millions) mid-1990	Per capita GNP[a] (1990)	Gini coefficient (1989)	Poverty (percentage of population)[b] (1989)	Terms of trade[c]	Life expectancy (years) (1991)	Adult literacy (%)
USSR	289.3	2,870	0.289	11.1	+19	69	98
Kazakh	16.8	2,600	0.289	15.5	+1	66	97
Kyrgyz	4.4	1,570	0.287	32.9	−7	69	97
Tajik	5.3	1,130	0.308	51.2	+50	66	98
Turkmen	3.7	1,690	0.307	35.0	−3	69	99
Uzbek	20.5	1,340	0.304	43.6	−24	72	99
Armenia	3.3	2,380	0.259	14.3	−7	71	96
Azerbaijan	7.2	1,640	0.328	33.6	−21	73	95
Georgia	5.5	2,120	0.292	14.3	−20	71	98
Belarus	10.3	3,110	0.238	3.3	−38	69	99
Moldova	4.4	2,390	0.258	11.8	+79	69	99
Russia	148.3	3,430	0.278	5.0	−18	70	99
Ukraine	51.9	2,500	0.235	6.0	−32	70	99
Estonia	1.6	4,170	0.299	1.9	−24	69	99
Latvia	2.7	3,590	0.274	2.4	−31	71	98
Lithuania	3.7	3,110	0.278	2.3			

Sources: columns 1–2, World Bank (1992, pp. 3–4); columns 3–4, Atkinson and Micklewright (1992, Table U13), based on Goskomstat household-survey data; column 5, Tarr (1994); column 6, World Bank, World Development Report 1993, pp. 249–50; column 7, UNDP, Human Development Report 1992.

Notes: (a) GNP per capita in U.S. dollars computed by the World Bank's synthetic *Atlas* method; (b) poverty is defined as the number of individuals in households with gross per capita monthly income less than 75 rubles; (c) impact on terms of trade of moving to world prices, calculated at 105-sector level of aggregation using 1990 weights.

Table 1.2. Inflation (change in consumer price index) 1991–2004 (percent).

	1991	1992	1993	1994	1995	1996	1997	1998	1999
Kazakhstan	79	1,381	1,662	1,892	176	39	17	8	7
Kyrgyz Rep.	85	855	772	229	41	31	26	36	12
Tajikistan	112	1,157	2,195	350	609	418	88	28	43
Turkmenistan	103	493	3,102	1,748	1,005	992	84	24	17
Uzbekistan	82	645	534	1,568	305	54	59	29	18

Source: EBRD Transition Report Update, April 2001, p. 16.

	1998	1999	2000	2001	2002	2003	2004
Kazakhstan	7	8	13	8	6	6	7
Kyrgyz Republic	11	36	19	7	2	3	6
Tajikistan	43	28	33	39	12	16	11
Turkmenistan	17	24	8	12	11	7	9
Uzbekistan	29	29	25	27	28	10	12

Source: EBRD Transition Report Update, April 2004, p. 17.
Notes: 2003 figures are preliminary actual figures from official government sources. Data for 2004 represent EBRD projections.

prices of energy imports. In practice, Uzbekistan benefited from the shift to world prices because it was able to reduce its dependence on imported fuel and because world cotton prices boomed during the first half of the 1990s, while Kazakhstan and Turkmenistan were unable to immediately benefit because the dominant exit route for their oil and gas exports was via the monopsonist Russian pipeline network.

The Central Asian republics were almost totally unprepared for the rapid dissolution of the Soviet Union in 1991.[4] As new independent states at the end of that year, they faced three major economic shocks: transition from central planning, dissolution of the Soviet Union, and hyperinflation. Dismantling the centrally planned economy created severe disorganization problems, which led to output decline everywhere in Central and Eastern Europe (Blanchard 1997). The dissolution of the Soviet Union added to these problems as supply links and demand sources were disrupted by new national borders and attempts to retain resources within these borders. In Central Asia the absence of any tradition of nationhood and the need to create new national institutions compounded these difficulties. Attempts to maintain existing commercial and political links by retaining a common currency fueled hyperinflation (Pomfret 1996, pp. 118–29).

Prices increased very rapidly in 1992, by more than 50% per month in all five countries (Table 1.2). The currency became the dominant economic issue in 1993,

---

[4] In the March 1991 referendum on the future of the Union, support for keeping the status quo was stronger in Central Asia than elsewhere in the USSR. When conservatives tried to oust Mikhail Gorbachev in the August 1991 coup, only the Kyrgyz republic's leader, Akayev, was quick to denounce the plotters, while other Central Asian leaders, notably the Uzbek republic's Karimov, welcomed the coup.

and four of the countries introduced national currencies—the Kyrgyz Republic in May, and Turkmenistan, Kazakhstan, and Uzbekistan in November. A national currency was a prerequisite for gaining control over inflation and hence establishing a functioning market economy in which *relative* price changes could be observed and could perform their allocative function. Tajikistan was torn by civil war and did not introduce a national currency until May 1995.[5]

A national currency may have been a necessary condition for macroeconomic stability and effective economic reform but it was not a sufficient condition, and each of the countries moved along a different reform path.

The Kyrgyz Republic is usually viewed as one of the most dynamic reformers among the former Soviet republics. It has been strongly supported by international institutions such as the IMF and World Bank, and in July 1998 became the first former Soviet republic to accede to the WTO. The Kyrgyz Republic was the first Central Asian country to succeed in curbing hyperinflation, bringing the annual inflation rate below 50% in 1995. Creating the institutions needed to support a functioning market economy was, however, more arduous, and important markets like the foreign exchange, domestic capital, and national labor markets are still not effective in allocating resources. Manufacturing output fell substantially during the 1990s, and the increased proportion of GDP that was made up by agriculture primarily reflected urban–rural migration as unemployed urban workers returned to their family's village. The only major growth pole has been the Kumtor gold mine. These structural problems may reflect the initial backwardness of the economy, not just in income levels but also in human capital, which has been exacerbated by substantial emigration.[6] The impetus for reform in the Kyrgyz Republic slowed after 1998 when the economy was hit by contagion from the Russian Crisis and by a domestic banking crisis, but reforms have been resumed in the twenty-first century.

Kazakhstan had a better base for creating a market economy, given its higher living standards and human-capital endowments, and it too was initially viewed as one of the more reformist Soviet successor states. Although macroeconomic control was attained more slowly than in the Kyrgyz Republic, with an annual inflation rate of 50% achieved in 1996, Kazakhstan did move fairly quickly with price liberalization and enterprise reform. In the mid-1990s, however, the privatization process and policies towards energy and minerals rights were associated with widespread corruption and a sense of casino or crony capitalism similar to that which emerged in Russia in 1995–96.[7] Kazakhstan's economy was the hardest hit in Central Asia

---

[5] Tajikistan had de facto a separate currency after November 1993 because it was the only country still using the Soviet ruble, but the national authorities did not control the money supply.

[6] Both the Kyrgyz Republic and Kazakhstan experienced large net emigration, predominantly of ethnic Germans and Slavs, many of whom had above-average education and skill levels.

[7] Two books on Kazakhstan by country specialists (Kalyuzhnova 1998; Olcott 2002 (which circulated earlier as a draft)) were both skeptical about the country's economic and political liberalization, in contrast to more upbeat assessments in earlier reports by international institutions and independent commentators (e.g., in the World Bank, World Development Report 1996). In its concentration of economic power

by the 1998 Russian Crisis, but, following a large devaluation of the currency and more importantly the upturn in world oil prices, Kazakhstan's economy began to grow rapidly after 1999.

Uzbekistan is often viewed as one of the least liberalized among economies in transition from central planning. To some extent, however, this reflects jaundiced views by the international financial institutions, with which Uzbekistan has been on frosty terms,[8] and a conflation of political and economic considerations. Although the political regime is authoritarian and illiberal, the economy has been gradually reformed since independence. Macroeconomic control was achieved more slowly than in the Kyrgyz Republic or Kazakhstan, with inflation only dropping below 50% in 1998 (Table 1.2). Price and enterprise reform proceeded slowly, but by 1996 practically all prices had been liberalized and housing and small enterprises had been privatized. Cotton and wheat, however, remain subject to state orders, and privatization of large and medium-sized enterprises has proceeded at a glacial speed. Nevertheless, the government has moved, albeit cautiously, to establish a market economy and has provided good governance, at least by the low standards of the region, in moderating corruption, providing infrastructure, and maintaining social expenditures.[9] By the second half of the 1990s the EBRD was ranking Uzbekistan ahead of Kazakhstan in its annual index of cumulative progress towards establishing a market economy.[10] The government, however, took a major step backwards in October 1996 when, in response to balance-of-payments problems following a decline in world cotton prices, draconian exchange controls were reintroduced. The

---

Kazakhstan resembles Russia, although an important difference to Putin's Russia is the personal wealth of the president and his relatives, which is more reminiscent of Soeharto's Indonesia. Since the turn of the century, it is unclear how strong the positions of the financial, economic, and media groups are, and whether the president is the biggest oligarch or the defender of the public interest against the ten megaholdings which control over four-fifths of the economy (a claim made, for example, in the speech opening Parliament on November 3, 2004).

[8] The paper by Gürgen et al. (1999, especially pp. 3, 4, 73) is typical in its assertion rather than substantiation of the contrast between the faster reformers, i.e., Kazakhstan and the Kyrgyz Republic, and the other Central Asian economies. The IMF has, however, continued to be an impartial collector of data, and empirical studies by some IMF staff, such as those by Taube and Zettelmeyer, are admirably objective. The World Bank has also had difficult relations with Uzbekistan, but has maintained its operational program. The EBRD tried to be more positive and held its 2003 annual meetings in Tashkent, to the dismay of many human-rights groups.

[9] Corruption is pervasive in Uzbekistan, but appears to be on a smaller scale than in other Central Asian countries—petty larceny rather than grand theft—and the government seems to have succeeded in creating a stable economic policy environment and providing physical infrastructure and law and order. EBRD (1999), reporting the results of a survey of 3,000 firms in twenty transition economies, found that almost half of the Uzbek firms bribed frequently (the third highest among the twenty countries), but when asked about the quality of governance under various headings Uzbekistan came out positively, ranking fourth behind Hungary, Slovenia, and Estonia, ahead of reform leaders like Poland and far ahead of Kazakhstan (fourteenth) and the Kyrgyz Republic (nineteenth); Tajikistan and Turkmenistan were not included in the survey, but would surely have ranked poorly on governance.

[10] In the EBRD's Transition Report 1998 (Table 2.2.1), the unweighted average of the EBRD's eight indicators (on an ascending scale of 1–4) for the Central Asian countries was 2.1 for Kazakhstan, 2.9 for the Kyrgyz Republic, 1.9 for Tajikistan, 1.5 for Turkmenistan, and 2.3 for Uzbekistan. This is, of course, a crude measure, and the exchange controls highlighted the government's distrust of market mechanisms.

Table 1.3. Growth in real GDP 1989–2004 (percent).

	1989	1990	1991	1992	1993	1994
Kazakhstan	0	0	−13	−3	−9	−13
Kyrgyz Republic	8	3	−5	−19	−16	−20
Tajikistan	−3	−2	−7	−29	−11	−19
Turkmenistan	−7	2	−5	−5	−10	−17
Uzbekistan	4	2	−1	−11	−2	−4

	1995	1996	1997	1998	1999	1999 (1989 = 100)
Kazakhstan	−8	1	2	−2	2	63
Kyrgyz Republic	−5	7	10	2	4	63
Tajikistan	−13	−4	2	5	4	44
Turkmenistan	−7	−7	−11	5	16	64
Uzbekistan	−1	2	3	4	4	94

Source: EBRD Transition Report Update, April 2001, p. 15.

	1998	1999	2000	2001	2002	2003	2004	2003 (1989 = 100)
Kazakhstan	−2	3	10	14	10	9	7	101
Kyrgyz Rep.	2	4	5	5	0	7	4	78
Tajikistan	5	4	8	10	9	10	6	66
Turkmenistan	7	17	18	12	5	11	9	110
Uzbekistan	4	4	4	4	4	1	3	110

Source: EBRD Transition Report Update, April 2004, p. 16.
Notes: 2003 figures are preliminary actual figures from official government sources. Data for 2004 represent EBRD projections.

consequence was a steadily widening gap between the official and the black-market exchange rate, leading to substantial resource misallocation. The negative effects of the exchange controls were slow to assert themselves, but became gradually more onerous until they were finally relaxed in 2003.

Turkmenistan is also classified as a slow reformer, and in this case indisputably so. The president has established an extreme personality cult and adopted populist policies aimed at minimizing fundamental change. Initially, he promised the people a range of free utilities and other services, to be paid for by natural-gas export revenues, but problems in receiving payment for such exports soon undermined these promises (Ochs 1997; Lubin 1999a). National resources have been frittered away on prestige projects, such as a magnificent presidential palace and a new national airport, and a large debt has been accumulated to fund import-substitution projects that are unlikely to ever generate (or save) foreign currency with which to repay the loans. Despite some promises of reforms after a major economic crisis in

1997, there is little evidence of change, either economically or politically.[11] Prices remain distorted, favoring import-substitution projects, especially in textiles and petrochemicals, and hurting farmers. After the president declared himself president for life, the EBRD took the unprecedented step of banning all public-sector loans to Turkmenistan, which underlined the increasing isolation of the country.

In Tajikistan the centrally planned economy was rapidly destroyed by civil war, rather than being reformed by a central government. A market economy emerged in the vacuum, but implementation of consistent economic policies was frustrated by the intermittent civil war throughout the 1990s. The economic disruption is captured in the huge decline in per capita output during the first half of the 1990s (Table 1.3), and even after peace was negotiated in 1997 the political situation remained fragile and the government's authority still did not cover the entire national territory. The poor security situation discouraged investment, and lack of unified control also deterred economic activity because separate agencies sought to raise revenue by taxes and fees. The government was kept afloat in the early and mid-1990s by military loans from Russia and, after 1997, by aid from the multilateral international financial institutions and from other donors. Since 1997 legislation has been liberal, but implementation is poor, and it is difficult to judge whether current policies should be assessed on the basis of the former or the latter.

1.2 Economic Growth Performance Since Independence

All of the Central Asian countries suffered a sharp drop in real output during the first half of the 1990s (Table 1.3), the impact of which on living standards was exacerbated by the cessation of intra-USSR transfers and by increased economic inequality. The initial decline in output is difficult to measure because of the problems of valuing Soviet-era output for which there was no demand after the end of central planning and because of quality changes and new products. Revaluation of energy products provided a boost to estimated GDP in Kazakhstan and Turkmenistan, which partly offset the decline in quantities. In Tajikistan the disruption of civil war led to an exceptionally sharp fall in output in 1992, which continued until 1995–96. With these caveats in mind, we can attempt to relate changes in real GDP to the initial conditions and policies described in the previous section.

Real GDP in the five countries followed very different time paths. Tajikistan is the easiest to explain, with the civil war destroying economic activity until the 1996 cease-fire, when real output had fallen to just over two-fifths of its level at independence. Growth rates have been fairly high since 1997, but this reflects recovery from a low base and by 2003 GDP was only two-thirds of its 1989 level. Turkmenistan, which had more abundant natural resources and enjoyed a decade of peace, was in

---

[11] Several CIS customers fell behind in payments for their gas and in 1997 Turkmenistan responded by cutting off deliveries, with a dramatic impact on its GDP (Table 1.3); deliveries were only resumed in 1999.

a similar position by 1997, albeit with a different time path. Turkmenistan's decline in real GDP was comparatively slow in 1992–93, accelerated in 1994–96, and went into collapse in 1997. Although growth accelerated in 1999 when gas exports were resumed and Turkmenistan benefited from rising energy prices in the early 2000s, there are questions about the reliability of Turkmenistan's economic data after the mid-1990s and it seems probable that, notwithstanding the high official growth rates, the economy has been in serious trouble and that this is due to poor and unsustainable economic policies.[12] The other three countries' experience is more complex and more interesting.

The Kyrgyz Republic saw real GDP decline by 45% between 1991 and 1995. This was due to the three shocks described in the previous section, the impact of which was not softened by possession of readily tradable natural resources. The decision to adopt the most radical economic reforms in the region and the most rapid macroeconomic stabilization also exacerbated the severity of the post-independence recession. The theory of rapid reform—which has been vindicated, to some extent, by Polish experience but is still a matter of debate—implies that after the pain the Kyrgyz Republic should have been best placed to grow once it had the institutions of a market economy in place. The Kyrgyz economy did indeed grow by 15% between 1995 and 1997, but it is unclear to what extent that was sustainable given the doubts about whether in fact the Kyrgyz Republic has a well-functioning market economy. Much of the economic growth originated in one project, the Kumtor gold mine, which boosted real GDP during the investment stage in 1996–97 and has added to real GDP since then. In 1998 economic growth was slower, due to the Russian economic crisis, domestic bank failures, and poor agricultural performance. The reform impetus slowed after 1998, when growth was anemic due to adverse weather conditions compared with those which abetted the bumper harvests of 1996 and 1997. In the early 2000s growth picked up, but it continued to be greatly influenced by Kumtor, where a landslide in 2002 was sufficient to knock the economy's growth down to zero (Table 1.3).

Kazakhstan's decline in real GDP in the first half of the 1990s was less than that of the Kyrgyz Republic, which may reflect the former's more abundant resources and perhaps its less radical reforms. After 1995 Kazakhstan's real GDP remained above that of the Kyrgyz Republic, but Kazakhstan did not enjoy the growth that the Kyrgyz Republic had in 1995–97. The Kazakhstan economy was then buffeted by the Russian Crisis in 1998 and real GDP was probably little different by the end of the century than it had been in 1995.[13] The proximate causes of the disappointing long-term

---

[12] The reliability of data will be an issue throughout this book, but, apart from the war years in Tajikistan, the situation is clearly worst in Turkmenistan. The figures quoted in this book are mostly from international institutions, and it is important to stress that, while these organizations adjust data for definitional consistency, the raw data come from national sources and international organizations have no way of correcting undisclosed collection or reporting biases.

[13] The decline in output and low inflation in 1998 and 1999 were related to a large real appreciation of the currency, which was reversed in April 1999 when the tenge was allowed to float. One positive feature

performance by the potentially best-placed new independent state in Central Asia were exogenous developments such as commodity price trends, interminable delays in establishing new oil-pipeline routes from the Caspian Basin to non-CIS markets, and the August 1998 Russian economic crisis. More fundamentally, the poor performance reflected a failure to truly reform the economy so that it could better weather such shocks. Perhaps even worse in terms of long-term growth prospects, central planning appeared to be being replaced by a rentier economy in which insiders live off the resource rents rather than generating new output. Towards the end of 1999 the economic situation changed dramatically as world oil prices began to increase and in 2000 a major new oil field, Kashagan, was discovered. During the first half decade of the 2000s Kakakhstan was clearly experiencing an oil-led boom, and its economy substantially outpaced the rest of Central Asia.

Uzbekistan's economic performance has posed the greatest puzzle among all former Soviet republics. The initial decline in real GDP was fairly moderate—at least by the awful standards of the former Soviet Union in 1992–93. This could be ascribed to the avoidance of reform, but such stability has proven short-lived in other nonreformers such as Belarus and Turkmenistan, whose unreformed economies continued to stagnate or decline in the late 1990s. Uzbekistan, in contrast, halted the decline in real GDP in the mid-1990s and even enjoyed modest economic growth during the second half of the decade. The relatively good performance between 1991 and 1996 was helped by buoyant world prices for Uzbekistan's two main exports, cotton and gold, although this appears to be only a partial explanation.[14] Both commodities' prices fell substantially in the second half of the decade, but Uzbekistan's GDP grew fairly steadily after 1995. Whether the gradual reform strategy is sustainable became more doubtful. The economy continues to grow in the twenty-first century and living standards are higher than they previously were, but the relative picture is quite different; whereas Uzbekistan felt it was performing far better than Kazakhstan in the 1990s, after the turn of the century it was ever more obvious that it was economically falling further and further behind its neighbor and rival for regional hegemony. Moreover, the growth rate began to slip in 2003 and 2004 despite an upturn in world cotton prices. Although the causes of political unrest, dramatized by the Andijan massacre in May 2005, are disputed, economic discontent was a contributing factor.

Two macroeconomic aggregates shed further light on comparative performance. The Soviet successor states suffered a drastic loss in public revenue, both absolutely and relative to the falling GDP, although there was a big range between Tajikistan with public revenue at 10% of GDP and Uzbekistan with 30% in 1995 (Table 1.4).

---

of these two years was that, despite widespread belief that Kazakhstan would default, the government continued to fulfil domestic and foreign debt-service obligations.

[14] Taube and Zettelmeyer (1998) and Zettelmeyer (1998) analyze the Uzbek puzzle and conclude that data deficiencies and favorable initial conditions and exogenous events only explain part of Uzbekistan's relatively good 1992–96 output performance, and policy must be given some of the credit. Spechler (1999, 2000) and Pomfret (2000c) also analyze Uzbekistan's policies and performance during the 1990s.

Table 1.4. Government revenue ("Rev.") and expenditure ("Exp.")
as percentages of GDP 1995–2002.

	1995		1996		1997		1998	
	Rev.	Exp.	Rev.	Exp.	Rev.	Exp.	Rev.	Exp.
Kazakhstan	22	26	17	20	17	19	18	25
Kyrgyz Republic	17	28	16	22	16	22	18	22
Tajikistan	10	17	12	18	15	19	11	14
Uzbekistan	30	33	34	36	30	32	31	33
	1999		2000		2001		2002	
	Rev.	Exp.	Rev.	Exp.	Rev.	Exp.	Rev.	Exp.
Kazakhstan	18	22	22	22	22	22	22	21
Kyrgyz Republic	16	20	14	18	16	18	18	21
Tajikistan	12	15	12	13	14	13	18	N/A
Uzbekistan	29	31	28	29	26	28	26	28

Source: Asian Development Bank, *Key Indicators*, 2003.
Note: N/A denotes not available in the source.

Table 1.5. External debt, as percentage of GDP 1993–2002.

	1993	1994	1995	1996	1997	1998	1999	2000	2001	2002
Kazakhstan	7	14	19	14	18	28	36	65	65	71
Kyrgyz Rep.	16	30	41	62	76	91	139	133	112	112
Tajikistan	23	20	51	66	95	94	117	104	100	95
Turkmenistan	6	9	7	32	66	79	N/A	N/A	N/A	N/A
Uzbekistan	5	5	18	17	19	21	28	32	41	58

Source: World Bank, "World development indicators," www.worldbank.org.
Notes: N/A denotes not available in the source; inherited external debt in 1992 was zero.

An important issue for Tajikistan, the Kyrgyz Republic, and, to a lesser extent, Kazakhstan was the rebuilding of their tax-raising capacity in the late 1990s and early 2000s. Uzbekistan, by contrast, maintained public revenues and expenditures, which partly explains better aggregate performance over the 1990s. After 1998, however, Uzbekistan addressed the opposite problem of reducing the share of government revenue and spending in GDP as part of cutting back the state's role in the economy.

For the two poorest countries, Tajikistan and the Kyrgyz Republic, government expenditures were not allowed to fall as far as public revenue. Faced with the dilemma of how to finance the budget deficit without inflation, the Kyrgyz Republic borrowed abroad to fund public spending. The consequence was a rapid buildup of external debt between 1992 and 1999 (Table 1.5). Tajikistan ran smaller budget deficits and funded them with more inflationary finance than the Kyrgyz Republic, but it too had a debt/GDP ratio over 100% by 1999. The Kyrgyz Republic's borrowing was largely from international financial institutions such as the World Bank and the IMF. Tajikistan's was mainly bilateral borrowing from Russia and, to a lesser extent, Uzbekistan for military purposes during the civil war.

The five countries' foreign trade is summarized in Table 1.6. These numbers need to be treated with caution, especially for the years 1992 and 1993 when the region was still using a common currency and trade within Central Asia and with important trading partners such as Russia and Ukraine went largely unmonitored. Even after the establishment of national currencies and functioning national customs services, the coverage of official trade statistics remained far from complete. Imports are under-invoiced or not declared. Small-scale traders (referred to as shuttle traders in the region) account for a large amount of imported consumer goods and other trade, but the recording of this trade is uneven.[15] Illegal trade is also important, with widespread smuggling and with the Afghanistan-originating drug trade passing through the five Central Asian countries. Even the data that are recorded are not always released, e.g., gold output and exports in Uzbekistan are state secrets and the Uzbekistan exports in Table 1.6 may be understated by as much as a billion dollars.

The Central Asian countries have open economies, in the sense of high trade/GDP ratios.[16] After the major shocks of the early 1990s, trade recovered in the Central Asian countries in 1994–97. In both the Kyrgyz Republic and Tajikistan, per capita values remained small and total trade declined between 1997 and 2002. The relatively superior export performance of Kazakhstan and Uzbekistan in the mid-1990s was due in part to favorable energy and cotton prices, and their divergent experience after 1997 is partly explained by low world cotton prices between 1997 and 2001 and by booming oil prices since 1999. Turkmenistan's exports are dominated by energy products and the 1995–96 values are inflated by overreporting of natural-gas exports to CIS destinations which were not paid for (the invoice value was recorded as exports, while the accumulating payment arrears were recorded as foreign assets); recognizing that the bills would never be paid in full, Turkmenistan stopped supplying gas in March 1997, after which export values (and GDP) collapsed until the gas flow was resumed in March 1999.[17]

---

[15] Pomfret (1999b, p. 32n) reports official estimates from Kazakhstan of shuttle trade accounting for a quarter of total imports in 1995, a third in 1996, and almost half in 1997, but these are based on heroic assumptions.

[16] Export/GDP ratios estimated by World Bank staff with 2000 data are Kazakhstan 59%, Kyrgyz Republic 42%, Tajikistan 81%, Turkmenistan 63%, and Uzbekistan 25% (Freinkman et al. 2004, p. 9).

[17] Turkmenistan's economic data are the least reliable in the CIS. According to nongovernment sources (reported in Pomfret (2001, p. 158)), gas exports fell from about a billion dollars in 1996 to $70 million in 1997, and this coincided with a poor cotton harvest due to which cotton exports fell from $332 million in 1996 to $84 million in 1997.

Table 1.6. International trade, 1993–2003 (millions of U.S. dollars).

	1993	1994	1995	1996	1997	1998	1999	2000	2001	2002	2003
Exports											
Kazakhstan	1,107	3,227	5,256	5,926	6,497	5,511	5,598	9,876	9,085	9,670	14,875
Kyrgyz Republic	360	339	483	506	609	509	454	504	476	486	622
Tajikistan	350	492	749	772	803	597	689	770	652	737	719
Turkmenistan	561	1,163	1,881	1,693	751	594	1,187	2,505	2,555	2,710	2,949
Uzbekistan	693	1,991	2,718	2,620	2,896	2,310	1,963	2,132	2,087	1,558	1,998
Imports											
Kazakhstan	1,704	3,285	3,807	4,247	4,302	4,373	3,686	5,048	6,478	6,584	9,377
Kyrgyz Republic	447	316	392	795	709	841	611	555	465	587	888
Tajikistan	532	545	810	668	750	711	663	671	680	710	881
Turkmenistan	586	904	1,364	1,313	1,228	1,007	1,476	1,788	2,210	1,819	1,964
Uzbekistan	918	2,455	3,030	4,854	4,538	2,931	2,481	2,067	2,293	2,07	2,510

Source: IMF "Direction of trade statistics."

1.3 Distribution

In all countries in transition from central planning to market-based economies, income inequality increased. For the Central Asian countries, given their low initial incomes and declining average incomes during the first half of the 1990s, the outcome was high poverty rates. The data are less convincing than for real output,[18] but in the most thorough attempt to assemble comparative data, Milanovic (1998) found that in 1993–95 the Kyrgyz Republic had the highest poverty rate of any Eastern European or former Soviet economy. Unemployment has also increased although this too is difficult to measure; more clear-cut was the decline in employment during the 1990s, especially in Kazakhstan.[19] These distributional considerations raise the important question of who have been the winners and losers from the transition from Soviet central planning to the more market-oriented national economies.

Average incomes fell and inequality increased throughout Central Asia during the 1990s, but there is ample evidence that there were winners as well as losers. Stories of profiteering and corruption are backed up by the presence of Mercedes and BMW cars in Almaty and Ashgabat. Everywhere members of the old elite in the capital cities were the people best able to protect themselves against economic hardship and to benefit from new opportunities, while most of the employees of the state enterprises in heavy industries and state farms lost their economic advantages.

The regional shifts are clearest and have been best documented in Kazakhstan. The coal mining oblasts (provinces) of Karaganda and Pavlodar had 16.6% of the national population and 29.3% of GDP in 1993, with per capita product about double the national level, but by 1998 they were producing only 19.1% of GDP, their population share had fallen to 14.8%, and per capita product was only 25–30% above the national level.[20] Meanwhile, the population share of Almaty, the Soviet-era capital city and economic and financial capital, and its surrounding oblast increased from 16.7% to 18.0% and share of GDP from 14.2% to 21.4%; per capita income in Almaty jumped from 40% above the national average in 1994 to more than double the national average in 1998. These are large changes over such a brief period. The petroleum-producing regions of Atyrau and Mangistau only increased their

---

[18] Falkingham (1999) analyzes the problems and pitfalls associated with Central Asian household-survey data. Anecdotal evidence supports the conclusion that poverty increased markedly in the Kyrgyz Republic during the early years after independence (e.g., Howell 1996a,b), but the poverty rates given by Milanovic are difficult to compare across countries with vastly different survey data.

[19] The number employed in Kazakhstan fell from 6.5 million in 1990 to 4.3 million at the end of 1995, when registered unemployment was reported at 4% (Bauer et al. 1997a, p. 3). The number employed in large and medium-sized enterprises, which still appears to cover over four-fifths of the employed workforce, declined from over 3,000,000 in 1997 to 2,015,000 in 1999 (*Kazakhstan Economic Trends* 2000 (January–March):113–14).

[20] Figures in this paragraph are taken from Table 1 in Esentugelov (2000, p. 23). A similar picture is drawn in IMF Staff Country Report 00/29, March 2000, pp. 21–23. De Broeck and Koen (2000, p. 12) report that the regional variation in the decline in industrial output during the 1990s was greater in Kazakhstan than in other large former Soviet republics.

combined share of GDP from 9.0% to 9.5%, implying that although Kazakhstan's growth was fueled by the hydrocarbon sector the real beneficiaries were in the commercial capital rather than near the oil fields. This pattern appears to have continued during the post-1999 oil boom. There is also a widely reported phenomenon of fifty to sixty "sick towns" that depended on a single large enterprise in the Soviet era (Bauer et al. 1997a, pp. 40–41; Rama and Scott 1999). The regional picture is less pronounced in the other countries, but in all of them the relative position of the capital city's residents has improved since independence.

Our best insight into the characteristics of winners and losers comes from the Kyrgyz Republic, which has by far the best set of post-independence household-survey data (Anderson and Pomfret 2003). Analysis of the 1993 household survey found that residence in the capital city and having tertiary education both significantly increased the probability of a household being above the poverty line, while no other factor had much of an effect. Given the very high poverty rate, this implies that a small group, presumably the old elite, had weathered the storm of the early 1990s better than anybody else.[21]

More sophisticated analysis of the 1993 and 1996 surveys using quantile regressions found more complex patterns of the determinants of household living standards (Anderson and Pomfret 2000). Residence in Bishkek was again the most important positive determinant of living standards, while the poor mountainous areas and especially the southern agricultural regions fell further behind. The other very clear result was that the costs of being a large household, in terms of reduced per capita expenditure, were larger in 1996 than in 1993, and this was especially true of households with many children. These results provide strong evidence of the decline in social protection offered by the state, and of the increased cost of raising children as benefits (such as kindergartens or school meals) previously provided by the state or the workplace have disappeared. Households with many adults or pensioners were also more poorly placed in 1996 than in 1993, indicating that the value of the generous Soviet-era pensions was being eroded, but they still helped to protect pensioners in poor households.[22] The impact of tertiary education was not clear-cut, although there was some evidence of a sorting effect whereby university-educated household heads appear to have moved their households up the income distribution between 1993 and 1996. The return to more vocational post-secondary education, which had been fairly high in 1993, especially in the mid-to-upper parts of the income distribution,

---

[21] The studies referred to in this paragraph are by Ackland and Falkingham (in Falkingham et al. 1997, pp. 81–99) and by Pomfret and Anderson (1999). Some form of multivariate analysis is desirable because variables such as ethnicity, location, education, and household size are connected. Simple cross-tabulations showing that, for example, Slav households fared better than Kyrgyz households may be confusing ethnicity with location, household size, or education because Slav households are more likely to be urban with a better-educated head and fewer children.

[22] The fiscal costs of defined-benefit pay-as-you-go pension schemes have, however, been a large burden, and the costs will increase further due to the future liability to post-1945 baby boomers. Kazakhstan instituted a personal-account system on the Chilean model in 1998, and the Kyrgyz Republic is seriously considering pension reform (Anderson and Becker 1999).

had disappeared in 1996, suggesting that state-enterprise employees with specific skills who were working their way up the seniority ladder in the planned economy have been big losers from transition. University graduates who were trained to think more broadly, even in the Soviet education system, have been better able to respond to the extreme disequilibrium of the 1990s than narrowly trained specialists.[23] Many of these patterns appear to characterize the evolution of income distribution in the other countries since independence. The evidence on these issues is analyzed in more detail in Chapter 8.

Changes in wealth distribution are likely to have been even more pronounced than changes in income distribution, although it is difficult to find data on wealth. Especially in Kazakhstan privatization transferred valuable public assets to a small group, but there is a feeling everywhere that those in power were able to use their position to obtain rents that were transformed into cars and other consumer durables or invested abroad. Privatization of the housing stock with priority to current occupiers favored the old elite, who had the best housing and, especially in the capital cities, could benefit from a tiny market in high-quality apartments to earn substantial rents from expatriates. For poor people, privatization of housing created new burdens on the household, which was now responsible for maintenance. In addition, the provision of heating, hot water, and other utilities was gradually shifted to a user-pay system.[24]

The distributional effects of the national economic strategies adopted during the transition from central planning can be modified by individual responses and by social policy. The increased cost of children has been associated with a declining birth rate; in the Kyrgyz Republic the crude birth rate was 32.0 per thousand population in 1985, 29.3 in 1990, and 27.5 in 1996. This will eventually lead to smaller families but will take decades to work its way through; meanwhile the current generation of children will grow up with poorer education than their parents, and there will be a significant number of children growing up outside family care.[25] Although private health and education provision is emerging and is in some respects more efficient than the old state monopoly, many people are excluded from these services by poverty. Reduced human capital will harm future growth prospects and

---

[23] This is not to deny that within the broader university degree the subjects of specialization probably made a difference. People with training in English or computer skills were better able to find employment after the collapse of the planned economy.

[24] Buckley and Gurenko (1997) show that imputed income from subsidized housing played a major role in reducing inequality in the Soviet Union. Finkel and Garcia (1997) analyzed options for pricing heating in the Kyrgyz Republic and found that many users in the capital city could not afford user fees set at any level. Outside the capital the underfunded heating system often failed, and this was associated with deteriorating health (Bauer et al. 1997a, p. 48).

[25] The increasing number of children outside the household system is a new phenomenon in post-independence Central Asia. Although orphanages existed in the USSR, they rarely catered to Central Asian children, who were taken care of within the extended family. The phenomenon of street children is still not fully accepted, let alone accurately measured; one symptom is the increased number of children being held in detention centers on vagrancy charges (Bauer et al. 1998, p. 108).

the emergence of an alienated underclass will challenge social stability, so there are strong reasons for active public policies.

Social spending has followed different national patterns. In the Kyrgyz Republic substantial foreign assistance enabled the government to maintain the share of public spending going to health and education, especially as donors encouraged investment in human capital, although the real amounts dropped with the decline in GDP.[26] In Kazakhstan, health care was one of the first casualties of independence, as the share of government spending going to health fell by about a third in 1992 and the percentage of GDP spent on health fell from 4% to 2%, where it stayed in subsequent years (Brooks and Thant 1998, p. 249). In Turkmenistan and Tajikistan social spending also declined as governments devoted diminishing aggregate public funds to pet projects and military spending, respectively. Uzbekistan stands out as the exception as the government there maintained domestically generated social spending (Pomfret and Anderson 1997) and introduced innovative measures to target social assistance (Coudouel and Marnie 1999), although there were growing complaints, especially after the educational reforms of the late 1990s, concerning falling standards.

1.4   The Situation in the Early 2000s

Table 1.7 provides a snapshot of social and economic conditions in the five Central Asian countries a decade after independence. The most striking feature is the much lower per capita output measured in current U.S. dollars in all five countries compared with the 1990 estimates reported in Table 1.1. The energy-rich countries, Kazakhstan and Turkmenistan, just about remain middle-income countries, although Turkmenistan's data are the least reliable in the region.[27] The Kyrgyz Republic, Uzbekistan, and Tajikistan have income levels comparable to some of the poorest countries in the world. Using PPP measures rather than those based on current prices and exchange rates gives a more positive picture with respect to income

---

[26] There is also anecdotal evidence of regional disparities as the northern regions are treated better than the southern regions. Conditions in the two southern oblasts are described by Howell (1996a,b). Center for Preventive Action (1999, pp. 180–81) quotes from an official 1997 report on Jalalabad oblast as follows:

> Since 1990, the education sector has had to cope with a severe cutback in financing. There have been virtually no allocations from the domestic budget for textbooks, school equipment or building maintenance. Teachers' salaries have fallen dramatically in real terms. Teacher morale and performance has been further undermined by the substantial delays in salary payments which are typically 2–4 months in arrears.

[27] Even Turkmenistan's *population* is uncertain. There has been no census since 1995; the figure of 4.8 million is the number of registered residents, but alternative extrapolations yield a de facto population of 5.4 million (The United Nations System in Turkmenistan, "Common country assessment, February 2004," p. 8). For basic demographic indicators such as life expectancy at birth, other sources believe the official figure (67 years) to be inflated. *The CIA Factbook 2003*, for example, reports life expectancy at birth of 61, and less than 58 years for men (data is available online at www.cia.gov/cia/publications/factbook/geos/tx.html). The same source notes that "Turkmenistan's economic statistics are state secrets, and GDP and other figures are subject to wide margins of error."

Table 1.7. Economic and social indicators, 2002.

	Population (millions)	Population aged under 15 (% of total)	Urban population (% of total)	Life expectancy at birth (years)	GDP (billions of $)
Kazakhstan	15.5	26	56	66	24.6
Kyrgyz Rep.	5.1	33	34	68	1.6
Tajikistan	6.2	37	25	69	1.2
Turkmenistan	4.8	35	45	67	7.7
Uzbekistan	25.7	35	37	70	7.9

	GDP per capita ($)	GDP per capita at PPP (international $)	ODA (millions of $)	ODA per capita ($)	Armed forces (thousands)
Kazakhstan	1,656	5,870	188.3	12.2	60
Kyrgyz Rep.	320	1,620	186.0	36.7	11
Tajikistan	193	980	168.4	27.2	6
Turkmenistan	1,601	4,300	40.5	8.5	18
Uzbekistan	314	1,670	189.4	7.4	52

Source: UNDP Human Development Report 2004; online statistical database at http://hdr.undp.org/ statistics (accessed July 21, 2004).

levels. In capturing well-being, PPP is a valid corrective to the understatement of the current-price GDP measures, but it must be emphasized that no PPP measures in Central Asia are based on detailed price data, which we would normally expect if they were to be treated as accurate guides. The issue of measuring economic well-being is taken up in greater detail in Chapter 7 after the individual countries' experience has been analyzed.

The demographic data in Table 1.7 bring out similarities and differences across the countries. The four southern states have higher birthrates, and hence younger populations, than Kazakhstan. They are also more rural. These characteristics reflect Kazakhstan's more diversified and more developed economy, and its more "European" society, while the other four countries tend to be more traditionally Central Asian with a stronger hold of Islam and of the extended family. The relatively high birthrate is responsible for the rapid population growth in the region, although again Kazakhstan is the exception. Kazakhstan's population in 2002 was less than in 1990, due to the substantial emigration of non-Kazakhs and the increase in male mortality rates in the 1990s. Some of these patterns also applied in the Kyrgyz Republic, but insufficiently to have a negative aggregate effect on the population. Tajikistan was also affected by emigration, as well as by the civil war. Uzbekistan and Turkmenistan both experienced rapid population growth after independence.

Official development assistance went in almost equal measure to four of the Central Asian countries, with Turkmenistan as the exception. This translates into much higher assistance per head of population for the two poor small countries:

the Kyrgyz Republic and Tajikistan. Turkmenistan did not seek much in the way of international assistance, and the despotic nature of its regime did not encourage offers of ODA. Uzbekistan also asserted its independence, although it continued to maintain relations with the main multilateral agencies. In April 2004, however, the EBRD suspended most of its assistance due to the country's record on economic and political reform, and in July 2004 the United States declared Uzbekistan ineligible for aid, citing lack of progress on democratic reform.

The GDP figures illustrate the significant shift in the balance of economic power in the region, especially after the post-1999 oil boom pulled Kazakhstan further and further ahead of the more populous Uzbekistan. At the time of independence the Soviet successor states largely inherited all of the assets on their territory at the time, which gave Uzbekistan the largest and best-equipped army in the region.[28] By 2002 Kazakhstan was able to support a larger army, and as the old Soviet equipment becomes obsolete it is likely that Kazakhstan's military is becoming better equipped than that of Uzbekistan.

Measuring the extent to which the Central Asian countries have become market economies is inherently more difficult than measuring vital statistics or material well-being. The EBRD assesses progress from a planned economy to a market economy in various areas on a scale of 1–4. The most commonly reported single number, the EBRD transition index, is a simple average of the disaggregated measures. It is a very rough measure, but it indicates a clear picture. In 2004 the five Central Asian countries were all among the bottom third of the twenty-seven countries covered by the EBRD. The Kyrgyz Republic and Kazakhstan, with scores just below 3, had made the most complete transition to a market economy, while Tajikistan and Uzbekistan scored significantly lower with 2–2.5, and Turkmenistan was the least reformed of all twenty-seven countries with a score of less than 1.5.

Table 1.8 reports two commonly used indices of the type of market-based economies that the Central Asian countries now have. Based on fifty independent indicators related to freedom to trade, property rights, and so forth, the Heritage Foundation assesses the degree of economic freedom on a scale of 1–5. When the Central Asian countries were first included in 1998, they all fell in the bottom group, "repressed" economies with scores of 4–5. By 2005 they had improved their scores, but very slowly: from 4.0 to 3.29 for the Kyrgyz Republic, from 4.23 to 3.66 for Kazakhstan, from 4.30 to 4.0 for Tajikistan, from 4.68 to 4.10 for Uzbekistan, and from 4.50 to 4.36 for Turkmenistan. In 2005 the Kyrgyz Republic and Kazakhstan both fell in the "mostly unfree" category (scores between 3 and 4), while the other three countries remained in the "repressed" category, ranking among the bottom 10% of all countries. This suggests that, although the centrally planned economy

---

[28] The Soviet Army's Turkestan Military Command was headquartered in Tashkent and large Soviet bases remained at Termez and Samarkand after the end of the USSR's involvement in Afghanistan. Although Uzbekistan inherited a good part of the military equipment on its territory, this was not universal, as some Russian officers refused to accept Uzbekistan's jurisdiction (Olcott 1996a, pp. 130–31).

Table 1.8. Indicators of economic freedom and of corruption, 2004–2005.

	Heritage Foundation Index Of Economic Freedom 2005	Transparency International Corruption Perceptions Index 2004
Kazakhstan	3.66 (130th)	2.2 (rank 122–128=)
Kyrgyz Republic	3.29 (97th)	2.2 (rank 122–128=)
Tajikistan	4.00 (144th)	2.3 (rank 114–121=)
Turkmenistan	4.36 (151st)	2.0 (rank 133–139=)
Uzbekistan	4.10 (147th)	2.0 (rank 133–139=)

Sources: Heritage Foundation, *2005 Index of Economic Freedom*, available at www.heritage.org; Transparency International (TI) Corruption Perceptions Index, available at www.transparency.org/cpi/2004/cpi2004.en.html#cpi2004 (both accessed in February 2005).
Notes: numbers in parentheses are the country's rank; the Heritage Foundation ranked 155 countries on a scale from 1 (free) to 5 (unfree); the TI Index is based on perceptions by businesspeople and country analysts on a scale from 1 (most corrupt) to 10 (least corrupt) (145 countries were covered in 2004).

has been largely displaced, the market economies that have been constructed offer very limited economic freedoms and these freedoms are only increasing slowly. According to the Corruption Perceptions Index reported by Transparency International, all five countries have high levels of corruption (with scores between 2 and 2.3 on the ten-point scale in 2004), which also indicates that they have poorly operating market economies.[29]

1.5 Conclusions

The five new independent states of Central Asia emerged from the Soviet Union with similar economic systems and some similarity of economic structure. By the twenty-first century their economic experiences were becoming sharply differentiated.

The two countries that were in the worst position when they became independent have perhaps done as well economically as they could have done in the circumstances. The Kyrgyz Republic adopted rapid and basic reforms, but due to its backwardness had difficulty actually establishing a well-functioning market economy. The severe decline in living standards may have been exacerbated by the rapid reform strategy, but this is unclear, as is the relationship between the degree of liberalization and the growth prospects for the 2000s. Tajikistan has had a grim economic experience since independence, but this was largely shaped by the civil war which waged on and off for most of the 1990s.

The biggest puzzle has been Uzbekistan, which is often characterized as a slow reformer, and during the 1990s had the best economic performance of all Soviet successor states. Perhaps Uzbekistan could have performed even better with a different

[29] By the TI index only Azerbaijan, Paraguay, Chad, Myanmar, Nigeria, Bangladesh, and Haiti had more corruption than Tajikistan and Turkmenistan. By the Heritage Foundation Index only Zimbabwe, Libya, Myanmar, and North Korea offer less economic freedom than Turkmenistan.

economic system, but the government did well enough on the policy front to limit the economic decline in the first half of the 1990s and to generate modest economic growth during the second half of the 1990s. This mainly seems to be due to good governance, at least by the low standards of the region. In the early years of the twenty-first century Uzbekistan's economic performance was less impressive, perhaps due to the increasing burden of exchange controls until they began to be eased in late 2003. The foreign-exchange controls introduced in 1996 were symptomatic of a distrust of market forces, and the broader failure to establish a well-functioning market economy is likely to restrict future growth.

For Kazakhstan and Turkmenistan the picture is dominated by their oil and gas reserves. In Turkmenistan gas wealth has clearly undermined the country's political and economic development, as an autocratic regime has appropriated the revenues and inhibited development of either civil society or a sustainable economic strategy. Kazakhstan, while also an autocratic regime under a single post-independence president, has a more developed civil society and a more nuanced record. Since the turn of the century, Kazakhstan has enjoyed an oil boom, which has pulled its living standards noticeably above those of the four southern Central Asian countries. Many countries' experiences have shown that oil can be a curse rather than a blessing when it comes to generating long-term growth with equity, and for Kazakhstan the downside of its transition to a market economy has been the increased corruption, which could lead to a "curse" outcome.

As with the other countries in the region, Kazakhstan's economic evolution remains a work in progress, with big changes not to be ruled out. The economic changes are in higher gear in Kazakhstan due to the frenetic pace set by the oil boom as world prices rose from less than $10 a barrel in 1998 to over $60 in 2005, and as exploration in the North Caspian revealed in 2000 the biggest new oil field in the world since the 1970s. In all five countries the greatest uncertainty, and potential catalyst for economic change, concerns the political regime.

By the early 2000s the five countries had established super-presidential systems with concentrated power and weak legislatures. Kazakhstan, the Kyrgyz Republic, Turkmenistan, and Uzbekistan were the only former Communist countries of Eastern Europe and the CIS to have an unchanged top leadership since the upheavals of 1989–91. As the region's autocratic rulers grow older and look over their shoulders at the 2003 rose revolution in Georgia and the 2004 orange revolution in Ukraine, and closer to home the 2005 tulip revolution in the Kyrgyz Republic, change looms but its form is uncertain. Possible alternatives to a more democratic future are that leadership will be kept in the family, as in Azerbaijan, or in the elite, as in Russia, or there could be reversion to civil war, as in Tajikistan. The outcome will be influenced by economic conditions and will have consequences for each country's economic future.

Part I

The National Economies

2

Uzbekistan: Economic Gradualism and Political Stability

Uzbekistan is the most populous of the Central Asian countries, and its capital, Tashkent, is the largest city in the region. Tashkent, with over two million people in 1991, was the fourth largest city in the USSR, and had been the metropolitan center of Tsarist Turkestan and of Soviet Central Asia. At independence Uzbekistan inherited important assets, including the best civil aircraft fleet, the military command (and significant military equipment), and the best administrative capacity in Central Asia.

Outside Tashkent, however, Uzbekistan's economy was (and continues to be) overwhelmingly rural and the poverty rate was second only to that of Tajikistan in the Soviet Union. The economy is heavily dependent on cotton, of which Uzbekistan is the world's fifth largest producer and second biggest exporter. Cotton is almost entirely grown on irrigated land, which requires extensive public management of the water system. Uzbekistan has been producing natural gas for a long time (it is currently ranked about tenth in world production) and has significant oil resources. Gold is also an important export earner. Other mineral resources include copper, molybdenum, tungsten, and uranium.

During the 1990s Uzbekistan was the most successful of all Soviet successor states in terms of output performance, and in 2001 it became the first former Soviet republic to have regained its pre-independence level of GDP. During the initial years of the twenty-first century, however, the economic picture looked dimmer, and the gloom was exacerbated by the boom conditions in Uzbekistan's neighbor and rival Kazakhstan. Uzbekistan's economic fortunes during the post-independence era can be divided into two periods: before and after the exchange controls introduced in October 1996 began to have deleterious effects. Removal of the exchange controls in the second half of 2003 inaugurated a third period too recent to be assessed here.

2.1 The Uzbek Paradox, 1991–97

Uzbekistan's performance during the 1990s was seen by many observers as a paradox, because it contradicted the conventional wisdom that a rapid transition from central planning was desirable. As President Karimov continually stressed, Uzbekistan's strategy was one of gradualism. Gradualism did not mean no change, and Uzbekistan's transition was more progressive than that of Belarus and Turkmenistan, two countries Uzbekistan is often lumped together with as the slowest reformers among the formerly centrally planned economies. The hallmark of Uzbekistan's economic policies was cautious recognition that economic change is inevitable, and a commitment to gradual reform in order to minimize negative or disruptive consequences of change.

Caution is reflected in macroeconomic policy. Immediately after independence, in 1992–93, Uzbekistan's leadership was suspicious of the big bang approach to stabilization pursued by Poland in 1990 and associated with Russia in 1992. The government's reluctance to embark on macroeconomic stabilization brought Uzbekistan into conflict with the IMF, but once the government had become convinced of the dangers of inflation and the merits of orthodox counter-inflation policies, it embarked, in January 1994, on a macrostabilization path that followed IMF blueprints fairly closely.

The national currency was introduced in July 1994 and supported by reductions in the growth rate of money supply over the next three years. Price controls were reduced and food rationing abolished, so that open inflation reached a peak in 1994 before declining to below 50% per year in 1997 or 1998 (depending on the data source). Foreign trade was liberalized and exchange restrictions relaxed. The fiscal deficit was cut from 10.4% of GDP in 1993 to 6.1% in 1994, and to 4.1% in 1995. The tax system was reformed and collection improved, while expenditure on supporting state enterprises and on consumer subsidies was reduced. Although Uzbekistan continued to be considered a slow reformer, by measures such as the EBRD's transition index it ranked above Kazakhstan in 1996. Arguably there was some unnecessary hardship due to the monetary confusion before July 1994 and the extended inflationary period in the mid-1990s, but the country's economic development suffered no irremediable damage.[1]

Price reform was cautious too, and this clearly delayed the introduction of market forces. Especially in 1992–94 significant parts of the economy remained characterized by shortages and queues rather than by market-clearing prices. Nevertheless, there were benefits, both in reducing the disruptive effects of sudden price liberalization on supply chains, which explains some of Uzbekistan's relatively shallow output decline during the first half of the 1990s, and in protecting people from sudden drops in real consumption. The benefits were, of course, not sustainable, as subsidies blew out the government budget, but the buying of time has nontrivial welfare benefits. The main consumption subsidies were abolished or reduced after 1995. By the end of the 1990s the major remaining price controls were on cotton, interest rates, and foreign exchange.

---

[1] The government seemed to be caught unawares by the rapid collapse of the ruble zone in November 1993, and issued a sum coupon which looked unimpressive and was explicitly temporary. Confiscatory elements of both the exchange of rubles for sum coupons and of sum coupons for sum in July 1994 and the nonconvertibility of the sum all undermined confidence in the currency and made monetary policy less effective. The IMF's mishandling of currency issues in 1992 added to the problem by undermining the credibility of the IMF's generally sound advice on monetary policy (Pomfret 2002c).

In 1992, although Uzbekistan was relatively cautious on price reform, the government moved quickly to privatize housing and small businesses, which to some extent picked up on traditions of home ownership rights and of the bazaar. Although housing and small-scale privatization proceeded apace, large-scale privatization and agrarian reform were limited in Uzbekistan. Whether this caution was wise or not depends upon the alternative. The more successful large-scale privatization programs in Central and Eastern Europe have been an integral part of the emergence of better-functioning market economies. On the other hand, large-scale privatization in Russia and Kazakhstan did more to exacerbate inequality and corruption than to promote economic growth during the 1990s. The former group of countries illustrates the benefits that Uzbekistan may have forgone by not pursuing faster privatization, but Uzbekistan has avoided the potentially serious risks of rapid privatization. Most importantly, in contrast to the latter group of countries, Uzbekistan's government has maintained control over natural-resource rents, which gave the government an important continuing source of revenue. The tension between maintaining control and creating a vibrant farm sector has, however, not been resolved. The 1998 amendment to the land code reaffirmed that land is state property, at the same time as it tried to create new categories of "private" farmers.

Financial-sector reform was limited by the same forces that stifled privatization. Commercial banking was legalized, and there were over thirty banks by 1998, but the state-owned National Bank of Uzbekistan, successor to the republic's branch of the Soviet foreign exchange bank, accounted for over 70% of loans (Akimov 2001). The Republic Stock Exchange Tashkent, the country's only stock exchange, opened in January 1994, but few shares are traded. The bond market was even slower to start, with the first treasury bills issued in March 1996.

Uzbekistan benefited from good governance in the economic sphere, at least by a narrow definition of economic management and by the generally low standards of the CIS. The natural-resource endowment may have been a positive initial condition, but both cotton and gold prices fell in the mid-1990s and the real test was the use made of the resource rents. Although some revenue was frittered away on wasteful public investment in industrial projects, the government did fairly well in maintaining health and education expenditure and in providing a social safety net (Pomfret and Anderson 1997).[2] The government acted innovatively and effectively in targeting social assistance through the decentralized *mahallah* scheme (Coudouel and Marnie 1999). Public building improved the cityscape in Tashkent and other towns,

---

[2] In 1998, when government expenditure amounted to 34.5% of GDP, 45.3% of this expenditure was allocated to health, education, and other social policies (*Uzbek Economic Trends* 2000 (January–March):89–90). Measures of inequality and poverty are even more dubious than the output measures reported in Table 1.3, but the evidence points to a relatively good performance by Uzbekistan. In 1989 the Uzbek Republic's poverty rate was the second highest in the USSR, exceeded only by that of the Tajik Republic (Table 1.1), but by the mid-1990s, according to the IMF (*World Economic Outlook* May 1998, Table 23, based on estimates by Branko Milanovic), Uzbekistan's poverty rate was the second lowest of the eight listed CIS countries.

without the grandiose aspirations of the Presidential Palace in Turkmenistan or the new capital in Kazakhstan. Transportation and other public services continued to function. Loosening of restrictions on small-scale activities and rising disposable income in the late 1990s, at least in urban areas, saw a revival of eating and drinking out, which recalled a past cultural heritage and raised the quality of life for many. Politically, the regime was unattractive to liberal observers, but in the 1990s President Karimov appeared to enjoy a degree of popularity for maintaining relative stability with social justice.

Corruption is endemic, but is widely accepted, with little perception that it has created a *nouveaux riches* class comparable to that of other CIS counties. Corruption and conspicuous consumption are both a matter of degree. An index of the quality of governance based on a 1999 business environment and enterprise survey of over 3,000 firms in twenty transition economies ranked Uzbekistan fourth, behind Hungary, Slovenia, and Estonia and ahead of Poland, the Czech and Slovak Republics, and all of the CIS countries included in the survey. In a similar 2002 survey Uzbekistan ranked third-least corrupt, behind Slovenia and Estonia, although caveats are highlighted in the text.[3] Anecdotal evidence also suggests that corruption in Uzbekistan is more like universal petty theft than the grand larceny of Kazakhstan or Russia. The potential rents from cotton and gold are large, but the ostentatious cotton magnates from Tsarist times (and the Brezhnev era) have not yet emerged on the same scale in modern Uzbekistan.

During the mid-1990s Uzbekistan emerged as a paradox among CIS countries. Although economic reform lagged that in the Baltics, Russia, or even the neighboring Kyrgyz Republic, Uzbekistan did not experience the deep decline in GDP suffered by all other CIS countries. The cumulative decline in GDP between 1989 and 1996 was the lowest among all former Soviet republics. Taube and Zettelmeyer (1998) examined the relative importance of various potential explanations of the "Uzbek puzzle" and, although measurement errors and favorable initial conditions played a part, their impact was dismissed as small in magnitude, and good policy and public investment were left as the major explanatory factors.[4]

---

[3] The results of the 1999 business environment and enterprise survey (BEEPS) are reported in the EBRD Transition Report 1999. The 2002 BEEPS is reported by Gray et al. (2004), who highlight the difficulties of measuring corruption; the third-place ranking is in the first summary table (on p. 12) of corruption as a perceived obstacle to doing business.

[4] In its March 2000 Staff Country Report ("Republic of Uzbekistan: recent economic developments," p. 5), the IMF discounted policy explanations of Uzbekistan's performance in favor of exogenous initial conditions:

> The main explanation for this performance is found in the set of initial conditions characterizing the Uzbek economy at independence. Not only was Uzbekistan comparatively unburdened by over-industrialization, but its endowment with easily marketable primary commodities (i.e., cotton and gold accounted for 60% of exports) allowed it to reorient quickly its exports after the collapse of the Soviet Union.

Although Uzbekistan may have been less burdened by industry than western Soviet republics, within Central Asia Tashkent was the industrial metropolis; the city had its full share of military-related industrial

The resource endowment was, however, fundamental to the balance of payments, the public-sector budget, and investment. Buoyant export earnings from cotton and gold contributed directly to GDP, and were a major source of government revenue.[5] Gas and oil production, leading to close to energy self-sufficiency, also helped to ensure that, contrary to the forecasts reported in Table 1.1, Uzbekistan during the 1991–96 period did not suffer from the shift from Soviet to world prices for primary products. The government kept tight control over the mining, energy, and cotton sectors. By a state order system which gave farmers a small fraction of the world price, resources siphoned from agriculture amounted to as much as a twelfth of GDP in 1996 (see Chapter 9). State control was associated with better (relative to neighboring countries), although still far from good, administration of the irrigation network on which agriculture depends.

An important difference between Uzbekistan and Russia or Kazakhstan was the degree to which resource rents were privatized.[6] The Uzbek government used the revenue to maintain public spending on education and health care better than in other CIS countries. Public investment in favored enterprises contributed to GDP, although the attempt to pick winners led to several failures and no obvious successes. Chemical and petrochemical projects in the desert were the biggest flops, but heavily subsidized cotton textile mills may also have been socially wasteful, even if they survived on the basis of distorted prices. The system of state orders for the two main crops was used to encourage reallocation of land from cotton to wheat, even though the foreign exchange savings from an additional hectare under wheat amounted to $500 less than the foreign exchange earnings from a hectare under cotton (Spechler et al. 2004, p. 180). The import-substituting nature of these projects illustrates the inward-looking development strategy, even though Uzbekistan was an open economy by measures such as the export–GDP ratio.

---

activity, including aircraft production, and Tashkent was also the center for production of agricultural machinery such as cotton harvesters, for which demand slumped in the 1990s with a switch to more labor-intensive harvesting techniques. While the emphasis on cotton and gold as favorable initial endowments is plausible for explaining the relatively shallow economic trough in the first half of the 1990s, it is difficult to reconcile with Uzbekistan's economic resilience when cotton prices fell by half and gold prices by almost a third between 1995 and 1999. Other negative shocks in the second half of the 1990s were the crises in 1997 in South Korea (the largest foreign investor in Uzbekistan) and in 1998 in Russia (Uzbekistan's largest trade partner).

[5] The mining sector is nontransparent. In 1989 gold output was 90 tonnes, about 30% of the Soviet Union's production, but by 1991 Uzbekistan's gold output had fallen to 70 tonnes. In spring 1992 an agreement was signed with Newmont Mining Corporation of the United States, which has been the principal foreign partner in Uzbekistan's gold mining. Gold and uranium are produced by the Navoi state enterprise, whose output and earnings are state secrets. The revenue goes not to the company but to the secret part of the state budget under the Ministry of Finance. According to the former British Ambassador Craig Murray (speech to Chatham House, London, on November 8, 2004), 10% of the sales revenue goes to bank accounts under the personal control of President Karimov, and this is the principal source of the president's personal fortune.

[6] Kalyuzhnova (2000) emphasizes the role of "the administrative method of management of economic life" in limiting the transitional recession in Uzbekistan, and she also analyzes the elaborate rent-seeking behavior of Uzbekistan's bureaucracy. Pomfret (2005e) also analyzes the political economy of economic policymaking in Uzbekistan during the 1990s.

Direct foreign investment into Uzbekistan was modest in total, but included some high-profile projects. Apart from Newmont Mining's involvement in gold production, practically all the foreign investment was in import substitutes such as Mercedes-Benz in trucks, British American Tobacco (BAT) in cigarettes, Coca-Cola in soft drinks, and Daewoo in cars. Daewoo decided in the early 1990s to make Uzbekistan its base for Central Asian operations, investing $100 million in a car factory which started production in 1995 and $45 million in consumer electronics and textiles joint ventures. The Daewoo car plant, in language familiar from Beijing Jeep in China or Proton Saga in Malaysia in the 1980s, was claimed to be a base for exporting to the region but its two cars and a minibus were sold only in domestic markets during the 1990s. The ubiquitous Daewoo cars, however, were a conspicuous sign of higher living standards during the second half of the 1990s.[7]

Economic success was accompanied by greater confidence in international relations. In the early years of independence President Karimov represented himself as a bulwark against Islamic fundamentalism, and continued to work with Russia in the Tajikistan conflict as well as in trying to maintain economic ties from the Soviet era (Bohr 1998). After a brief period of economic nationalism tinged with isolationism in late 1993, Karimov started to exert a more positive leadership role in Central Asia during 1994 and then on the world stage. Relations with the United States warmed considerably as Karimov took opportunities to denounce Iran and vote with the United States at the United Nations.[8] In July 1996 Presidents Clinton and Karimov met in Washington.

2.2   The Reintroduction of Exchange Controls

Up until the summer of 1996 relations between Uzbekistan and the IMF and World Bank had been thawing. Uzbekistan was still seen as a slow reformer, near the bottom of most liberalization league tables such as that in the World Bank's World Development Report 1996, but there were signs of improvement. In particular, Uzbekistan was committed to liberalizing its foreign exchange regime and establishing convertibility for current-account transactions. In autumn 1996, however, the government reneged on this commitment by reintroducing draconian exchange controls.[9]

---

[7] The symbolism was also fairly egalitarian, because the little Tico (which cost not much over $1,000 at black-market exchange rates in 1999) was less opulent and exclusive than the imported Mercedes and BMWs which appeared in Kazakhstan and to a lesser extent in Turkmenistan and the Kyrgyz Republic. Car production in Uzbekistan increased from 82 in 1994 and 300 in 1995 to 25,358 in 1996, 64,908 in 1997, 54,456 in 1998 ("Republic of Uzbekistan: recent economic developments," IMF Staff Country Report No. 00/36, March 2000, p. 40), and 58,800 in 1999 (*Uzbek Economic Trends* 2000 (January–March):105), but then stagnated as the Daewoo parent company went bankrupt.

[8] The most notable denunciation of Iran was at the May 1996 ECO summit in Ashgabat, which consequently broke up a day earlier than planned. In the United Nations, the United States found itself on occasion with only two supporting votes, Israel and Uzbekistan.

[9] The operation of Uzbekistan's trade and exchange controls is described in Rosenberg and de Zeeuw (2000), in "Republic of Uzbekistan: recent economic developments," IMF Staff Country Report No. 00/36, March 2000, pp. 85–94, and in Spechler (2003).

The exchange controls appear to have been a drastic reaction to balance-of-payments pressures, triggered by a drop in the world price of cotton (see Section 9.1), rather than part of a considered strategy. Resort to controls to deal with an adverse external shock was symptomatic of the delayed structural reforms, which made the economy less flexible. Gleason (2003b) argues that Uzbekistan's success between 1993 and 1995 in achieving oil self-sufficiency, increasing natural-gas exports, and boosting food self-sufficiency by shifting crop acreage from cotton to wheat all helped to ameliorate the transitional recession and "resulted in delaying structural reforms" because the government felt less pressure to act. The exchange controls were strongly criticized by the IMF, and the Uzbekistan government took pride in asserting its independence by defending the policy.

Other elements of Uzbekistan's gradual transition remained essentially unchanged, and economic performance continued to be good by CIS standards as growth became positive in 1996 and accelerated in 1997 and 1998 (Table 1.3). Around the turn of the century Uzbekistan became the first former Soviet republic to regain the pre-transition level of GDP. Inflation was brought below 50%. A mass privatization program initiated through Public Investment Funds with World Bank aid had little impact, and neither did a case-by-case approach to privatizing thirty large enterprises (only one cement company had been privatized, through foreign purchase, by late 1999). Creation of new small and medium-sized enterprises was also slow, apart from small-scale restaurants and other service activities. Uzbekistan's record in new enterprise creation may, however, have been superior to that of most of its neighbors. Estimates of de novo firms' share of GDP by Havrylyshyn and McGettigan (1999, p. 8) are 35% in the Kyrgyzstan, 30% in Uzbekistan, 20% in Kazakhstan, and 15% in Tajikistan and Turkmenistan.

A worrying sign was a growing external imbalance, not fully reflected in official statistics, but by 1999 frequently referred to by officials as a crisis. Some negative external developments, such as declining cotton and gold prices and the 1998 Russian Crisis, contributed, but the major problem was the import substitution strategy exacerbated by the foreign exchange policy. Production for export was discouraged by policies directing capital to import-competing projects and skewing relative producer prices in favor of such activities. As the gap between the official exchange rate and the black-market rate widened from 100% in autumn 1998 to 300% a year later, voluntary exports through official channels became less and less attractive. The external debt increased in 1998 and 1999; although debt-service ratios were not yet high (Table 1.5).[10]

In many respects Uzbekistan's experience began to mimic that of many newly independent countries of the 1950s and 1960s: it enjoyed early economic success,

---

[10] Frosty relations with the IMF and World Bank meant that Uzbekistan contracted little debt to these institutions. This may be because the international financial institutions viewed Uzbekistan as a poor credit risk. On the other hand, skeptics of the IMF/World Bank role in transition economies have seen Uzbekistan's reluctance to borrow as a cause of those institutions' frostiness—a nonborrower is a poor client.

but ran into subsequent problems after pursuing import-substitution policies and ignoring the resource-misallocation costs. An overvalued official exchange rate discouraged production of traded goods, while the large black-market premium encouraged rent-seeking activities. The controls encouraged smuggling, both of imports and exports, and enforcement of import restrictions and exchange controls diverted resources from productive use. Capital was allocated mainly by government directive, and the outcome was declining productivity of capital. By 1999, official estimates of the ICOR (i.e., the units of additional capital required to increase the output stream by one unit) were around 6 and the IMF estimate 8.3, compared with ICORs for well-functioning economies of 3–4.

The viability of the government's strategy depended heavily on its continued implicit tax on cotton and gold. After 1996, the foreign exchange controls helped to hide the full extent of the difference between world prices and prices set in domestic currency as transfers out of agriculture continued to be large despite falling world cotton prices. Rosenberg and de Zeeuw (2000) estimate that the multiple exchange rate regime in the late 1990s transferred about 16% of GDP from exporters to importers, with the Central Bank making a substantial profit as intermediary. Supply of these commodities was believed to be relatively price inelastic, which is likely to be true in the short term but is less plausible for the longer term. Apart from the continued misuse of public resources by directing credit and foreign exchange to specific enterprises, the government continued to spend relatively wisely by maintaining health and education spending and extending the social support delivered via the *mahallas*. Nevertheless, wise use of GDP is not a substitute for misuse of productive investment in promoting future economic growth.

2.3   The Economy in the Early 2000s

From 1997 to 2002 Uzbekistan's GDP grew at 3–5% per year. Although that would have been a respectable performance in the earlier transition period, it looked less positive when compared with other transition economies emerging from their transitional recessions in the late 1990s. More particularly, it became increasingly apparent after 2000 that Uzbekistan was falling economically behind its rival for regional hegemony, Kazakhstan.

Uzbekistan's economic malaise could be traced to the exchange controls which muffled price signals and added a significant level of regulation to stifle entrepreneurial initiative in the traded-goods sectors. The negative effects of the continuing existence of state procurements for cotton and wheat became more pronounced over time, as production patterns were distorted and farmers sought unofficial marketing channels.[11] The government relied on the state order system to transfer resources from the cotton sector to the state budget, and the foreign exchange

---

[11] Low farmgate cotton prices meant low wages for cotton picking (or reversion to the Soviet pattern of forcing students and others to harvest the crop). The contrast with wages in the market-driven Kazakhstani farm sector encouraged the most skilled cotton pickers to cross the border to South Kazakhstan at harvest

controls helped to mask the size of the gap between world prices and farmgate prices. Although the government was in principle committed to rolling back the state order system, its revenue dependence led it to resort to subterfuges. Thus, although the percentage of wheat and cotton subject to state order was reduced to 30% in the late 1990s, this percentage was calculated on the basis of expected harvests whose values were heavily exaggerated; for example, state orders ended up applying to 90% of the actual 2002 cotton harvest (EBRD Transition Report 2003).

More fundamentally, Uzbekistan's experience illustrates the dynamic dangers of gradual reform as the government became reliant on controls to assure its own revenue and to generate the rents that keep its clients in line. As the economy's performance lagged and the government's popular support waned, it became more reliant on regional and sectoral elites, who can deliver stability (and repression) as long as the semireformed market economy is not liberalized.

The years 1996–2002 were characterized by minimal economic reform and increasing political repression. Karimov's popularity and reputation for maintaining stability may have been declining since the late 1990s, but with restricted freedom of expression that is difficult to gauge. After a series of assassinations of public officials in 1997, the government arrested hundreds of people in a 1998 crackdown (Lubin 1999b). After the explosion of five bombs in downtown Tashkent in February 1999, killing several people and injuring over a hundred and with the biggest one outside the Cabinet of Ministers building apparently targeted at the president, another crackdown targeted "religious extremists" (Whitlock 2002, pp. 242–64). In August 1999 some 650 Islamist gunmen were caught entering Uzbekistan. Attempts to bomb the insurgents' bases hit the wrong targets, killing several Kyrgyz civilians and Tajik cows and undermining Uzbekistan's reputation for military effectiveness. Border closure measures, justified by the need to keep out terrorists, increased the cost of cross-border trade, at the same time as increased controls in Uzbekistan increased the incentives for arbitragers to import goods from the more open markets of the Kyrgyz Republic or Kazakhstan.

The need to retain control over the rents from the cotton sector meant that the biggest gap between claims of establishing a market economy and the reality of public policy was in the area of land reform. The large collective farms from the Soviet era were renamed *shirkat*, but their operation has changed little as the staff and management are appointed by the regional government and remain an integral part of the power structure. Individual members of the *shirkat* have little incentive to work hard or to innovate and productivity remains low, apart from the time spent on the small (0.25 hectare) plot of irrigated land that households are allowed to cultivate for their own use or for small-scale marketing. The category of *dehkan* small-scale farms is exempt from state orders and enjoys inheritable unrestricted possession of land, but the land cannot be sold or sublet. Moreover, even on leased

---

time (see Section 9.1), despite the risk they faced in doing so and the harassment that illegal or semilegal migrant laborers were subjected to.

"private" land farmers must grow what they are told to and sell to prescribed buyers at fixed prices, with payment into bank accounts from which they have difficulty withdrawing cash. In sum, most of the irrigated arable land remains in farms whose official descriptions changed (e.g., from kolkhoz to *shirkat*), but over which the former state-farm managers or local administrators retain considerable authority.[12]

Poor economic performance since the mid-1990s has impeded the government's ability to match its claimed commitment to social sectors with delivery of social services. In education there have been increasing complaints of inefficiency, corruption, and falling standards. In 1997 the government announced replacement of the eleven-year Soviet school system by a nine-year system followed by two-year colleges preparing students for university or providing technical training. In 1999 funds were allocated to building new colleges with the goal of completing the reform by 2009. There are, however, shortages of textbooks and other materials.[13] More importantly, the college system is rife with corruption, as grades are openly traded for bribes in well-organized markets, especially in the new colleges, but also in many universities and secondary schools, where underpaid teachers feel the need to supplement their state salaries of about $50 per month. The government fears that relaxing its grip on the education system by allowing private schools or colleges might undermine political stability.

Health-sector reform was initiated in 1996 with a presidential decree that signalled a shift away from hospitalization towards primary health care and a reduction in the number of tiers of health facilities. This is a positive shift from the Soviet system's overemphasis on capital-intensive hospitals and specialist services and towards greater reliance on general practitioners and access to outpatient facilities. Between 1996 and 2000 patient admissions to hospitals decreased and the average length of stay fell from 14.8 days per person to 12.1 days (United Nations Uzbekistan, "Common country assessment 2003," p. 30). As with education, however, there are concerns about the effectiveness of reform and the quality of services, as public-sector resources available for the health sector decline and accountability mechanisms are weak. Private financing of health has increased both officially through the introduction of a prepaid rather than a free system and also unofficially as people pay to gain preferential treatment, raising concern about access to health care for the poorer and most vulnerable groups in society. Health problems such as drug addiction and the spread of HIV/AIDS have become more serious since independence, although data are unreliable.

After September 11, 2001, some saw a window of opportunity for reform as the United States provided aid and backed renewed IMF and World Bank engagement

---

[12] There may be regional variation in how the farm sector is evolving. The account here draws heavily on Trevisani's (2004) fieldwork in Khorezm, but the patterns of central control appear to be repeated nationwide.

[13] Uzbekistan adopted the Latin script in 1996, which added to the need to replace worn-out or obsolete textbooks.

in Uzbekistan. An IMF Staff Monitored Program agreed in January 2002 foreshadowed agrarian reform, banking-sector improvements, trade liberalization, and moves towards currency convertibility, but little of this was implemented and an IMF mission in September saw few grounds for satisfaction. Indeed, some measures such as the tariff hikes in May 2002 and increased restrictions on small and medium-sized enterprises (SMEs) were backward steps. A November 2002 decree allowing renationalization of any business which had changed its activities since privatization without prior permission effectively gave local authorities carte blanche to harass SMEs.

Whether the tighter controls and declining economic performance of the 1996–2002 period were a trend or part of a cycle that will be reversed is unclear. Starting in early 2002 the government used tight monetary policy to gradually reduce the black-market premium on foreign currency. Inflation halved to 12% in 2003. In June 2003 the government committed itself to abolish the restrictions on foreign exchange availability for current-account transactions before the end of 2003. The commitment was honored, although a requirement to preregister all import contracts with the Agency for Foreign Economic Relations meant that bureaucratic hurdles on access to foreign currency remained.[14]

In the run-up to the official removal of foreign exchange controls, the government introduced various trade barriers to protect domestic producers of import substitutes who might be hurt by increased competition. The restrictions were particularly strict on the shuttle traders who went on shopping trips to China, Turkey, and neighboring countries, and who stocked many of the stalls in the bazaars. The government even sought to close the bazaars in November 2002. The immediate effects of the restrictions were higher prices for many consumer goods, and increased purchases in border areas of Kazakhstan or the Kyrgyz Republic of such goods, which were brought legally or illegally into Uzbekistan.[15]

In 2003 the government did introduce some measures that may signal a freeing up of the economy or improvement in efficiency. State procurement of wheat and cotton was increased to 50% of the crop, but was applied to the actual harvest rather than the expected harvest, which should reduce the actual burden and improve transparency. The government began serious moves towards reforming delivery of energy and water. Power-sector tariffs were increased by 60% in 2002 and by 40% in 2003, although they were still well below cost-recovery levels, and a metering program

---

[14] When the formal move to convertibility, i.e., compliance with IMF Article VIII, was announced in October 2003, the official exchange rate was 975 sum/$ and the black-market rate was 1,700. The excess demand for foreign exchange implied by this black-market premium was choked off by the banks through long delays in processing requests for foreign exchange, a de facto limit of $5,000 on availability of foreign currency, and requiring completion of long forms of which people were distrustful, fearing the information might be passed on to the government and used to their disadvantage.

[15] The main effect seems to have been the displacement of a legal tax-paying shuttle trade by an illegal bribe-paying shuttle trade. The International Crisis Group (ICG 2004a, p. 17) reports that $350 in bribes could ensure that a car full of goods from the Kyrgyz Republic could reach Tashkent without a problem. For those without cash, smuggling can be profitable but dangerous as border guards shoot to kill.

and other steps to improve collection rates was under way. The mahallahs, which had been providers of decentralized social assistance, suffered from reduced funding in the early 2000s, reflecting the pressure on the state budget of funding the quasi-fiscal deficits of the energy sector, and they increasingly became seen as an instrument of political control rather than of social support. In 2003 the government announced its aim of moving towards more targeted social assistance. In sum, the collectivity of reforms described in this paragraph suggest a renewed commitment to measures aimed at more efficient delivery of public services, but also a reality of very slow and gradual change.

At the same time, ever-tightening security measures stifle economic activity. Even in their attenuated post-2002 form the bazaars were harassed by the authorities, who saw them as hotbeds of illicit activities. Closure of bazaars in March and November 2004 was associated with the worst rioting since independence.[16] The violence in Andijan in May 2005 was triggered by the imprisonment of small businessmen whom the authorities claimed to be religious fundamentalists.

The system of official residence permits, *propiskas*, remained from the Soviet era. Enforcement has varied as Tashkent's population swelled from just over 2 million at independence to around 3.5 million a decade later, but in July 2004 the mayor of Tashkent announced a cleanup which was accelerated after the July 30 bomb attacks on the U.S. and Israeli embassies and on the office of the Prosecutor General. People expelled from the city for lack of *propiskas* included skilled workers who had been living there for years, and all were deprived of fundamental labor rights, e.g., by law people losing their jobs are entitled to two months' pay but this was denied to the illegals.[17]

Borders, especially in the Ferghana Valley, have been subject to irregular and unannounced closures, which became more general after March 2004 when bombings and street battles in Bukhara and Tashkent left about fifty dead. Security was given as the official reason for these border controls, but they also imposed high costs on the pervasive small-scale cross-border trade in the Ferghana Valley. After masonry bridges were blown up to prevent Uzbekistan residents from going to the market at Kara-Suu in the Kyrgyz Republic, the locals established rope bridges and pulley systems which allowed cross-border trade to continue to some extent, but also claimed several lives. Near Osh at a spot where the border is a narrow stream the Uzbek border officials helpfully placed a plank across the stream and charged each person using the plank 100 sum.[18]

---

[16] The details of both sets of events are unclear. The March 2004 violence, ascribed by the government to Islamic extremists, featured four days of gun battles in Tashkent and Bukhara, in which fifty or more people died, and two suicide bombs in Tashkent's Chorsu bazaar. The November 2004 riots in Tashkent and in towns in the Ferghana Valley were more spontaneous and directly related to new regulations on small-time traders.

[17] See the report "Tashkent Mayor: 'Non-official' residents threat to security," posted at www.eurasianet.org on October 27, 2004.

[18] The bridge stories are reported in Megoran et al. (2005).

The current situation is difficult to monitor but the Kara-Suu (near Osh) and Dordoi (in Bishkek) markets in the Kyrgyz Republic had by 2004 become the largest in Central Asia and were catering overwhelmingly to customers from Uzbekistan. The merchants at the Kara-Suu market were largely ethnic Uzbeks with Kyrgyz citizenship who acted as wholesalers between merchants from western China and shuttle traders from Uzbekistan. Despite the official restrictions from Uzbekistan, this business was so profitable that similar markets developed in other towns in the southern Kyrgyz Republic, such as Jalalabad and Uzgen, and in Khojand in northern Tajikistan, all located close to the Uzbekistan border. Ironically, Uzbekistan was now outsourcing the small-scale entrepreneurial activities which had characterized the first phase of transition from central planning, and in which Uzbekistan had been the leader in Central Asia in 1992.

The country's human-rights record has left it increasingly isolated. The EBRD's 2003 annual meetings were held in Tashkent as a signal of the institution's increased attention to Central Asia as the EBRD's Eastern European and Baltic clients were about to join the European Union, but the drawback for Uzbekistan was that the EBRD set targets on human-rights issues, such as the elimination of torture, that the government was not prepared to meet. EBRD involvement in Uzbekistan was substantially reduced in 2004, and the only multilateral institution left with an active program in Uzbekistan was the Asian Development Bank. The United States also cited human-rights concerns when its aid was cut back in July 2004.[19] Uzbekistan redirected bilateral relations towards Russia, and to a lesser extent China, because these countries placed little emphasis on their allies' human-rights records.

Nevertheless, Uzbekistan's economic strategy and prospects remain hard to categorize. In January 2005 President Karimov announced a program of economic reforms envisaging deeper liberalization of the economy and extension of the private sector. Key reforms to the financial sector, the tax system, and the protection of property rights have the potential to improve significantly the operation of the economy. An IMF mission in February–March 2005 "was encouraged by the comprehensive economic reform program," expecting that these measures "would enhance Uzbekistan's medium-term growth prospects."[20]

---

[19] The State Department announced an $18 million cut in U.S. aid, but in the next month, as Defense Secretary Rumsfeld visited Afghanistan, the chairman of the U.S. Joint Chiefs of Staff, Richard Meyers, visited Tashkent and announced a $21 million increase in U.S. military assistance, over the $39 million already committed, to Uzbekistan. See "Top US general tours Central Asian capitals, dispenses aid to Uzbekistan," *Eurasia Insight*, posted at www.eurasianet.org on August 13, 2004, and Camelia Entekhabi-Fardi, "Rumsfeld addresses security concerns on lightning trip to Afghanistan, Azerbaijan," *Eurasia Insight*, posted at www.eurasianet.org on August 12, 2004.

[20] This upbeat assessment (from IMF Press Release No. 05/60, released March 15, 2005) contrasted with the previous press release (No. 03/189, released November 12, 2003), which followed a visit by IMF Deputy Managing Director Shigemitsu Sugisaki, that expressed concern:

> that much remains to be done to improve the business climate and achieve the government's objective of creating a market economy. In particular, the external and domestic trade restrictions imposed since mid-2002 are dampening growth and will limit the

2.4 Conclusions

In the uncharted waters of transition, a wait-and-see approach was not a bad option, especially for a new country, previously isolated far from European or Asian role models of market economies and development strategies. Any government of a newly independent country, all of whose economists were Soviet trained with no experience of a market economy, was bound to make mistakes, although to outsiders the reprise of the ISI policies adopted by newly independent countries in the 1950s and 1960s is depressingly familiar. Import substitution is not a viable strategy for promoting long-run growth, and the severe exchange controls imposed in 1996 were a major policy error with ever more dire consequences. The cautious approach to reform means that there is still time to loosen overstrict regulation and to reverse the bias against exports, much as South Korea did in 1964 after a decade of mild import substitution. The longer that change is delayed, however, the more severe the shock of reform will be and the more unpredictable and uncontainable the negative consequences.

One benefit of delay is that Uzbekistan's economic policymakers have now been exposed to market economies and to non-Soviet economics by international travel and a variety of training programs. Nevertheless, reform seems to be difficult to push through. One argument is that the system put in place during the decade after independence created opportunities for self-enrichment by a small elite who are now wary in case any change might undermine their hold on power or their sources of income,[21] but this view of the politics of partial reform (drawing on Hellman (1998)) fails to explain the cycles of Uzbekistan's policy reform and nonreform. Given the autocratic nature of the state, the outcome will depend critically on the role of the president—is he the leader of the corrupt elite or the good emir surrounded by bad courtiers?—and a source of uncertainty is the lack of succession arrangements. The ICG (2003) suggests that the president's poor health may be stymieing reform as would-be successors are locked in a power struggle that has pushed economic policymaking into the background.

Meanwhile, the economic situation is fueling discontent. The bomb attacks outside main public buildings in downtown Tashkent in 1999 were ascribed by the government to Islamic extremists, as are every other sign of public discontent, such as four days of street fighting in March 2004 and a series of suicide bombs in July 2004. Increasingly frequent and larger-scale demonstrations cast doubt on this explanation and they in fact appear to be more closely related to economic distress

---

beneficial economic impact of the exchange liberalization. Cash shortages, as well as government wage and pension arrears, are also depressing economic activity.

[21] This view is set out in, for example, ICG (2004a, p. 1). Vested interests resisting reform include the former state-farm managers (Pomfret 2000b) and state-enterprise managers, but because of the lack of large-scale privatization there is no group comparable to the Russian oligarchs.

and opposition to the brutality of the regime. In November 2004, thousands of rioters took to the streets in several towns in the Ferghana Valley and in Kashkadarya province.[22] Most dramatically of all, in May 2005 troops fired on a crowd in Andijan resulting in a death toll of 179 by official estimates, and perhaps many more (Akiner 2005). The government may be correct that militants organize some of the demonstrations of discontent, but the economic and policy situation provides a fertile breeding ground.

---

[22] In Kokand a crowd reported to be 6,000 strong burned police cars and beat up tax inspectors ("Signs show Uzbek stability buckling under economic stress," posted at www.eurasianet.org on November 16, 2004). The same article reports that the official suicide rate masks a substantial increase in actual suicides, and that people who have lost the will to live are easy recruits for extremists seeking suicide bombers.

3

Kazakhstan: Oil-Boom Economy

Kazakhstan has large oil and natural-gas reserves, substantial gold deposits, and rich unmined veins of copper, chrome, and other minerals, as well as enough developed farmland and pasture to feed itself. Yet, these resources were poorly utilized during the first decade after independence. The inheritance of a weak state with a precarious ethnic balance between Kazakhs and Russians created substantial economic uncertainty. Mass migration during the first half of the 1990s contributed to economic decline, and disappointing inflows of foreign capital held up development of the oil and mineral sectors (Tables 3.1 and 3.2).

3.1   A Two-Part History

In the initial years following independence, Kazakhstan's leadership was preoccupied with nation building in the context of real prospects of secession or internal conflict. Economic policy in 1992–94 was driven in large measure by President Nazarbayev's attempts to maintain economic contacts with Russia. Kazakhstan was the last Soviet republic to formally declare its independence in 1991 and its leader was the most assiduous in trying to construct a viable successor organization to the USSR. Kazakhstan followed Russia's radical reforms, notably the price liberalization of January 1992 and early privatization measures, but initially macroeconomic stability was not pursued, and even if it had been desired was hamstrung by retention of the ruble until November 1993. In 1994 pluralism briefly flourished, before the process of political repression began to take shape and Kazakhstan became noticeably less democratic than Russia. Despite statements to the contrary, economic reform was put largely on hold for the remainder of the decade.[1] The 1999 referendum that allowed President Nazarbayev to stand for another seven-year term and the ensuing election were blatantly rigged.[2]

In the mid-1990s Kazakhstan's privatization process took a similar turn to Russia's as a voucher scheme was displaced by asset sales. Between September 1995

---

[1] For example, trade reform commitments included in 1998 IMF-supported programs were not implemented. Kazakhstan, however, maintained its commitment to current-account convertibility, unlike Uzbekistan and Turkmenistan which responded to economic difficulties by introducing draconian exchange controls in 1996 and 1998, respectively.

[2] See Kolstø (2004, p. 170) on the 1999 election, and Melvin (2004) on the comparative authoritarianism of Kazakhstan, the Kyrgyz Republic, and Uzbekistan.

Table 3.1. Kazakhstan: DFI, 1992–2003 (millions of U.S. dollars).

	1992	1993	1994	1995	1996	1997
DFI	100	473	635	964	1,137	1,320
	1998	1999	2000	2001	2002	2003
DFI	1,143	1,584	1,278	2,796	2,138	2,500

Source: EBRD Transition Report 2003, p. 65.

Table 3.2. Kazakhstan: immigration and emigration, 1991–2003 (thousands).

	1991	1992	1993	1994	1995	1996	1997
Immigration	171	162	111	70	71	54	38
Emigration	228	327	333	481	310	229	299
	1998	1999	2000	2001	2002	2003	
Immigration	41	41	57	54	58	65	
Emigration	144	165	156	142	120	74	

Source: International Organization for Migration, www.iom.kz/eng/migr/obsh.php.

and the end of 1996 many of the most valuable state enterprises were sold. In this period the government's attention also began to focus more narrowly on oil-sector development, and became associated with wealth accumulation by the elite. Externally, Kazakhstan came to be seen less as one of the reformist CIS counties and more as an example of a corrupt Soviet successor state.[3] The economy was hit by several negative exogenous shocks in the late 1990s, notably low oil prices and the August 1998 Russian Crisis. Given the country's economic potential, Kazakhstan's performance during the 1990s was disappointing.[4]

Following a large currency devaluation in 1999 and an upturn in proven oil reserves and in oil prices, Kazakhstan entered a boom period in the early twenty-first century. In 2000, 2001, and 2002 Kazakhstan experienced double-digit economic growth (Table 1.3), led by a boom in foreign trade (Table 1.6) fuelled by oil exports (Table 3.3). This extraordinary boom continued as oil prices climbed over $60 per barrel in 2005, and the dominant question for Kazakhstan's economic future is whether oil will turn out to be a curse or a blessing. A "curse" outcome could arise if corruption and rent seeking become so deeply ingrained that growth outside oil

---

[3] In 1996 Kazakhstan ranked below neighboring Uzbekistan, a self-styled gradual reformer, on the EBRD's transition index.

[4] The poor outlook is reflected in articles in *The Economist* which argued that there was no more than a 20% chance of finding recoverable oil in Kazakhstan's waters ("Hoping for a gusher," August 28, 1999) and derided the idea "that this impoverished country is about to turn into a Saudi Arabia" ("Priming the pump," May 27, 2000).

Table 3.3.   Kazakhstan's oil and gas: output and exports.

	1998	1999	2000	2001	2002	2003
Oil production (mmt)	25.6	29.4	35.4	39.3	47.3	51.3
Oil exports (mmt)	20.4	23.7	29.4	31.7	39.3	44.3
Oil exports (millions of $)	1,650	2,164	4,429	4,463	5,157	7,300
World oil price ($/bbl)	13.1	18.0	28.2	24.3	24.9	28.9
Natural-gas production (bcm)	7.9	9.9	11.5	11.6	13.1	14.2

Sources: "Republic of Kazakhstan: selected issues and statistical appendix," IMF Country Report No. 03/211, July 2003, p. 8 (oil) and p. 72 (gas); "Republic of Kazakhstan: selected issues," IMF Country Report No. 04/362, November 2004, p. 22.

Note: the source projects oil production in 2010 of 96.7 mmt (millions of tonnes) and natural-gas production of 39.3 bcm ("bcm" denotes "billions of cubic meters", "bbl" denotes "billions of barrels").

extraction is prevented, or if volatility due to oil-price fluctuations leads to poor macroeconomic management.[5] On the other hand, booming oil revenues present an opportunity for Kazakhstan, free of the financial constraints facing their southern neighbors, to improve the physical and institutional infrastructure so that living standards are raised and economic growth can become self-sustaining.

3.2   Macroeconomic Performance during the 1990s

Kazakhstan suffered a severe recession in the first half of the 1990s as GDP fell by over two-fifths between 1991 and 1995. The decline halted in 1996 and 1997, before GDP suffered a further drop in 1998. Anemic performance in 1999 ended a decade of poor macroeconomic performance (Table 1.3). This could not be explained by war as in most of the CIS economic disasters.[6] Indeed, with its high initial income and human capital and its abundant natural resources, Kazakhstan might have been expected to do much better.

The most plausible explanation is in terms of disorganization—a theory of transitional recession popularized by Blanchard (1997) and applied to Kazakhstan by de Broeck and Kostial (1998). Kazakhstan's government moved quickly towards price liberalization in January 1992, but it failed to follow up with the institutions required for a well-functioning market economy. Thus, the functioning, albeit inefficiently, coordinating mechanisms of central planning were followed by a coordinating void. Tardiness in bringing the hyperinflation of 1992–93 down to moderate

---

[5] A sustained oil boom might also have deleterious effects on other sectors of the economy by drawing off resources and via Dutch disease mechanisms (i.e., an appreciating exchange rate makes production of other traded goods unprofitable) or by discouraging investment in human capital. Yet there are oil-driven success stories (e.g., Norway, Alaska, or Alberta); whether oil is a curse or a boon seems to be most closely related to institutional factors such as the degree of democracy, which does not augur well for Kazakhstan with its autocratic government.

[6] The worst CIS performers during the 1990s, measured by the level of real GDP in 1999 relative to 1989, were Moldova, Georgia, Ukraine, Tajikistan, and Azerbaijan, all of whom saw their GDP cut by over half (EBRD Transition Report Update, April 2001, p. 15; see also Ofer and Pomfret 2004, p. 12).

inflation levels also contributed to the poor functioning of the market economy, although inflation was more or less under control by 1997 (Table 1.2).

Physical disintegration was exacerbated because, among the Soviet republics, Kazakhstan was one of the most tightly integrated into the Union economy. In particular, its mineral wealth was associated with single-enterprise towns dependent on production chains involving suppliers, smelters, and end users elsewhere in the Soviet Union (usually in Russia).[7] The fledgling oil industry in western Kazakhstan relied on Russian pipelines (see Section 3.4), but Kazakhstan's own major refineries in Pavlodar in the northeast and Shymkent in the south were linked by pipelines to Siberian oil fields. The chaotic privatization of large enterprises in 1995–96 added to the confusion, although in the longer term providing clearer ownership rights may have encouraged reduction of the physical problems.[8]

Kazakhstan experienced high emigration during the 1990s, as its population fell from over 17 million at the time of independence to less than 15 million a decade later (Table 3.2). According to the final Soviet census in 1989 the population consisted of roughly two-fifths Kazakhs, two-fifths Russian, and one-fifth other ethnic groups. The Russians, who had been the largest group in the republic a decade earlier, were concentrated in the capital city, Almaty, and in northern and eastern regions bordering the Russian Federation. Among the other groups were large contingents of ethnic Germans and Koreans who had been shipped to Kazakhstan by Stalin, who feared their potential to be a fifth column, supporting invaders from the west and east. Most of the Germans took advantage of German citizenship laws to emigrate to Germany in the early 1990s. The German and Russian emigration, both of which contained a disproportionate number of the country's well-educated and skilled people, constituted a substantial brain drain in the early post-independence years.[9] The exodus slowed substantially with the Russian Crisis in 1998, but even in 2000 annual net emigration was still over 100,000; it only began to drop substantially with the post-2000 oil boom.

Emigration complicates comparison of Kazakhstan's economic performance because output comparisons across transition countries are usually by total output rather than per capita GDP, so that Kazakhstan's relative performance may look worse than it was. In addition, the biases of all GDP estimates for transition economies probably overstate the extent of the initial recession. Other indicators of well-being reinforce the impression that Kazakhstan did not perform as poorly

---

[7] Rama and Scott (1999) analyze the labor markets in one-company towns.

[8] Table 1.3, however, illustrates the lack of short-term benefits at the macroeconomic level. Hoff and Stiglitz (2004) argue that the disregard for legality or fairness in Russian- or Kazakhstan-style privatization had long-run negative consequences for the emergence of the rule of law.

[9] About a million Russians and 700,000 Germans left Kazakhstan during the 1990s (Kolstø 2004, p. 170). There were smaller flows of Ukrainians, Belorussians, and Tartars to other parts of the CIS, and of Jews to Israel (Becker et al. 2005, p. 108). The emigration was to a small extent offset by immigration of Kazakhs from the former USSR and Mongolia; the UNDP (Human Development Report, Kazakhstan 2000, p. 6) estimated the number of repatriations over the 1990s to be 260,000.

as the GDP estimates suggest, and that this gap between estimates and reality was bigger for Kazakhstan than for neighboring CIS countries (Chapter 7). Nevertheless, whatever its absolute or relative magnitude, Kazakhstan's output performance in the 1990s was well below potential.

The 1998 recession followed the Russian Crisis. Although the Russian Crisis was an exogenous negative shock, Kazakhstan's susceptibility to contagion reflected to some extent the failure to create a vibrant market economy that could withstand such a shock. The government responded with a large devaluation, which as in Russia helped to kick-start the economy in 1999 and 2000. Starting in 2000 Kazakhstan enjoyed a period of rapid economic growth, which coincided with an upturn in oil prices. In May 2000 the government paid off its debts to the IMF ahead of schedule, as a signal of the health and financial strength of the economy.

The post-1999 oil boom raises the question of whether or not the growth is sustainable in the event of oil-price reversals. A major concern is the institutional environment. In the 1990s the situation deteriorated from a promising pluralism in 1994 to crony capitalism in 1995–96. The privatization process, described in the next section, was widely identified with burgeoning corruption and deteriorating standards of governance. A second, and related, concern is the role of oil wealth. Oil has driven economic growth since 2000, and proven resources guarantee a substantial flow of oil until at least the middle of this century (see Section 3.4), but oil was the biggest and most corrupt part of the alienation of public resources.

3.3 Privatization

The first Privatization and Denationalization Act was passed in June 1991, but Kazakhstan only started to work seriously on privatization in 1992. In the first phase housing was privatized through a coupon scheme. For most households the number of coupons was sufficient to purchase their apartment or house, so that the outcome was essentially reversion to existing occupiers. In this phase small consumer service businesses—such as retail outlets, catering, laundries, saunas, etc.—were sold by auction, usually to the existing operators.

The second stage of privatization began in 1993 with the issue of vouchers with which citizens could buy shares in Investment Privatization Funds (IPFs) which would buy shares in medium and large state enterprises. The scheme was a mix of Czech and Russian voucher schemes, intended to ensure a fair denationalization of state assets, and Poland's IPF scheme, intended to forestall excessive fragmentation of ownership. In practice, there were conflicts over the fairness of voucher allocation, which was biased in favor of rural residents and hence in favor of Kazakhs,[10] and over the competence of the IPFs to act as governing boards or mutual funds. The

---

[10] In part this was a reaction to the first phase of privatization, which was considered to have favored other ethnic groups because Russians had held better jobs associated with better housing allocations and Uzbeks and other minorities had run the small service businesses.

vouchers became heavily concentrated in a handful of IPFs (Olcott 2002, p. 138). These deficiencies contributed to some amassment of wealth, but the process of privatization was slow[11] and to some extent was overtaken by spontaneous alienation of state assets by anybody in a position to steal them.

In November 1993 the government experimented with offering shares in large enterprises to foreign purchasers. Philip Morris purchased a 49% share in the Almaty Tobacco Factory for $313 million. RJR Nabisco purchased 90% of the Shymkent Confectionery Factory for $70 million. Unilever purchased 90% of the Almaty and Karaganda Margarine Plants for $60 million. In 1994 and 1995 the State Property Committee earmarked other large enterprises for sale, but the process of privatization by sale really took hold after September 1995.[12]

In the third stage of privatization, companies were sold in part or whole, or contracted to the management of individual investors for a specified period, under an individually negotiated agreement, "making this the most corrupt stage" according to Olcott (2002, p. 139). The lack of transparency was exacerbated by the speed with which many of the deals were concluded.[13] Table 3.4 provides details (from Kalyuzhnova 1998, Table 5.1) of twenty-five sales, which raised almost $7 billion between September 1995 and October 1996. At the same time as individual deals were concluded with speed, the overall process moved slowly as many of the enterprises listed for sale failed to attract buyers. In June 1997 the government announced that shares in thirteen of the largest remaining state enterprises would be offered for sale on the stock exchange before the end of 1997,[14] but a year later only three were fully tradable (Olcott 2002, p. 141). The government also vacillated on how to deal with natural monopolies, until, in December 1998, Nazarbayev announced that the railways, power transmission lines, and oil and gas pipelines would remain in state hands. Case-by-case privatization has continued, relatively slowly since 2000, because with the oil boom the government is less desperate for revenue, and perhaps more transparently.[15]

---

[11] By the start of 1995 only a third of vouchers had been used (Kalyuzhnova 1998, p. 76). Verme (2001, pp. 60–61) reports that between April 1994 and September 1995 eighteen auctions were held in which 169 IPFs participated and about 1,000 medium-sized enterprises with around 400,000 employees were privatized.

[12] According to Verme (2001, p. 61) only five large enterprises had been sold by the end of 1995.

[13] According to Sander Thoenes in an article entitled "Kazakhstan's sale of the century":

Speed differentiates Kazakhstan's privatization more than anything. One company asked a consultancy to submit a proposal for a three-week legal and commercial investigation for a bid. Two days later the consultancy found that the company had already won the bid.

Financial Times (London), October 25, 1996 (quoted in Kalyuzhnova (1998, p. 78))

[14] These included Halyk Savings Bank (the country's largest), Borly coal mines, the largest trade center in Almaty, two oil companies, and a number of metal producers (Olcott 2002, p. 286 n. 38).

[15] In late 2002 the state raised $199 million when it sold its residual 34.6% stake in the copper mining company Kazakhmys through public tender. In April 2003 the state's 31.8% stake in Aluminium of Kazakhstan was sold to Corica, a subsidiary of J&W Holding AG (Switzerland) for $21 million. In May

The third stage coincided with a period of increased interest in oil exploitation, and sale of rights. Despite the early Tengiz agreement with Chevron and formation of the Agip-led OKIOC consortium in 1993 to exploit offshore Caspian oil, the involvement of foreign majors in exploration and exploitation was delayed by renegotiation of agreements and by opposition from the "oil barons" of western Kazakhstan. In 1996 Mobil purchased half of the state's original 50% share in Tengiz, to the dismay of Chevron. In August 1996 Hurricane Hydrocarbons of Canada bought into the Kumkol oil field in central Kazakhstan. In the year starting in spring 1997 a series of oil and gas contracts were signed (Table 3.5) as the government came to an accommodation with regional barons.[16] The most important outcome was new injections of capital into the OKIOC consortium to explore the potentially rich offshore fields.[17] In this period Russian oil companies were notably absent, but the following years saw large increases in Russian and Chinese investment in Kazakhstan's energy sector.[18]

In Kazakhstan the sales of 1995–97 were seen as disposing of state assets at giveaway prices to well-connected people or foreigners. The October 1997 replacement of Kazhegeldin as prime minister was connected to his failure to realize enough revenue from the sales. However, the policy of case-by-case privatization continued under his successor, Balgymbaev, and Kazhegeldin's dismissal may have reflected intra-elite battles over the spoils. Groups associated with Kazhegeldin, notably Trans-World, fared less well after 1997.[19] Some privatization contracts were reassigned to groups associated with Balgymbaev or President Nazarbayev's

---

2003 the auction of the state's 25.1% share in an oil exploration joint venture with the Chinese National Petroleum Company (CNPC) and Aktobemunaigas was won by CNPC for $150 million.

[16] Luong (2004a, p. 203), writing about the 1997 decentralization legislation, explains this legislation in terms of clearing up contractual inconsistencies which had arisen from oil and gas investors' accumulation of legal obligations to both central and regional governments during a de facto decentralization period (1995–98) in Kazakhstan's institutional development.

[17] In September 1998 Kazakhstan sold its share of the consortium to Phillips Petroleum and Inpex. In summer 2001, after Agip became sole operator, the consortium was renamed AgipKCO (Agip–Kazakhstan North Caspian Operating Company).

[18] By February 2003 LUKoil had invested $1 billion in Kazakhstan, with a 15% stake in the Karachaganak gas field, a 50% stake in Turgay (Kumkol), a 5% stake in Tengiz, and a 15% share in the CPC (Rutland 2003, p. 49); and in April 2003 LUKoil and Kazmunaigas signed a joint venture agreement to develop the offshore Khvalynskoe field. In 1997 CNPC obtained a 60% share in the Aktyubinsk Oil Company. In early 2003 two Chinese state firms offered British Gas $1.23 billion for its 16.7% share in the Karachaganak oil and gas venture but existing shareholders exercised their rights to preempt the bid; later in the year CNPC took control of the North Buzachi oil field, and in December 2003 Sinopec bought a 50% share in three large exploration blocks near Tengiz.

[19] Trans-World Metal Corporation, Japan Chrome, Ivedon International, and White Swan are sister companies owned primarily by a group of Russian metal traders, headed by an Israeli, David Reuben, reportedly with close ties to Kazhegeldin. Sale of the Pavlodar and Aksu aluminum facilities to the Trans-World Group was especially controversial (Olcott 2002, pp. 161–63; Richard Behar "Capitalism in a cold climate," *Fortune*, June 12, 2000). Although Trans-World's influence waned after 1997, it received substantial compensation ("Trans-World settles with Kazakhstan," *Financial Times*, February 8, 2000). After Kazhegeldin's fall from power, one of the original partners, Aleksandr Mashkevich, attempted to grab company assets, reportedly with President Nazarbayev as a silent partner (Olcott 2002, pp. 139–40).

Table 3.4. Kazakhstan: privatization by sales (millions of U.S. dollars): twenty-five cases, 1995–96.

Enterprise	Date	Buyer	Basis	Value[a]
Pavlodar Aluminium	09.14.95	Whiteswan	50%	169.6
TNK Kazchrom	10.15.95	Japan Chrome	52%	582.6
Karaganda Metallurgy	11.15.95	Ispat-International		838.6
AO Zheskazganskii GOK	12.08.95	Novaresources SG	40%	45.4
AO Sokolovo-Sarbaiskoe GOPO	02.13.96	Aivedon International	49%	124.7
AO Torgaiskoeboksitovoe-rudoupavlenie	04.05.96	Whiteswan	51%	13.2
AO Krasnootyabrskoe-boksitovoerudoupavlenie	04.05.96	Whiteswan	51%	29.2
AO Keregitas	04.05.96	Whiteswan	51%	19.7
Karagandinskaya TES 2	04.17.96	Ispat-Karmet	Property	42.5
AO Ermakovskaya GRES	05.02.96	Japan Chrome	53%	259.7
AO Zheskazgan Svetmet	05.24.96	Samsung Deutschland	40%	351.2
Karaganda Shakhta Ugol	06.18.96	Ispat-Karmet	Property	195.0
Ekibastuskaya GRES 1	06.26.96	AES-Suntree Power	Property	554.0
Almatyenergo	07.31.96	Tractebel	Property	358.4
Shymkent oil refinery	07.??.96	Vitol Munay	94%	230.0
Pavlodarskaya TES 1	08.08.96	Whiteswan	Property	113.7
Zheskazganskaya TES	08.08.96	Samsung	Property	107.2
Zambylskaya GRES	08.27.96	Vitol Munay	Property	124.1
GAO Yuzhneftegas	08.28.96	Hurricane Hydrocarbons	89.5%	930.0
AO Sary-Arka Pollimetall	09.19.96	Nakosta	39%	28.6
Razrez Vostochnii +34% of Razrez Stepnoi	09.25.96	Japan Chrome	Property	317.6
Razrez Bogatyr +66% of Razrez Stepnoi	10.18.96	Access Industries Inc.	Property	801.2
Razrez Severniy	10.18.96	Sverdlovenergo	Property	233.5
AO Lisakovskii GOK	10.24.96	AO Esil	51%	46.0
Karagandinskaya GRES 2	10.??.96	Independent Power Corp. plc	Property	418.8
Total				**6,934.5**

Source: Kalyuzhnova (1998, pp. 79–83).

Notes: [a]value includes all buyer liabilities, including guaranteed investments, guaranteed future contributions to the state budget, bonus, debt repayment, wage arrears, budget and non-budget arrears, royalties, etc.

Table 3.5. Kazakhstan: privatization by sales (millions of U.S. dollars): energy-sector privatization or long-term management contracts, spring 1997–98.

Enterprise	Date	Buyer	Basis	Value
Karazhanbasmunai	03.97	Triton-Vuko Energy Group	94.5%	90
Mangistaumunaigaz	05.97	Medeo Energy Corp.	85%	N/A
Aktyubinskmunaigaz	06.97	Chinese National Petroleum Co. (CNPC)	60%	4,000
Uzen Oil Fields	07.97	CNPC	60%	9,500
Mangistaumunaigaz	01.98	Central Asian Petroleum	65%	248
OKIOC	09.98	Phillips Petroleum	State share	*ca.* 500

family, although the most persistent rumors concerned large direct payments to top leaders during the Balgymbaev era.[20]

Outside the country, initial euphoria at making bargain purchases was quickly tempered by operational difficulties, hidden commitments, and concern about the state's ability to recontract. After the Belgian energy group, Tractebel, acquired a twenty-year management contract for Almatyenergo in 1996, it experienced difficulty in obtaining fuel and maintaining electricity supplies in the winter of 1996–97 (the nadir of Kazakhstan's transition), and never made a profit (Olcott 2002, pp. 164–65). After threats and counterthreats Tractebel finally pulled out in early 2000.[21] After the U.S. company AES bought a power plant in Ekibastuz in 1996 and then invested about $70 million in the facility, the national grid operator KEGOC unilaterally split the grid into two parts making it impossible for AES to deliver electricity to its southern customers so that in 1998 AES made big losses in Kazakhstan (Kalyuzhnova 2003, p. 161). Hurricane Hydrocarbons's profits from the Kumkol oil field were undermined by commitments to supply the Shymkent oil refinery at fixed prices and a number of social obligations whose magnitude the Canadian company failed to appreciate when entering into the deal in 1996 at an apparent bargain price of $120 million (in contrast to the much higher total value of the deal reported in Table 3.4). The July 1996 sale of the Shymkent oil refinery was initially to a Dutch company, Vitol, but in early 1997 Vitol backed out and a former subsidiary Kazvit took over the contract. Other high-profile deals with reputable foreign companies fell through in opaque circumstances, such as a 1995 contract with Placer Dome of

---

[20] A suit filed in London in fall 1997 by an international businessman named Farhat Tabbah accused Balgymbaev, three U.S. businessmen, and a subsidiary of Mobil of cheating him out of millions of dollars. Although the suit failed, it stimulated U.S. investigations which led to a high-profile trial of one of the U.S. businessmen (James Giffen, a former Adviser to President Nazarbayev) under the Foreign Corrupt Practices Act and to the conviction of a second of the U.S. businessmen (Bryan Williams, a former Mobil executive), who was sentenced to 47 months in jail for failure to declare monies received from Giffen in his tax return. The two high Kazakhstan officials implicated in the U.S. cases are referred to only as KO1 and KO2.

[21] In May 2000 a buyout was agreed that turned over Almatyenergo to Access Industries, a group headed by Len Blavatnik, a businessman with close ties to Nazarbayev.

Canada to exploit the Vasilkovskoe gold mine, or the Deutsche Telekom offer for 49% of Kaztelekom which fell through in January 1997.[22]

A number of the deals involved corrupt practices. Cases before the U.S. courts concern a series of payments by U.S. oil companies during the period 1995–2000, which allegedly led to millions of dollars being paid through a U.S. intermediary into offshore accounts of senior Kazakh officials.[23] In 2003, a former Mobil executive was imprisoned for tax evasion related to monies he received in connection with the 1996 sale of a 25% share in the Tengiz oil field to Mobil. ChevronTexaco officials are being questioned by the U.S. Justice Department about Texaco's 1997 agreement to develop the Karachaganak field, and contracts involving Amoco and Phillips have also been cited in U.S. judicial proceedings. In connection with its ill-starred management contract for Almatyenergo, Tractebel reportedly paid $55 million through the Eurasian Bank, whose chairman Aleksandr Mashkevich was subsequently charged with money laundering and investigated for bribery by a Belgian judge.[24] When the government sold a share of Vasilkovskoe, the country's most attractive gold mine, fees and signing bonuses were reported to be worth $35 million (Olcott 2002, p. 167).

Despite the problems, Kazakhstan has been relatively successful among CIS countries in attracting DFI. Chevron began negotiating for the Tengiz oil field in 1990, in what was the biggest DFI deal in the history of the USSR, but otherwise DFI was sluggish in the first half of the 1990s. The sales of 1995–96, creation of a "one-stop" State Investment Committee in November 1996, and a generally more inviting environment encouraged greater DFI, although it remained overwhelmingly in the energy and metals sectors. From 1996 to 2000 DFI exceeded a billion dollars a year and since 2001 it has exceeded two billion dollars (Table 3.1), with over 85% going to natural-resource activities.[25] In manufacturing some of the earliest investors have made further investments, e.g., Philip Morris built a $340 million tobacco factory in 2000 and now controls 80% of Kazakhstan's tobacco market (Olcott 2002, p. 145), but the amount of DFI in manufacturing is small.

The method of large-scale privatization and of allocation of oil and mineral rights undermined the institutional quality of the economy as Kazakhstan moved down

---

[22] The 1995 Vasilkovskoe contract was itself controversial in that the government had announced a tender process but then signed with Placer, to the consternation of other interested parties. Rio Tinto, which had been negotiating since 1992, was especially displeased. In a March 1999 testimony to the U.K. House of Commons Select Committee on Foreign Affairs, Rio Tinto stated that Kazakhstan did not offer "an acceptable investment climate." A 60% share in Vasilkovskoe was finally sold in 2000 to Floodgate Holding, a company registered in the Dutch Antilles, although some reports claimed its real owner was an Israeli diamond dealer (Olcott 2002, pp. 166–67).

[23] For more details see Seymour M. Hersh "The price of oil; what was Mobil up to in Kazakhstan and Russia?" *New Yorker*, July 9, 2001, pp. 48–65.

[24] See Steve Le Vine's article "Kazaks face money laundering charge," *Wall Street Journal*, July 6, 2001.

[25] Data from EBRD Transition Report 2003; cumulative DFI 1989–2002 of $13,568 million or $938 per capita is the highest in the CIS, although less than DFI in Poland, Hungary, and the Czech Republic.

the rankings of good governance or freedom from corruption.[26] More positively, however, the cumulative impact has been to diminish the state's hold on economic activity.[27] The private sector accounted for a mere 25% of GDP in 1995; this share increased to 40% in 1996, 55% in 1997, 60% in 1999, and 65% in 2002 (EBRD Transition Report 2003, p. 158). Whether the privatized enterprises are more efficient than state-owned enterprises remains an open question.[28]

3.4   The Oil, Gas, and Minerals Sectors

The oil and gas sectors suffered from several handicaps during the 1990s. The preexisting pipelines were controlled by Russian state-run oil and gas pipeline monopolies, Trasneft and Gazprom, which discriminated against Kazakh oil.[29] The ownership status of the principal oil field, Tengiz, was disputed and only resolved, together with some easing of the pipeline problems, when Russian shareholder participation was agreed. Prospecting for new reserves under the potentially oil-rich North Caspian was delayed by disagreements over delimitation of national territories and by domestic wrangles over selling exploration rights to foreign firms possessing the technology to explore the offshore fields. The turnaround in 2000 was highlighted by rising oil prices and the discovery of the Kashagan offshore field, which is the largest oil field outside the Middle East but has difficult exploitation conditions. Although Kazakhstan only reached agreement with Russia in 2002 over delimitation of the Caspian Sea bed, oil fields explored in the late 1990s will come online in the first decade of the twenty-first century with huge potential production levels. The pipeline issue is also taking time to resolve, but since 2001 the situation is becoming more favorable to Kazakhstan.

The Tengiz field, with recoverable reserves of 6–9 billion barrels, is the largest active field in Kazakhstan. After the dissolution of the USSR, the government of Kazakhstan took over the state's share in the TengizChevron joint venture, but Russia

---

[26] Kazakhstan has, for example, gradually slipped down the list in Transparency International's Corruption Perceptions Index, ranking 100th out of 133 countries in 2003 ("Global Corruption Report 2004," Transparency International, Berlin). Other high-profile cases of corrupt practices involved the sale in 1999 of forty jet fighters to North Korea, after which the director of the export agency was assassinated and his successor imprisoned for twenty years, and an illegal sale in 2000 of a $1.5 million military plane to the Congo for $35,000 by a businessman who ended up with a twelve-year prison sentence (Redo 2004, p. 106).

[27] Doubts remain about whether the government is comfortable with this outcome. The state oil and gas company, Kazmunaigas, has become a more significant player during the oil boom, as the tool for the government to claw back some of its lost ownership share in this key sector. A law passed in 2003 requires Kazmunaigas to have at least a half-share in all future projects. There is an echo here of the Russian situation but the situation is less dramatic than the Putin government's recapture of Yukos assets.

[28] Kalyuzhnova et al. (2003), using industrial survey data from 1996 to 1998, found no difference in efficiency, apart from within the subgroup of export-oriented firms where there was some evidence of privatized firms' superior efficiency.

[29] The goal of receiving national treatment from the Russian pipeline operators has been a driving force behind Kazakhstan's desire for some form of regional trading arrangement that includes Russia (see Chapter 10).

claimed rights to part of the oil and also controlled the only existing pipeline, rights of access to which were not committed to in the original agreement. The Russian state-owned pipeline company, Transneft, engaged in monopsonistic practices such as artificially high assessments of technical losses, arbitrary long-route allocations, and other discriminatory pricing including absence of a quality bank that would recognize the higher quality of Tengiz oil; the net effect was that transit tariffs for Kazakhstan's crude were typically double those for Russian crude.[30] Operations at Tengiz were also dogged for most of the 1990s by disputes over ownership shares, as Mobil and LUKoil were brought into the joint venture.[31]

The Kumkol fields in central Kazakhstan suffered even more from high transport costs. Developed by Hurricane Hydrocarbons of Canada, which was renamed PetroKazakhstan in 2003, the Kumkol field produces over 7 mmt per year, but its expansion has been constrained by transport costs of around $12 per barrel.[32] The firm has been exporting oil by railcar to China and to the Trasneft Russian pipeline system, and in 2003 signed an agreement to sell 1 mmt per year to Tehran in exchange for Iranian crude at a Gulf port. In October 2005 China's National Petroleum Corporation purchased PetroKazakhstan for $4.2 billion, presumably sealing the direction of exports from this field.

The opening of the first privately owned and commercially operated pipeline in autumn 2001, the CPC, provided an alternative route through Russia, thus cutting transport costs from Tengiz in half.[33] Other producers in Kazakhstan have also benefited from the CPC. In early 2003 a 450 km pipeline was completed to link the Aktobe oil field, operated by the Chinese National Petroleum Company, to the CPC. Aktobe's production was expected to rise to 6 mmt by 2005, from around 2.5 mmt in the late 1990s. The CPC's existence also led to reductions in the costs of using the Transneft pipeline, but doubts remain over whether the CPC pipeline will provide

---

[30] IMF estimates from "Cross-border issues in energy trade in the CIS countries," IMF Policy Discussion Paper PDP/02/13, December 2002. See also "Republic of Kazakhstan: selected issues and statistical appendix," IMF Country Report No. 03/211, July 2003.

[31] Chevron was reportedly unhappy at Mobil's buying into Tengiz, but in 1997 Chevron itself sold a 5% stake in the joint venture to LUKoil. Delays in the late 1990s and early 2000s in agreeing upon new investment were related to the increased number of principals and Chevron's wariness of its partners.

[32] The $12 calculation is reported in "Republic of Kazakhstan: selected issues and statistical appendix," IMF Country Report No. 03/211, July 2003, p. 9, and also by Gaël Raballand (a World Bank economist) and Ferhad Esen (a petroleum economist in the research department of a French bank). Raballand and Esen (N.D.) estimate that the costs would have been reduced to $8 if PetroKazakhstan could have joined the CPC, but it was induced by the Kazakhstan government to sign on to construction of a 700 km link to the existing pipeline network, which will reduce its transport costs to $9.5 per barrel.

[33] The CPC is half owned by Russia (24%), Kazakhstan (19%), and Oman (7%), and the other half is divided among ChevronTexaco (15%), LUKoil (12.5%), ExxonMobil (7.5%), Rosneft/Shell (7.5%), Agip (2%), British Gas (2%), Kazakhstan Pipeline Ventures (1.75%), and Oryx Caspian Pipeline (1.75%). After the dissolution of the USSR, the CPC (then consisting of Transneft, Kazakhstan, and Oman) was awarded the rights to transport oil from Tengiz to the Black Sea, but negotiations dragged on how much Chevron should pay towards construction. After Mobil bought 25% and LUKoil/Arco 5% of Tengiz, the Tengiz partners together with other investors took a half-share in the CPC.

Table 3.6.   Kazakhstan's oil and gas: actual export routes for
Kazakhstan's oil, 2000–03 (millions of tonnes).

Routes	2000	2001	2002	2003
Western Kazakhstan–Europe (Druzhba)	1,171	2,145	3,493	163
Western Kazakhstan–Europe	349	496	327	417
Western Kazakhstan–Kaliningrad	7	323	592	292
Western Kazakhstan–Odessa	8,195	8,082	6,857	7,137
Western Kazakhstan–Primorsk	0	0	1,003	1,483
Baku–Supsa	4,900	5,870	6,205	6,293
Western Kazakhstan–Odessa	2,341	2,296	1,020	12
Baku–Novorossiisk	561	2,306	2,752	2,716
Western Kazakhstan (Druzhba)–Gdansk	0	0	0	3,463
Atyrau–Novorossiisk (CPC)	0	934	10,998	12,983
Atyrau–Samara–Novorossiisk	1,707	3,430	3,248	3,300
Kumkol–Chinese border	584	1,414	2,023	3,500
Aktau–Baku–Batumi	3,640	4,600	5,470	5,537
Western Kazakhstan–Novorossiisk	594	655	408	136
Turkmenistan–Novorossiisk (different routes)	191	5	481	77
Tengiz–Feodosiya	3,976	3,388	363	489
Aktobe–Talinn	0	43	85	0

Source: Raballand and Esen (N.D.).
Notes: routes in italics include pipelines; other routes involve railcars.

true competition in the long term or whether Russia will enforce monopsonistic practices.

The alternative export routes for Kazakhstan's oil in the early 2000s are listed in Table 3.6, which illustrates the dramatic impact of the CPC. Other planned or potential pipeline links with Turkey, China, Iran, and South Asia will increase Kazakhstan's options and substantially undermine Russia's pipeline power (Table 3.7). The Ceyhan pipeline agreement signed in 1999 is the most advanced project, despite lengthy delays associated with financing, environmental concerns, and political disagreements. The 1,760 km long Baku–Ceyhan pipeline became operational in 2005 and will eventually have a capacity of one million barrels of oil per day. Initially, it will mainly serve Azerbaijan, but as Kazakhstan's Caspian oil output increases it is expected that substantial amounts will be exported via the Turkish port of Ceyhan, especially if Azeri production begins to decline at the same time. Construction of a 988 km pipeline from Atasu in central Kazakhstan to the Chinese border began in September 2004 and will have an initial capacity of 200,000 barrels per day upon completion at the end of 2005—compared with 20–30,000 barrels per day reaching the Chinese border by rail before 2004. This project, like the Unocal trans-Afghanistan pipeline, was initially planned in 1997. The logic of both of these projects—supplying energy to the rapidly growing oil-importing countries of south and east Asia—is strong, and was reinforced as oil prices climbed from around

Table 3.7. Kazakhstan's oil and gas: alternative pipeline routes.

	Destination	Status	Capacity	Comments
Atyrau to Samara	Russia (and Europe)	Preexisting; plans to rebuild and upgrade	15–16 mmt	Controlled by Transneft (Russian pipeline monopsony)
Caspian Pipeline Consortium	Black Sea; Russia's Novorossiisk-2 terminal	Agreed 1993; first flows 2001	28 mmt	From Tengiz; currently independent
Trans-Caspian	Mediterranean; Ceyhan (Turkey)	Agreed 1999; Baku–Ceyhan completed May 2005		Aktau–Baku by tanker
Atasu to Chinese border	China	Construction began September 2004; completed December 2005	10 mmt	Most expensive option; eventual links to Caspian fields
To Iran	Indian Ocean	Shortest route to saltwater, but barred to U.S. companies		
Via Afghanistan	South Asia	Proposed 1996–97		Shelved during Taliban era

$10 per barrel in 1998 to over $50 in 2005. A pipeline connection to Iran's ports makes similar sense in terms of delivering Caspian oil to markets east of Suez, but the Iranian option is blocked by U.S. sanctions against participation by U.S. companies.

The largest gas and gas-condensate field is Karachaganak in west Kazakhstan.[34] Exports in the early 2000s of around 6 mmt went to Gazprom in Orenberg at well below Russian market prices, and even further below European market prices. As with the oil pipelines, however, the Russian company took a less aggressively monopsonistic position after 2001, and a 2002 agreement to create a joint venture, Kazrosgaz, with Gazprom led to more attractive prices for Kazakhstan's gas exports and access to Western European markets.[35] Also, as with oil, new gas fields could be exploited once Caspian Sea demarcation issues were resolved. A January 2005 agreement resolved a border dispute with Russia over the Imashevskoye natural-gas

[34] Karachaganak is being developed by Agip, Texaco, LUKoil, and British Gas. In early 2003 two Chinese state firms tried to purchase British Gas's 16.7% share for $1.23 billion, but the other partners exercised their right to preempt the sale.

[35] Kazakhstan has some bargaining power because Gazprom's lucrative pipeline services for gas from Turkmenistan and Uzbekistan rely on transit rights through Kazakhstan.

Table 3.8.   Kazakhstan's oil and gas: major oil and gas projects with foreign involvement.

Field	Participants	Reserves (proven/probable)
Aktobe	70% CNPC, 30% KMG	1.0 bbl
Emba	85% KMG	0.7 bbl
Caspian shelf	LUKoil 50%	
Karachaganak[a]	32.5% Agip, 32.5% British Gas, 20% ChevronTexaco, 15% LUKoil	2.6 bbl oil, 1,000 bcm gas
Kashagan (Caspian shelf)[b]	20% Agip, 20% ExxonMobil, 20% Shell, 20% TotalFinaElf, 10% Inpex, 10% Conoco-Phillips	15.0 bbl
Kumkol[c]	Hurricane (PetroKazakhstan), LUKOIL	0.6 bbl
Mangistau	60% CAPC	1.0 bbl
Tengiz	50% ChevronTexaco, 25% ExxonMobil, 20% KMG, 5% LUKOIL/BP	9.0 bbl
Uzen	90% KMG	1.0 bbl
Other offshore		8–10 bbl

Source: based on estimates provided to an IMF mission in July 2004 and reported in "Republic of Kazakhstan: selected issues," IMF Country Report No. 04/362, November 2004, p. 22.
Notes: "KMG" denotes "Kazmunaigas," "CAPC" denotes "Central Asian Petroleum Corporation" and "BP" denotes "British Petroleum"; [a]primarily a gas field; [b]production expected 2007; [c]purchased by the Chinese National Petroleum Corporation in October 2005.

field, Kazakhstan's second largest, by agreeing on equal rights to the field, which will be developed by Gazprom and Kazmunaigas.

Oil output is set to expand substantially in the coming years.[36] A three-year $3 billion investment program in Tengiz was launched in 2003. Meanwhile, the even bigger offshore Caspian field of Kashagan, discovered in 2000 and estimated to contain 45 billion barrels of which 8–13 billion are recoverable with existing technologies, should begin production in 2006. Other oil and gas fields are being actively explored and exploited by foreign companies (Table 3.8). Unexplored areas of the north Caspian are expected to also contain large fields. World energy prices are difficult to predict, but the IMF is forecasting annual oil exports of 84 mmt, earning $10 billion, and natural-gas production of around 40 bcm by 2010 and, although government revenue from product sharing is always back-loaded, it could amount to around $165 billion over the next forty-five years.[37] Unless these forecasts turn

---

[36] To understand the heightened expectations since the late 1990s, see the survey by Ruseckas (1998), who in 1997 placed Kazakhstan's total proven oil reserves at 10 billion barrels and considered $18 per barrel as a reasonable, but perhaps optimistic, world price over the life of the reserves.

[37] IMF staff estimates reported in "Republic of Kazakhstan: selected issues and statistical appendix," IMF Country Report No. 03/211, July 2003, pp. 15–16.

out to be far above the mark, the coming decades will see a huge stimulus to the economy and great potential for economic development.

3.5 Agriculture

The agricultural sector is a major part of the economy, employing over a third of the labor force despite accounting for less than 10% of GDP. Kazakhstan is a substantial food exporter—selling grains, meat, and fruit and vegetables primarily to Russia and other CIS markets—and a minor cotton exporter. It is a net importer of sugar (from outside the CIS) and of milk (from Russia). If the experience of the better-documented Eastern European economies' food trade is a guide, the post-transition pattern is of traditional primary products being exported and processed-food products of higher perceived quality being imported.[38]

The farm sector was in deep crisis throughout the 1990s (Gray 2000). Between 1992 and 1995 input prices were liberalized while important output prices remained controlled, leading to farm losses and resort to barter.[39] Direction by local authorities led to farms concentrating on activities which they knew to be loss-making, while the continued extension of loans to loss-making farmers sunk them ever deeper into debt. Imposition of heavy penalties for tax arrears also distorted farmers' incentives to repay their creditors. Most farms became indebted and the problem was exacerbated by drought conditions in much of the country during the 1996–98 seasons. Grain production in 1998 was 6.5 million tonnes compared with 30 million tonnes in 1992, and the number of cattle fell from 9 million to less than 4 million over the same period (the figures come from the United Nations "Common country assessment—Kazakhstan: achievements, issues and prospects," Almaty 2003, p. 9).

Reversal of the price squeeze began in 1999, when the government introduced a price support system for wheat and then extended it to other goods. This led to a dramatic increase in the numbers employed in agriculture, from 1.3 million in 1999 to 2.4 million in 2001, although some of this increase is due to statistical reclassification of the shadow economy ("Republic of Kazakhstan: selected issues and statistical appendix," IMF Country Report No. 03/211, July 2003, p. 760). Moreover, price support is an inefficient response leading to accumulated grain stocks. Even if relative prices have become more rational in the twenty-first century, the legacy of the price policy errors of the early transition years remains in the debt overhang.

---

[38] For an analysis of Kazakhstan's agricultural trade in 1997, see Weber (2003, p. 395). The anticipated flood of farm products from Eastern Europe into the European Union did not materialize in the 1990s, and indeed the net food trade balance was in the other direction; Swinnen (2003) explains this in terms of product differentiation and the premium consumers will pay for higher perceived quality and reliability.

[39] De Broeck and Kostial (1998, p. 41) estimate that in 1993 the price of inputs used in agriculture increased 18.8 times while output prices rose 8.8 times. Fertilizer application rates in the wheat sector collapsed; in 1992 150,000 tonnes of nitrogen, 315,000 tonnes of phosphates, and 10,000 tonnes of potash were used, while in 1994 the corresponding numbers were 65,000, 50,000, and 6,000 (Meng et al. 2000, p. 710).

The 1995 Farm Reform established the principle of state ownership of land, with private use rights under long-term (99-year) leases. The government adopted a fresh approach to restructuring in 1998, based on acceptance of the need for bankruptcies that would lead to changes in ownership and management. In 2003 the government announced several new agriculture initiatives, most of which reflected statist attempts to modernize infrastructure, relocate farmers and publicize output targets (Nursenkova 2004). The overall impression is that the government has still not resolved the issue of how the farm sector should be organized in the market-based economy.[40]

The proximate problem facing the farm sector today is lack of investment to improve the infrastructure and permit quality upgrading. The capital–output ratio, labor productivity, and total factor productivity (TFP) all continued to decline in the second half of the 1990s and early 2000s, when productivity growth had become positive in other sectors.[41] Much of the farm produce is spoilt or has become over-priced before reaching its primary market. The fruit and vegetables and processed-food products are often uncompetitive with imported goods because of poor storage, processing, or packaging. The government earmarked 1 billion dollars for a three-year program (2003–05) for restoration and development of the agriculture sector, which may help, but is unlikely to be sufficient even if it is well-used. In microcosm and with its own specific problems, the agricultural sector typifies the failure of the non-oil economy to adapt to and flourish in a market-based environment. The travails of the farm sector are not yet over, because Russia's imminent accession to the WTO will likely work against Kazakhstan's farmers who will face increased competition from non-CIS suppliers to the Russian market.[42]

3.6 Is Economic Diversification Necessary to Avoid the Natural Resource Curse?

The industry policy being formulated in 2002–03 includes sector- and even firm-specific assistance to promote diversification and non-oil development.[43] In May 2003 the government announced as priority areas sectors with linkages to the oil-extraction sector, high-value-added sectors (such as space, nuclear, and information

---

[40] Land tenure arrangements posed particular problems for the pastoral sector, where seasonal migration patterns were disrupted by changes in access rights.

[41] According to IMF estimates, TFP in agriculture declined by an annual average of 1.8% during the period 1996–2001, when TFP growth averaged 5.8% in industry, 9.5% in construction, and 4.0% in services, and labor productivity fell by 8.2% per year in agriculture while it was increasing by more than TFP in the other sectors. See "Republic of Kazakhstan: selected issues and statistical appendix," IMF Country Report No. 03/211, July 2003, p. 23.

[42] The increased trade in farm products after Kazakhstan's own WTO accession, which is likely to closely follow Russia's, should yield an overall net benefit through lower prices to consumers, while only seriously harming domestic producers of sugar (Weber 2003).

[43] See "IMF Staff Report for the 2003 Article IV consultation," May 7, 2003, p. 14. See also "Republic of Kazakhstan: selected issues and statistical appendix," IMF Staff Country Report No. 03/211, July 2003, pp. 37–55.

technology), and agriculture (EBRD Transition Report 2003). Three institutions will provide financial support to private-sector development: the Development Bank, the Investment Fund, and the Fund for Innovation. However, all are small.[44] The efforts of the government to support non-oil sectors suggests a commitment to the idea, underlying Dutch disease arguments, that these activities have positive externalities lacking in the oil sector (see Section 9.6).

To date, however, there is little evidence of a resource curse operating through the mechanism of a negative impact on non-resource sectors.[45] Government intervention in agriculture during the oil-boom years has had greater positive impact than any negative relative price effect from high oil prices or via the exchange rate. Indeed, the Kazakh tenge depreciated in real terms from 1999 to 2002,[46] i.e., long after the crisis-induced recession of 1998–99. A stronger real-economy argument may be that relative-factor-price effects led to a lower return to investment in human capital, but this is difficult to observe; the transition from communism had a much stronger negative effect on the value of human capital than any observed in the twenty-first century. Transmission of an oil curse through price volatility is also difficult to assess because so far Kazakhstan has only experienced the boom part of the cycle; in principle, the government is taking appropriate income-smoothing steps through the establishment of an oil fund, but the key question concerns the independence of the oil fund and its management during the bust phase of the cycle.

3.7 The Social Sectors

Kazakhstan inherited the Soviet system of universal social-assistance programs, including generous pensions. In the early and mid-1990s the budgetary demands were substantial, many programs were characterized by lengthy payment arrears, and assistance was poorly targeted. Initial attempts at pension reform in 1996 were stymied amidst mass protests. By 1997 the social programs accounted for 10% of GDP and almost four-fifths of government expenditures. Pension reform was introduced in 1998 and over the next four years the government attempted to streamline other programs. By 2002, however, government spending on social-assistance programs had shrunk to 5.4% of GDP, or a quarter of total government expenditures, and over four-fifths of this spending went to pensions. In January 2002 the government introduced the state-targeted social-assistance program, which provides

---

[44] In July 2003 the Development Bank's capital was $270 million, the Investment Fund's authorized capital was $148 million, and that of the Fund for Innovation was less than $20 million. The Export Insurance Corporation had less than $50 million. The combined capitalization of all of these institutions amounted to less than a fifth of the oil fund's assets and less than a tenth of the country's gold and foreign-exchange reserves ("IMF Staff Report for the 2003 Article IV consultation," May 7, 2003, p. 5).

[45] There have been positive linkages to the construction sector and some tradables ("Republic of Kazakhstan: selected issues and statistical appendix," IMF Country Report No. 03/211, July 2003, pp. 19–36), but these are small. Kalyuzhnova et al. (2004) also find little evidence of Dutch disease effects in Kazakhstan.

[46] "Republic of Kazakhstan: 2003 Article IV consultation," IMF Staff Report, IMF Country Report No. 03/210, July 2003, p. 11.

means-tested assistance to individuals and families living below the poverty line in each oblast. The government also announced a substantial increase in funding for social-assistance programs over the 2002–07 period, which is aimed at eliminating income poverty.

As in all Soviet successor states the pension system has been an area of controversy during the transition. In 1996, Parliament tried to reform the system by introducing voluntary pension contributions, but people were unwilling or unable to save in this system. As the minimum pension fell to the equivalent of about $10 and even this was rarely paid on time, there were mass protests by pensioners. The government finally determined to remove all arrears by the end of 1997, and to fundamentally restructure the system along the lines of Chile's pension reforms. A residual public system was retained for workers who had accumulated years of service,[47] but the principal pillar of the system introduced in January 1998 was a system of mandatory savings. Kazakhstan's pension reform is one of the most sweeping in all transition economies, and although harsh on the current cohort of pensioners is intended to benefit future generations.[48]

The new pension system was expected, as a positive side effect, to contribute a boost to the development of the financial sector, although the investment rules were very conservative until rule changes in 2003 brought pension management in line with general asset management. It is worth emphasizing that, especially since the economic boom began at the turn of the century, Kazakhstan's financial-sector development has far outstripped that in other Central Asian countries. The insurance and mortgage markets have flourished, and real-estate markets are active, especially in the cities of Almaty, Astana, and Atyrau. Kazakhstan's banks effectively took over the Kyrgyz Republic's banking sector after 1999. In 2004 the government announced its intention to bring Kazakhstan's banking legislation in line with that of the European Union.

Since the 2002 reforms, Kazakhstan's social protection system's main components are the social-assistance program and other allowances, housing benefits, and the pension system. The targeted social assistance has been successful in reaching the poorest people, and according to the World Bank's 2002 poverty assessment it halved the poverty headcount from what it would have been without the program. The targeted social assistance helps poor people to smooth consumption over time and to deal with devastating income shocks, but there are concerns that the amounts allocated are too little to address severe poverty. The average value of the transfer

---

[47] The net cost of the residual system is forecast to decline from 5.7% of GDP in 1998 to less than 2% of GDP by 2016.

[48] According to "Streamlining social security in Kazakhstan," *The CACI Analyst*, April 23, 2003 (Central Asia and Caucasus Institute of the Johns Hopkins University), over half of the country's 1.7 million retirees received less than $40 per month in 2003. By 2002, however, pension-fund assets amounted to $1.4 billion, which was, at 6% of GNP, a larger share than in any other transition economy (cf. 4.5% in Hungary, 3.5% in Poland, and 0.8% in Bulgaria), although much lower than Chile's 54% (Chan-Lau 2004, p. 18).

to recipient families in 2002 was 4,330 tenge per head, which is 8% of the official poverty line. Funding for the program is by oblast, and oblasts with higher local revenues have more to spend on assistance than poorer oblasts, which exacerbates the funding problem.

Housing benefits, which are intended to benefit the poor, appear not to be very successful in achieving this goal. About 5% of the population receives such allowances to assist with utility bills and household maintenance, but they have a poor targeting record in terms of helping the most needy.[49] Other social-assistance measures such as insurance against death, disability, and other life events are being consolidated, e.g., by a law on mandatory social insurance which became effective in January 2005, and are also not targeted, although because benefits are unrelated to previous income they tend to be progressive as lump-sum payments are relatively more beneficial to poor recipients.

Expenditure on education and health dropped substantially during the 1990s. Expenditure on education from the public budget was equal to 3–4% of GDP in every year from 1994 to 2003, which signified a sharp drop in total expenditure before GDP started to grow after 1999. As elsewhere in Central Asia, the drop in preschool places was especially pronounced. Private education institutions have emerged, especially offering vocational training and tertiary education. These developments at the start and the end of the educational process have increased inequality of access. Similar changes have occurred in the health sector, where public expenditures have been around 2% of GDP, but the private health sector has expanded. The gray area between free and paid medical services has been associated with a high level of unofficial payments to medical workers.

In sum, during the 1990s, despite the social traumas of the transition from central planning, the government's stance on social issues was quite weak. Expenditures were allowed to fall substantially, and only in the area of pensions, where burgeoning costs and accumulating arrears required action, did the government take action. The pension reform, however, ended up being radical and perhaps the most far-reaching and successful in any transition economy. Around the turn of the century the government's attitude to social policies became more proactive; in the first half-decade of the 2000s the social protection system was redesigned in generally desirable ways, and after 2002 more funds were allocated to these programs.

3.8 Conclusions

Kazakhstan at independence had a promising future in terms of strong fundamentals as a middle-income country well endowed with human capital and abundant natural resources. In the medium term, however, the country faced formidable difficulties associated with nation building and ethnic diversity. These heightened the potential

---

[49] These assessments are from Volume 1 of the World Bank report "Dimensions of poverty in Kazakhstan," Report No. 30294-KZ, November 9, 2004.

for oil and mineral wealth to be a curse rather than a blessing. The various elements are intertwined, as policy errors in the 1990s such as the flawed privatization of large enterprises and corrupt process of allocating oil and mineral exploitation rights hindered establishment of a well-functioning market economy and threatened to leave the country with a form of crony capitalism, which is inimical to equitable growth.

In the early twenty-first century the outlook began to appear more promising, as new oil discoveries, alternative pipeline routes and soaring oil prices fuelled an oil boom. Although the benefits were unevenly spread, the oil boom reversed the depressing economic picture of the 1990s and saw Kazakhstan pull away from its central Asian neighbors in economic prosperity, at least in the principle cities. By 2005 Almaty was noticeably more affluent than Tashkent or Bishkek. The political situation, however, remains opaque. President Nazarbayev won the 2005 election with over 90% of the votes. Opinion polls suggested that the president would have won a fair election, but the unwillingness to disavow vote rigging does not augur well.

The oil boom of the twenty-first century provides a golden opportunity to overcome the errors and missed opportunities of the 1990s. The immediate effect has been to increase incomes and resources available to the social sectors. Kazakhstan, which has long had higher per capita incomes than its Central Asian neighbors but which suffered anemic growth in the 1990s, has since 2000 become clearly the richest country in the region. The oil revenues will be beyond anybody's dreams of a decade earlier, but will they be used to promote long-term economic development and growth with equity or will they enrich a self-perpetuating elite who can prevent any political or institutional reform that will challenge their control of the revenue stream?

4

Tajikistan: Civil War and Its Aftermath

Tajikistan's political situation has been so unstable that it has dominated the country's economic development since independence. The open civil war of 1992–93 simmered on for several years before peace negotiations held in December 1996 and early 1997 led to the June 1997 Agreement on Peace and National Reconciliation. During this period about 50–100,000 people lost their lives and over half a million people were displaced as a result of warfare, mostly in the hot-war period of 1992–93 when atrocities were committed by all sides.[1] Even after the peace agreement the central government did not have full control over the territory, and until 2001 bandits were operating within 50 km of the capital city. Between 2001 and 2004 President Rakhmonov appeared to have stabilized his power, creating a powerful presidency with limited opposition, much as in the other Central Asian countries, but it had taken a decade longer in Tajikistan and the stability was less assured.

Political conditions meant that Tajikistan did not introduce a national currency until May 1995. The first serious reform program, with support from the international financial institutions, was only introduced in 1996 and this was partially reversed later in the year as the security situation deteriorated. Economic progress was massively disrupted by the civil war. Even after the 1997 peace agreement, the economy suffered from the 1998 Russian Crisis and from a cruel mix of floods and droughts in 1998–2000. In these conditions the economy went through dramatic decline during the 1990s, and Tajikistan was among the poorest countries in the world by the turn of the century. The rapid growth that could be expected in the recovery from civil war only really began in 2000, and even by 2003 GDP had only reached two-thirds of its 1989 level—by far the worst economic performance in Central Asia (Table 1.3).

The dire state of the national economy was illustrated by the growth of migrant labor in the early twenty-first century. Much of this movement, which is primarily to Russia, is undocumented, but estimates run as high as a million Tajiks working

---

[1] These are numbers commonly cited, but without documentation. The true numbers will never be known, especially in the early post-independence years when Tajikistan had no effective government and there were no outside observers in the country. The UNHCR estimated that 20–60,000 people died between June 1992 and February 1993, and that in this period 486,000 people left their homes, of which 90,000 fled to Afghanistan.

temporarily abroad, and remittances have become a major source of income for those remaining in the country.

4.1 The Political Background

Tajikistan is divided into distinct geographic areas, and regionalism has been a major feature of post-independence political history. The capital Dushanbe was predominantly a Russian city until the 1980s when rural–urban migration brought Tajiks into the city, and then in 1992–93 most of the Russians emigrated. The northern province of Sugd (formerly Leninabad) is the most economically developed part of the country, separated from the rest of the country by high mountains, which are impassable in winter. A road tunnel begun in the Soviet era remains unfinished, despite Iranian offers of financial and technical assistance.[2] The southern province of Khatlon was created in 1993 by amalgamating Kulyab and Qurgan Teppe; the latter had been developed as a cotton-producing area by major irrigation projects in the 1960s, and many workers from the poor mountain region of Gharm had been brought into the region to work on the cotton farms. The east of the country, including Gharm and the autonomous region of Gorno Badakhshan, is mountainous, sparsely populated, and only loosely under central government control.

The civil war that broke out as Soviet rule dissolved was a struggle for power with regional and ideological dimensions (Pomfret 1995, pp. 98–102). The incumbent leader, Rakhmon Nabiyev, represented the northern elite, which had dominated the Tajik Soviet republic since the 1930s in association with cadres from Kulyab.[3] The opposition consisted of Islamic parties and democratic forces opposed to neo-Communist rule, but it also had a regional dimension, with its main strength in Gharm, Gorno Badakhshan, and Qurgan Teppe. In May 1992, after seven weeks of demonstrations in Dushanbe, a coalition Government of National Reconciliation was announced. Nabiyev remained president, but he was ineffective and increasingly lived in the Russian garrison. The regional leaders in Khujand (Leninabad) and Kulyab openly declared that they would not accept the government's authority, and adopted the name Popular Front. By June, intercommunal differences between Popular Front and opposition supporters were being settled violently. In September

---

[2] Iranian interest in Tajikistan stems largely from the common linguistic roots in Farsi, in contrast to the Turkic languages of the other Central Asian countries' titular nationalities.

[3] Nabiyev, who had been first secretary of the Tajik Republic from 1982 to 1986, replaced his ineffectual successor, Kakhar Makhkamov, in a November 1991 election intended to consolidate the northern elite's grip on power. In January 1992, contrary to the pattern in all other former Soviet republics, the ruling party, which had renamed itself the Socialist Party of Tajikistan in September 1991, reverted to calling itself the Communist Party of Tajikistan. Akbarzadeh (1996) suggests that, if he had been more astute in hijacking the opposition's nationalist ideology, as other Central Asian leaders did in 1991–92, and less resistant to accepting the country's Islamic heritage (unlike President Karimov in Uzbekistan, he refused to swear the presidential oath on the Koran), Nabiyev might have survived. Nabiyev died in mysterious circumstances in May 1993. Akiner (2001) emphasizes the importance of the division of power whereby the northerners dominated politically and Kulyabis dominated the security services, because after civil war broke out the Presidential Guard would become more important than the president.

1992 the Popular Front conquered Qurgan Teppe, and in the same month Nabiyev was deposed as the opposition took formal control of the national government in Dushanbe. Pro-Nabiyev forces occupied Dushanbe in October, but were driven out again in two days. At a November meeting of the Supreme Soviet in the northern city of Khujand, a strongman from Kulyab, Emomali Rakhmanov, was chosen as the new leader. With the help of Russian and Uzbek troops, tanks, and military aircraft, forces loyal to Rakhmanov recaptured Dushanbe in December, and by the end of January 1993 the Popular Front was militarily victorious all over the country.

The viciousness of some civil war episodes reflected deep interregional hatreds.[4] The Gharmis who had moved to the cotton fields of Qurgan Teppe were resented by groups longer-established in the south, and some of the most bitter fighting and worst massacres of the war involved Kulyabis and Gharmis from Qurgan Teppe. The Badakhshanis were disliked and even hated by the dominant Leninabad/Kulyab group, who despised their dialect, considered their Ismaili brand of Islam heretical, and generally considered them to be barbarous mountain people. As a consequence of the rural–urban migration of the 1990s, the fighting within Dushanbe was largely between groups who related to their region of origin and were swept up by the Leninabad/Kulyab versus Gharm/Qurgan Teppe/Bhadakhshan rivalry.

The fighting subsided in 1993. The losers regrouped in northern Afghanistan as the United Tajik Opposition (UTO), and in spring 1994 negotiations began between the UTO and the government, although they moved slowly and were deadlocked in 1995–96. In September 1994 a UN-monitored cease-fire was arranged, and in November 1994 Rakhmonov was elected president. In 1995 many displaced people returned to their homes, and in early 1996 the government began to implement economic reforms. Later in 1996, however, renewed fighting broke out across the country. In December peace negotiations were resumed between the government and the UTO, and an agreement was finally signed in Moscow in June 1997.

The 1997 Agreement granted amnesty to the UTO members (and to fighters in the Popular Front, which supported President Rakhmonov), incorporated large numbers of those who had fought in the war into the national armed forces, and offered 30% of government posts at every level to the opposition. Many opposition members were, however, unhappy with the agreement and refused to join the post-1997 government, and many fighters refused to submit to the central government. In November 1998 an armed rebel force, led by a disaffected former Popular Front officer, invaded Tajikistan's northern province (Sugd) from Uzbekistan.[5] A decision

---

[4] A BBC correspondent in Central Asia, Monica Whitlock (2002, pp. 156–81), vividly describes the situation in the south and in Dushanbe between April 1992 and January 1993.

[5] The invasion was led by Makhmud Khudoberdyev, a Popular Front commander in the 1992 war and later an army colonel, who had turned against President Rakhmonov in 1997 and fled to Uzbekistan. The force of about 1,000 fighters briefly captured all administrative buildings in the regional capital of Khojand, before being repulsed. Gleason (2001, p. 1,094) cites official reports of 114 Tajik government troops and 220 rebels killed, 451 Tajik government troops and 215 rebels wounded, and 75 rebels taken prisoner. Although Uzbekistan's President Karimov condemned the attack, Tajikistan's government

by the government to demobilize 4,000 former opposition fighters in 2000 added to the problems as many of these former soldiers became unemployed and may have been tempted to join armed opposition forces or bandit gangs. In 2001 several high-ranking government officials and ministers were assassinated, including the deputy minister of the interior in April and the minister of culture in September, but this proved to be the zenith of armed opposition. Prominent rebel leaders were killed by government forces in 2001, and law and order was more or less restored by the end of 2001.

The outcomes of the 1999 presidential and 2000 parliamentary elections were viewed by opponents as consolidating the power of elites from the Kulyab district. Between 2001 and 2004 President Rakhmonov worked systematically to reduce the power of local warlords, including those in the Popular Front who had helped to put him in power in 1992. This process culminated dramatically with Ghaffor Mirzoyev, whose base is in Kulyab and who had been in charge of the Presidential Guard since 1995 until he was dismissed in January 2004.[6] The power of the main religious opposition group, the Islamic Renaissance Party (IRP), has also been undermined in recent years, despite the 1997 power-sharing agreement. In 2003 two IRP leaders were arrested on what appeared to be trumped-up charges and in 2004 they were sentenced to sixteen and nine years in prison.[7] Some reports emphasize that pressure on the IRP may have driven activists into more extreme Islamic organizations, including some ethnic Uzbeks as much opposed to the Karimov regime in Uzbekistan as to Tajikistan's President Rakhmonov (ICG 2004b, pp. 8–12).

The result of these political maneuvers has been a powerful presidency much as in the other Central Asian countries, but one which has been cemented almost a decade later than elsewhere and which may be more vulnerable to armed revolt. Since 2001 President Rakhmonov has tried to fill government posts with loyal supporters, often from his own village of Danghara (ICG 2004b, pp. 1–5). While the reduction in the power of warlords is good for governance, a narrower power base limits the available competent administrators and increases discontent among excluded regional groups, arousing fears that the civil war may be reignited.[8] A referendum in 2003 lifted the

---

accused Uzbekistan of being behind the plot and attempting to destabilize the Sugd region with its large ethnic Uzbek population.

[6] In January 2004 Mirzoyev was removed from his position as head of the national guard and reassigned to being head of the Tajik Drug Control Agency and chair of the Tajik Olympic Committee. On August 6, shortly before his scheduled departure to the Athens Olympics, he was arrested on nine charges including abuse of power, illegal possession of weapons, tax evasion, and murder. According to the BBC report, the accusations included using drug enforcement helicopters to ship heroin from Afghanistan and possession of a private armory, which included antiaircraft missiles.

[7] Shamsiddin Shamsiddinov, deputy chairperson of the IRP, was sentenced to sixteen years for serious crimes—including forming a criminal group, illegal border crossing, polygamy, murder, and treason— and another senior IRP member, Qurbon Rahimov, was sentenced to nine years for rape of a minor (although Rahimov was 61 and in poor health at the time of the alleged attack).

[8] The political situation is complex. Russia and Uzbekistan dress their intervention in terms of resisting Islamic fundamentalism, but the leader of the IRP, Abdullo Nuri, appears to be hamstrung by his commitment to a secular democratic state and his fears that opposing Rakhmonov will only lead to the

Table 4.1. Output of selected items in Tajikistan
1991, 1997, and 2002 (thousands of tonnes).

	1991	1997	2002
Seed cotton	826	175	516
Cotton lint	247	104	N/A
Wheat	153	559	701
Potatoes	181	128	357
Grapes	121	127	81
Rice	26	44	50
Barley	51	23	36
Maize	60	30	55
Coal	313	9	27
Petrol (crude)	100	26	16
Gas (millions of m^3)	93	42	33
Cement	1,013	36	89
Wheat flour	756	322	293
Aluminum	380	189	N/A

Source: Asia Development Bank data, reported in Sharma (2004, Table 9.2).

term limits on the president, allowing Rakhmonov to run for reelection in 2006 and to continue in office until 2020, when he will be seventy. Rakhmonov came to power as a regional warlord, but by 2004 appeared to have reinvented himself as a national leader without obligation to his regional base.

4.2 Economic Performance

Output fell drastically during the civil war period, 1992–97. Manufacturing output in 1997 was only 27% and agricultural output 50% of the 1990 level. The decline was especially large for products requiring any kind of marketing chain, such as cotton, coal, cement, or commercially milled flour, and less pronounced for home-consumed crops, such as wheat (Table 4.1). The post-1997 recovery was also uneven, with sectors like cotton regaining some but not all of the lost output, but other sectors such as coal and cement had not recovered five years later.

Especially during the war years 1992–97, the industrial sector was plagued by outright theft, not just of private property but especially of state property and even of bank assets (Umarov and Repkine 2004, p. 202). As the country was divided under competing armies, military authority was used to sell off enterprises and equipment; much of what was of any productive value left the country. The absence of new investment meant that any physical assets remaining by the end of the 1990s were likely to be obsolete or so poorly maintained as to be worthless. Destruction of the

complete sidelining of the IRP. The pro-democratic forces in the UTO have practically disappeared. The regional aspects of the civil war have left the opposition regions disaffected, but also groups in the formerly powerful north resent the victory of their former junior partners, the Kulyab-based southerners. The Mirzoyev affair suggests that by 2004 there may even be disaffected groups in Kulyab.

physical infrastructure was immense in some areas, especially Qurgan Teppe in the south and in Dushanbe and the surrounding Regions of Republican Subordination.

The only significant industrial enterprise to survive the 1990s was the aluminum smelter that had been built in the final years of the Soviet era as the centerpiece of the South Tajik Territorial Project. Although production was erratic and maintenance poor, the smelter survived as a prime earner of foreign currency and thus as the economic prize for the central government. Details of the aluminum industry are state secrets, but its significance is reflected in the share of nonferrous metals in total industrial output, which increased from 8% in 1991 to 31% in 1996, and 56% in 2000.[9]

Hydroelectric power, generated from the Nurek power station just south of the capital, also remains under central government control and is an important export. The exports go to Uzbekistan, mostly in barter arrangements for gas and electricity. Control over the power station and the barter earnings has enabled the government to use power supply as a political weapon, maintaining a degree of public support by charging low tariffs, and by lax collection. These quasi-fiscal activities were, however, adjusted in 2002 as utility tariffs were raised and collection rates increased.

In contrast, the central government has lost control over the cotton sector, and considerable liberalization has taken place. Farmers are free to sell their cotton directly to foreign buyers. The cotton ginneries were completely privatized in 2001. In practice, however, in the two main cotton-growing regions, Khatlon (60% of output) and Sugd (30%), local officials use their control over inputs to enforce output quotas, which are sold through them at artificially low prices (Luong 2004b, p. 221), raising revenue at the local level in much the same way as the central government has done in Uzbekistan.

Trade in drugs and weapons is rampant, linked to perhaps 30–50% of all economic activity. One aspect of these quasi-legal or outright illegal activities is the participation of many officials, which undermines the rule of law and contributes to the country's poor governance. The social consequences will be analyzed in Section 4.4 below.

4.3 Economic Policies

More than elsewhere it is important to distinguish between legislation and statements of principle on the one hand and actual progress in reforming the centrally planned economy on the other hand. Liberalization of domestic prices and foreign exchange was fairly rapid and extensive in 1992, but rather than a conscious policy of big bang transition this reflected loss of government control in the most severe part of the civil

---

[9] Official data from the Tajik Statistical Committee, reported in Umarov and Repkine (2004, p. 203). Aluminum output in the 1990s is understated because hundreds of tonnes were smuggled out of the country under the protection of bribed officials. The only other functioning nonferrous metal activity in 2000 was a small gold mine.

war.[10] Macroeconomic stabilization was exceptionally slow. Tajikistan continued to use the Soviet ruble even after all other countries abandoned the currency in 1993, and the elsewhere worthless Soviet banknotes ended up in Tajikistan. Inflation was still over 400% in 1994, by which time most Soviet successor states had seriously addressed hyperinflation. A national currency was finally introduced in May 1995, but the Tajik ruble depreciated rapidly. Only in October 2000, after replacement of the Tajik ruble by the somoni, was inflation brought down to the reasonable level of 12% in 2002.

Privatization was much slower than elsewhere, with small-scale privatization only completed in 1999 (Umarov and Repkine 2004, p. 208). Privatization of medium and large enterprises only really began in 1998, and proceeded slowly. However, as mentioned earlier, much spontaneous, forced, or illegal privatization took place. In agriculture, privatization probably occurred faster than elsewhere in Central Asia because the war situation disrupted supplies to state farms. Presidential decrees authorizing privatization of land reflected both recognition of the actual situation and a way of encouraging farm production. In retail trade, which is almost entirely privatized, the main development was the emergence of new enterprises, especially the shuttle traders whose activities were legalized in 1996 and who accounted for three-quarters of employment in the retail-trade sector by 1999 (Umarov and Repkine 2004, p. 210). In both agriculture and trade, however, the new production units struggled in the face of declining domestic demand and their lack of access to credit, as well as the considerable government regulations imposed on small and medium-sized enterprises.

Trade policy has been liberal, but even low tariffs are often evaded. In the 1996 reforms, remaining export taxes, export surrender requirements, and export and import licenses were abolished. Between 1999 and 2002 import tariffs fell by three-fifths, and in 2002 they were unified at 5% with few exceptions. In 2001 Tajikistan applied to join the WTO. There was a minor reversal in 2003, when the government sought to align its tariffs with those of other members of the Eurasian Economic Community and this led to an increase in the average tariff from 5% to 7.7%. In 2004 the government removed the final restrictions on currency convertibility for current-account transactions. The extent of evasion is by its nature unknown, but under-invoicing of imports is believed to cost the government $250–300 million per year in lost revenue.

Foreign debt was a major problem in the first decade after independence, and by the end of 2002 the debt amounted to $982 million, or 82.3% of GDP.[11] About four-fifths of the total external debt is public or publicly guaranteed, and 45% of this portion is multilateral. Much of the bilateral debt was incurred from Russian assistance during the civil war. In December 2002 debt owed to Russia, the largest

---

[10] State orders for cotton were formally ended before the 1996 crop.

[11] Data in this paragraph are from the IMF's "Republic of Tajikistan," IMF Country Report No. 04/17, January 2004.

creditor with 65% of Tajikistan's bilateral debt, was restructured, and arrangements were also made with other bilateral creditors. Combined with faster growth, this reduced the debt/GDP ratio to 72.8% by the end of 2003. A larger debt-reduction step occurred during the October 2004 visit by Russian President Vladimir Putin, who wrote off a large part of the bilateral debt in return for military-base rights in Tajikistan. Multilateral debt was mostly incurred after the end of the civil war. At the May 2003 Consultative Group meeting, donors pledged $900 million over the next three years, twice the amount pledged over the previous cycle, but disbursements are conditional on improved reform implementation.

Increased foreign remittances and higher prices for the traditional exports of cotton and aluminum helped to promote growth in 2003, but merchandise exports were running into obstacles due to the poor transport infrastructure and border restrictions. The physical infrastructure, massively destroyed during the civil war, is in a terrible state, exacerbated by worsening interstate relations with Uzbekistan, through which all international rail and much road transport must pass.[12] In 2004 there were long delays at road borders. In winter the road from Dushanbe to Khujand is impassible (and even in summer it is in poor shape), so that much of the overland transport between the country's two largest cities must pass via Uzbekistan. All flights between Tajikistan and Uzbekistan have been suspended, and people in Khujand wishing to travel abroad were in 2004 making the four to five hour road trip to Batken's airport in the Kyrgyz Republic. New road links to northwest China and northern Afghanistan are expected to provide some minor relief from this constraint in the second half of the decade.

Nevertheless, good trade policies and improved transport infrastructure will only have a positive impact on trade flows and economic growth if the government reduces the red tape that boosts the costs of international trade. The multiple border checks on trucks entering Tajikistan include requirements for sixteen to twenty inspections and documents, some of which are little more than excuses for the inspectors to collect bribes. The requirement that every imported good must satisfy national standards applies even to imports like Mercedes cars, which are individually inspected for quality at the border entry point. Failure to harmonize standards even within organizations like the Eurasian Economic Union mean that medicines from India or China, which have met Russian or Kazakhstan's standards, are still required to satisfy Tajikistan's standards.

---

[12] Uzbekistan's transit regulations have also caused problems. Tajikistan's wine and grape exports have been destroyed by a requirement that the full value of the shipment must be deposited when the goods enter Uzbekistan; during the 1990s the deposit was often not returned by the Uzbekistan government, which retained it in lieu of delinquent debt repayments by Tajikistan. Imports, such as natural gas from Turkmenistan, are also affected by Uzbekistan's transit policies, to the extent that in 2004 Turkmenistan and Tajikistan were considering a gas pipeline route via northern Afghanistan in order to bypass Uzbekistan.

4.4 Social Indicators and the Quality of Life

Social indicators in the Tajik Republic tended to be the worst in the Soviet Union, but in many respects they have declined substantially since then. Declining standards of education and health-care provision have especially hurt the poor, as the better off can afford to pay to obtain better services. Social protection measures had become ineffective by the end of the 1990s, and pensions had fallen to about a third of the value of salaries.

As in other successor states kindergarten provision declined; preschool enrolment rates dropped from 16% in 1989 to 5.5% in 2000. More distinctively, the proportion of 15–18 year olds enrolled in education fell from 40% in 1989 to 23% in 2000, a rate matched only by Moldova among Soviet successor states (Falkingham 2004, p. 163). Many school buildings are in poor condition. A World Bank survey of 1,845 schools found that a quarter of them lacked heating, a quarter were without water supply, and over a third without toilets.[13] The Soviet-era curriculum was largely unchanged during the 1990s, and curriculum reform has been hampered by lack of funds to purchase textbooks.[14] The four institutions for teacher retraining were, in 2003, closed for lack of funds, and there is an estimated shortage of 10,000 teachers at all levels.[15]

As elsewhere in Central Asia, Tajikistan inherited the Soviet health system, which was comprehensive but centralized and inefficient. The civil war accentuated the gap between the inherited structure and a desirable structure, as Tajikistan appeared to have an oversupply of hospitals, beds and even trained personnel, but with an almost complete absence of medical equipment, supplies and pharmaceuticals (World Bank 2000, p. 9).

Lack of infrastructure investment or maintenance has left the country exposed to natural disasters. Pumping stations are clogged with silt and pipes are corroded, to the extent that the poor quality of drinking water contributed to a typhoid outbreak in Dushanbe in October 2003.[16] After heavy rain in July 2004 led to flooding of the Varzob River, the main source of water for Dushanbe, the government sent vehicles around the capital broadcasting advice not to drink or bathe in the polluted water coming out of household taps.[17] Typhoid outbreaks have also occurred outside the capital (e.g., in the village of Kolkhozabad 120 km south of Dushanbe more than

---

[13] Another survey of Khatlon found that over half of the schools did not have access to water; see the government's 2003 progress report on Tajikistan's Poverty Reduction Strategy, available as IMF Country Report 04/280, August 2004, p. 29.

[14] The problem was exacerbated in Uzbek-speaking areas of the country because new books from Uzbekistan use the Latin script while Tajikistan retains the Cyrillic script.

[15] This number is from the government's 2003 progress report on Tajikistan's Poverty Reduction Strategy, available as IMF Country Report 04/280, August 2004, p. 30.

[16] Previous typhoid outbreaks in 1997, which infected 8,900 people of whom 95 died, and in 2002 also appear to have been due to contaminated drinking water.

[17] Konstantin Parshin, "Floods fuel concern about Public Health Crisis in Tajikistan," *Eurasia Insight*, posted at www.eurasianet.org on July 16, 2004.

fifty people contracted typhoid in late 2004), but these cases are less likely to make the news headlines.

The 1999 Tajikistan Living Standards Survey, based on the LSMS methodology described in more detail in Chapter 7, revealed the greatest inequality and the highest levels of poverty in Central Asia. The Gini coefficient for per capita expenditure was 0.47, slightly higher than the Kyrgyz Republic's 0.46 and much higher than Kazakhstan's 0.35 or Tajikistan's own 0.31 in 1989 (Table 1.1).[18] Poverty rates depend on the poverty line used, but with a benchmark of 15,111 Tajik rubles (roughly equal to the poverty line of $2.15 at purchasing power parity that is frequently used in transition economies) 65.4% of the population was living in poverty. There were large variations between the most poverty-stricken regions (GBAO and Khatlon) and those with the fewest poor (Dushanbe and the RRS).

Poverty and social disintegration have contributed to a major drugs problem. With 1,400 km of porous borders with Afghanistan, Tajikistan has become, since the early 1990s, a major transport route for opium, and more recently heroin. The civil war provided a fertile ground for the drugs trade as the competing factions financed their military activities from drug money, and this continued after the 1997 peace agreement. In 2000, following a crackdown by the Taliban regime, opium production plummeted in Afghanistan, but the harvest rebounded rapidly after the fall of the Taliban regime, from 16 tonnes in 2001 to 3,600 tonnes in 2003 (equivalent to about 300 tonnes of heroin, worth as much as $30 billion in western markets). According to UN estimates, this was about three-quarters of the world's opium production, and with tightened security on the borders of Iran and Pakistan the majority passes though Central Asia, mostly via Tajikistan and then the Kyrgyz Republic.[19] In Dushanbe heroin cost $1,500–6,000 per kilogram, depending on quality, while in Europe the price is $30–100,000 per kilogram and as much as $300,000 at retail. Huge potential profits plus poverty have brought many Tajiks into the drug trade, and as much as a third of the population is thought to be dependent on the drug trade.

Most of the local traffickers are paid in kind, creating about 20,000 addicts in Dushanbe alone. Street prices, with low-grade heroin available in Dushanbe for $2 a dose, are low enough to displace vodka, but high enough to lead addicts into crime. Women and girls have been especially used as couriers, because they were thought to appear less suspicious; negative consequences include increasing abuse of females at borders, criminalization of females, and transition to people-trafficking for the sex trade. Another negative consequence of the burgeoning drugs trade is the spread of HIV, whose primary mode of infection in Central Asia is intravenous drug injection. The ambivalent attitude of the authorities—who on the one hand support nongovernmental organizations' distribution of clean syringes but on the other hand often treat drug-takers as criminals subject to police harassment—has led to the lack of a consistent policy, and uncontrolled, and unmonitored, spread of

---

[18] The Kyrgyz and Kazakhstan Ginis are from their 1996 LSMS surveys (see World Bank 2000, p. 19).

[19] There is also an important drug route through Turkmenistan, but data on that are extremely sparse.

HIV. The government's official position is strict, with heavy penalties, including the death penalty, for participating in the drug trade, but high officials are among the participants.[20]

Another symptom of economic failure is the massive emigration, especially of males seeking temporary work abroad, mainly in Russia but from about 2004 also to Kazakhstan. Since many of the workers have a precarious legal status and fear repatriation, their numbers are difficult to assess, but estimates of the number of Tajiks working in Russia in 2002 are around 800,000, sending remittances of $400 million to their families back home—an amount exceeding the government's budget.[21] Tajik workers in Russia have been subjected to frequent crackdowns, in part due to local resentment of foreigners but sometimes as part of national policy. In November 2002 high-profile summary deportation of two hundred Tajiks by military aircraft, in flagrant disregard of the 2000 bilateral agreement on visa-free travel, appeared to be connected with Tajikistan's improved relations with the United States after September 11, 2001. The Tajik government is in a difficult position: because so many of its citizens depend upon remittances to make ends meet, they do whatever they can to ease the way for migrant workers, making official protests to Russia against the deportations or lack of rights for temporary workers and trying to facilitate the movement of workers, e.g., in January 2003 passenger rail fares to Russia were cut by about a sixth. The continuing importance of good relations with Russia were underlined in March 2003, when Tajikistan's government was the only one in Central Asia to criticize U.S. military action against Iraq.

4.5 Conclusions

Tajikistan's rapid growth in the five years after 1999, ongoing reforms, and much-improved internal security are all positive signs. On the other hand, Tajikistan remains the poorest country in Central Asia, and many problems remain acute. The economy relies heavily on earnings from aluminum and cotton exports (which accounted for 55% and 28% of total export earnings in 2003), and the only other serious potential foreign exchange earner is hydroelectricity. Institutional change has been slow, and governance remains poor. The physical infrastructure, heavily damaged by civil war, is still in poor shape. Social collapse is highlighted by the drug problem and the migration which both divide the once-strong family structure.

The severity of the economic problem is reflected in the extent to which Russia was able to gain control of the country in 2004. In October 2004 President Putin agreed to write off $240 million of the $300 million owed to Russia in return for a

---

[20] Tajikistan's ambassador to Kazakhstan was twice caught carrying substantial quantities of heroin into Kazakhstan before being expelled ("At the crossroads: a survey of Central Asia," *The Economist*, July 26, 2003, p. 15.

[21] Figures reported in "Russia, Tajikistan spar over illegal labor migration," posted at www.eurasianet. org on January 9, 2003.

permanent Russian base and control over Soviet-era antimissile facilities in Tajik-istan. At the same time, large Russian companies undertook what were essentially cash-for-shares moves to gain control over some of the commanding heights of the economy; Rusal undertook to invest $600 million in an aluminum smelter and $560 in the Rugun hydro dam, and Unified Energy System (UES) committed to invest $250 million in the Sangtuda hydro dam with an agreement to invest a further $480 million. These numbers should be seen in the context of a country whose GDP at market prices was little over one billion dollars.

5

The Kyrgyz Republic:
The Region's Rapid Reformer

The Kyrgyz Republic was one of the poorest of the Soviet republics. The economy was not highly industrialized, but much of the industry that the republic did have was tightly integrated into the Soviet military–industrial complex, which left the republic especially vulnerable after the dissolution of the USSR. The largest single enterprise was a sugar refinery which owed its existence to Soviet foreign assistance and regional policy; once transportation costs were taken into account and Cuba was abandoned, it made no sense to be refining sugarcane in the southeast part of Central Asia for distribution across the former Soviet economic space. Dissolution of the USSR left the sugar refinery and many of the military-related factories high and dry. The economy during the 1990s was characterized by substantial urban–rural migration as town dwellers returned to their family villages, and by the reemergence of subsistence and informal activities.

The options available to the newly independent Kyrgyzstan—the names Kyrgyzstan and Kyrgyz Republic, the country's official name since 1999, will be used interchangeably in this book—were limited. Its main natural resource is the water flowing down from some of the world's highest mountains, but harnessing this for hydroelectricity generation requires large investments with long payback periods and grids to take the electricity to reliable markets. In practice, during the 1990s, water only led to quarrels with downstream neighbors, who needed it for irrigation but were unaccustomed to paying anything like an economic price for water. The single exploitable resource was gold in the Kumtor mine, which came to play a dominant part in the monetized economy after production came on stream in 1997, but whose physical life is limited.[1]

Whether due to limited options or to the chance event that the incumbent leader had come from the Academy of Science rather than through the Communist administrative hierarchy as in the other Central Asian countries, the Kyrgyz Republic had by 1993 become the most liberal country in the region and the one most closely aligned with the "Washington Consensus" view of transition advocated by the IMF

---

[1] The mining industry also produces some nonferrous metals (antimony, mercury, rare earth), and there are undeveloped deposits of gold, tin, tungsten, and other metals. Coal deposits and possible oil fields remain unexplored.

and the World Bank. In May 1993 the Kyrgyz Republic became the first Central Asian country to leave the ruble zone and issue its own national currency, and thereafter it was the first to bring hyperinflation under control. Its price and trade reforms were the most sweeping in Central Asia, and in 1998 it became the first of all the Soviet successor states, including the Baltic countries, to accede to the WTO.

The results were not as good as expected, even though the economy began to register positive growth in 1997. Inequality had increased and poverty was widespread. The adverse costs of rapid loss of purchasing power are illustrated by Howell's (1996a,b) harrowing picture from the southern provinces of the Kyrgyz Republic of families cutting down fruit trees, slaughtering livestock, and keeping children out of school in order to maintain subsistence consumption levels. The economy was hurt by the 1998 Russian Crisis and by a concomitant domestic banking crisis. During the late 1990s reforms were put on hold.

The major source of the economic problems was the failure to create an environment in which market forces could produce socially desirable outcomes. Despite formal progress in establishing institutions related to the rule of law and other market-supporting institutions, in practice, market-unfriendly institutions such as the importance of personal contacts and the ubiquity of corruption dominated.[2] In the public sector, the initially tolerant president resorted to ruling by decree when he encountered obstacles in the mid-1990s. Subsequent elections, while not as outrageously manipulated as in Turkmenistan or Uzbekistan, were not fair.

Macroeconomic management was also flawed, as price stability was achieved without bringing the budget deficit under control. Assistance from multilateral institutions, by far the highest in Central Asia, was being used to support current consumption rather than to generate future growth. An economic crisis was triggered in 1998 by the Russian Crisis and Kazakhstan's subsequent devaluation, and by domestic bank failures. This was followed by currency depreciation, import contraction and fiscal adjustment in 2000–01, scaling back of external borrowing, and a 2002 debt restructuring by the Paris Club.

After the turn of the century, with a more sustainable macroeconomic policy, reforms were resumed, especially in areas of deregulation and reduction in bureaucratic red tape. Economic growth was not smooth, but it was higher in 2000–04 than it had been in 1998–99. Economic recovery was helped by robust growth in Russia and Kazakhstan, and after 2000 labor migration to those two countries and workers' remittances became significant. Nevertheless, popular frustration remained strong. Although President Akayev himself was not seen to be profiting as blatantly

---

[2] In the 1999 BEEPS survey, on the headline measure of perception of corruption as an obstacle to doing business, Kyrgyzstan was rated the worst of the twenty transition economies covered—and this was in the face of serious competition for the wooden spoon from war-torn and failed states such as Georgia, Moldova, Bosnia, and Romania. In the 2002 survey, which covered twenty-six transition countries, Kyrgyzstan moved up to sixteenth place on the same measure, but it still ranked below the three other Central Asian countries (Uzbekistan, Kazakhstan, and Tajikistan) in the survey (see Gray et al. 2004, p. 12).

as Nazarbayev in Kazakhstan, the president's family, especially his daughter and son-in-law, were perceived to be benefiting economically from their political connections. The frustration also had a regional dimension in a country divided by high mountains: in the poorer southern part of the country, people complained that the political system favored northern groups closer to the president. When political unrest mounted in March 2005 it began in the south, but it became a national phenomena, dubbed the "tulip revolution." After President Akayev resigned, agreement was reached between the leading opposition leaders from the south (Kurmanbek Bakiyev) and the north (Feliks Kulov) to run on a common ticket in the July 2005 election.

5.1 Creating a Market Economy

The Kyrgyz Republic was the most explicit of the Central Asian countries, and to some extent of all former Soviet republics, in following the transition from central planning advocated by the IMF and the World Bank. After initial hesitation in early 1992, the government adopted a big bang approach to price liberalization and macroeconomic stabilization. Practically all price controls were rapidly removed, apart from those on public transport, electricity, and municipal services.[3] International trade was liberalized as export controls were removed, and trade barriers were low.

In 1990–91 the Kyrgyz Republic suffered from a substantial decline in transfers from within the USSR, and it had few domestic sources of funding for public spending. In the early 1990s the fiscal deficit was financed by inflation, but by early 1993 it was being supported by foreign aid. Inflation was brought down fairly rapidly, although as mentioned above this was largely done by relying on foreign assistance to cover the budget deficit rather than by establishing a sustainable fiscal balance. Nevertheless, the general budget deficit was reduced from a peak of 17% of GDP in 1995 to 9% in 1996, although it edged back up to 10–11% of GDP in 1999–2000 (Mogilevsky and Hasanov 2004, p. 227).

The extent of the real decline in public spending is difficult to measure given the hyperinflation and monetary disorder of the early 1990s, but it was huge. In U.S. dollar terms, the value of public spending fell by 90% between 1991 and 2000.[4] The government tried to cushion the impact of reduced direct support via social policies or subsidies for state-owned enterprises and consumer goods by relaxing pricing of public services such as district heating,[5] gas, public transport, water, irrigation,

---

[3] Many services were, however, not paid for, so the presence or absence of price controls was irrelevant. The electricity monopoly, for example, estimated nonpayment of around 40%.

[4] This is the preferred measure in World Bank (2004, Volume I, p. 13) and, although it suffers from questions about the appropriate ruble–dollar exchange rate in 1991, it is perhaps the best measure of change according to a fairly stable unit of account.

[5] District heating is the supply of heating to urban buildings from a central boiler. The system inherited from the Soviet era is extremely inefficient, often running through uninsulated pipes. In the Kyrgyz

and electricity. These quasi-fiscal operations increased, especially in 1995–97 when there was some reform fatigue in the country. The subsidies to users of the public services took the form of discounts and lax collection, as well as noneconomic pricing. They were funded by running down assets and accounting sleight of hand.[6] The imputed cost of these quasi-fiscal activities, according to World Bank (2004) estimates, peaked at 17% of GDP in 1999. Understandable as such subterfuges might have been in the situation of rising poverty and general economic hardship, adding new price distortions to the economy and running down infrastructure assets was neither desirable nor sustainable.

Privatization was fairly rapid. Housing and small enterprises were mainly transferred to current occupiers and operators. Large and medium-sized enterprises were transferred into private ownership through a voucher scheme. By the end of the 1990s the private sector was producing three-fifths of GDP.[7] The relative ease of privatization in the Kyrgyz Republic was assisted by the lack of valuable assets to be contested. Even among the small enterprises privatized in the early transition years, most failed to survive for more than two years (Anderson and Pomfret 2001). By far the largest and most successful enterprise in the country is the Kumtor gold mine, which was developed as a joint venture between Cameco of Canada, which had the necessary expertise, and the government. Among the few other dynamic enterprises, the most successful retailing and media were associated with the president's family, who were believed to have received special privileges.

Agrarian reform was more difficult because of population pressure on the land and suspicion of the creation of a rich peasant (*kulak*) class. Various measures of arable land per person in the late Soviet era all indicate population pressure in rural Central Asia, but an added problem in the Kyrgyz Republic was the regional variation. Irrigated land per person was much less in the southern districts of Jalalabad and Osh than in the mountain areas or the northern districts (Table 5.1). A further complication in the south was the ethnic tensions over land: the worst outbreak of violence in Central Asia during the Gorbachev era followed a reallocation in 1990 of land tilled by ethnic Uzbeks to ethnic Kyrgyz, and several hundred people were killed in the ensuing interethnic riots.

Nevertheless, reform did proceed as the state farms were dismantled, and the approximately 500 collective and state farms averaging over 2,500 hectares per farm at the time of independence have been replaced by over 60,000 farms averaging

---

Republic it is mainly significant for Bishkek and Osh, and covers a diminishing proportion of households. The best solution is to allow the system to atrophy, but there is an equity issue as the decrepit district heating network is increasingly left serving poor urban dwellers who cannot afford to purchase alternative sources of heating for their homes.

[6] The largest quasi-fiscal operations concerned electricity provision by the state monopoly supplier Kyrgyzenergo. During the late 1990s income from releasing water to the downstream countries, Kazakhstan and Uzbekistan, was treated as revenue to Kyrgyzenergo, rather than as state revenue from exporting a public resource.

[7] These are the rounded figures quoted in EBRD Transition Reports. In the Kyrgyz Republic the extensive unofficial sector makes it likely that the private share was even larger.

Table 5.1.   Land resources and population by oblast
in the Kyrgyz Republic, January 1, 1995.

	Total land (thousands of ha)	Cultivable land (thousands of ha)	Irrigated land (thousands of ha)	Rural population (thousands)	Cultivable land per person (3/5)	Irrigated land per person (4/5)
Jalalabad	2,791.9	159.1	6.7	820.5	0.19	0.12
Issyk-Kul	4,390.7	187.8	136.8	418.5	0.45	0.33
Naryn	4,411.8	133.0	110.9	261.7	0.51	0.42
Osh	4,208.1	259.2	129.2	1,408.5	0.18	0.09
Talas	1,443.9	120.0	88.9	202.4	0.59	0.44
Chui	2,428.8	446.9	273.1	745.5	0.60	0.37
Kyrgyz Rep.	19,674.8	1,306.0	835.6	3,857.1	0.34	0.22

Source: Bloch and Rasmussen (1998, p. 115), based on national official data.

about 20 hectares per farm (World Bank 2004, Volume II, p. 130). By early 2002 about half of the arable land was cultivated by individual farmers, a fifth was owned individually but managed under a reformed collective structure, a quarter was held by the community-based Land Distribution Fund, and the remaining 5% was in the hands of about twenty state research farms (Cord et al. 2004, p. 177).[8] The successor organizations operated at first with long-term leases. Following a 1998 referendum, private land ownership was legalized, but a five-year moratorium was placed on transactions involving land. By 2003 land was private property in a meaningful sense, and a land market was functioning.

The general problem in the 1990s was the lack of preparedness for the transition to a market economy. This was, of course, true to some extent in all formerly centrally planned economies, but Frunze, as the republic's capital was then known, was a particularly sleepy and backward Soviet capital. Attempting a big bang transition was far more fraught in this setting than in Warsaw or Prague or than in Tallinn or Moscow. Mogilevsky and Hasanov (2004, pp. 228–29) provide evidence on one symptom: the legal instability. They show that the lack of experience of policymakers, administrators, lawyers, and others led to laws quickly needing redrafting, and the subsequent legal uncertainty is especially acute for legislation directly affecting enterprises and business.

Licensing and certification requirements remained prevalent, increasing the costs of doing business. The banking system also remained weak. In 1998–99, when growth, which seemed to have been reestablished in 1996–97, slowed to 2–4%,

---

[8] Giovarelli (1998) reports very large differences in productivity between individually owned and state or collective farms: although the two groups each cultivated about half of the ploughed land by 1996, the individual farms' output was worth 12.25 billion sum, while that of the state and collective farms was worth 3.05 billion sum. This may partly reflect the geographical pattern of ownership, with individual farms dominant in the fertile Chui Valley in the north and state and collective farms dominant in the poorer south (Mudahar 1998, pp. 45–46).

the main symptom of economic problems in the Kyrgyz Republic was the failure of three of the four largest banks. Banking-sector assets fell from $160 million before the crisis to $90 million by the end of 2000 (Pomfret 2004, p. 89). The August 1998 Russian Crisis was one trigger, but the banks' weak balance sheets were also related to their relationship with Kyrgyzenergo and the uncertain status of that company's balance sheet due to the government's quasi-fiscal operations. When the banking system was restructured in the early 2000s, it was dominated by banks from Kazakhstan.

The aftermath of the 1998–99 banking crisis saw an apparent slowdown in major reforms, but more importantly the government addressed the underlying macro-economic imbalances. Between 1999 and 2001 the general government deficit was reduced from 11% of GDP to 5% of GDP, and the quasi-fiscal deficit was reduced from an estimated 16% to 7% of GDP (World Bank 2004, Volume I, p. 10). The latter reduction was associated with important structural reform, especially in energy supply. Electricity tariffs were increased by over a fifth in each year from 2000 to 2002, and at the same time the number of users eligible for special tariff reductions was reduced and the tariff structure was modified to mitigate the impact on the poor.[9] In 2001 the government divided Kyrgyzenergo into a generating company, a transmission company, and four distribution companies in order to increase transparency. The subsequent increase in aggregate reported losses highlighted the complexity of the preexisting in-kind collection and offsets by which the distribution segments had been deprived of capital in order to focus limited funds on maintaining upstream facilities.

5.2   Developments in the Real Economy

The initial transition period was characterized by substantial economic decline and deindustrialization. In the 1992–95 period, Kyrgyzstan was exporting machinery and equipment, while the output of the machine-building sector declined sevenfold (Mogilevsky and Hasanov 2004, p. 233), reflecting the destruction of the nation's physical capital stock. During the 1990s private investment was small, apart from a spike in 1995–97 associated with the Kumtor gold mine. This reflected low domestic savings rates and failure to attract DFI, apart from this single project. Starting in 1999 public investment began to increase as the World Bank, Asian Development Bank, and other donors funded the Public Investment Programme, which financed infrastructure spending on roads (especially the Bishkek–Osh road connecting the north and south of the country), irrigation systems, and electricity transmission lines.

The workforce also declined over the 1990s. The population growth rate declined from 2.0% per year in 1979–89 to 1.2% in 1989–2001, due to a decline in the birth rate, from 3.0 in 1989 to 2.0 in 2001, and to emigration. Between 1989 and 1999,

---

[9] Nevertheless, the average billed tariff in 2002 was still no more than half of the cost-recovery level (Pomfret 2004, p. 96).

Table 5.2. Kyrgyz Republic labor force data, 1989 and 1999 (thousands).

	1989	1999
Population	4,290.4	4,850.7
Working-age population (WAP)	2,118.1	2,541.4
Labor force (LF)	1,795.0	2,006.9
Participation rate (WAP divided by LF)	84.7%	79.0%
Unemployment rate (percentage of LF)	3.1%	14.4%
Workforce employed	1,738.6	1,717.9

Source: Mogilevsky and Hasanov (2004, p. 241), based on Kyrgyz National Statistical Committee data.

393,500 people, 8.6% of the population, emigrated. Although part of the emigration reflected a desire of ethnic minorities to move to countries where their ethnic group was the majority, much of the emigration and the decline in the birth rate was driven by economic motives. The nature of the population change meant that the share of working-age people increased, as a disproportionate number of elderly people emigrated and fewer children were born. At the same time participation rates fell, from 85% in 1989 to 79% in 1999, reflecting some voluntary return to the household (some of this was also involuntary because provision of kindergarten services declined), and workers commuting to jobs in Kazakhstan or Russia.[10] The official data reported in Table 5.2 show that despite a larger working-age population in 1999 than in 1989, due to the lower participation rates and increased unemployment, the number of people actually employed was slightly lower in 1999 than a decade earlier. The number of hours worked may have declined even more because of the practice of including part-time workers among those employed.[11]

The rise of the unofficial economy makes it difficult to measure the actual employment situation. The official unemployment figures understate the number of people losing their jobs, because low benefits and strict eligibility conditions weaken the incentives to register as unemployed (Babetski and Maurel 2002).[12] Especially during the mid-1990s and during the 1998 crisis, people resorted to informal employment in services or street trading, and many turned to subsistence farming as a coping mechanism. The phenomenon of urban–rural emigration may be interpreted as a correction to the overindustrialization of the Soviet era or as a symptom of the relatively good performance of the agricultural sector in the post-Soviet era. Between 1996 and 2000 the only two sectors in which employment increased were

---

[10] Unless otherwise stated, figures in this paragraph are from Mogilevsky and Hasanov (2004).

[11] In the Soviet era people classified as full-time workers may have worked less than part-time workers a decade later. According to an old joke, in some Soviet factories the managers pretended to pay the workers, and the workers pretended to work.

[12] One sign of the reporting bias in the official unemployment data is the position of the capital, Bishkek, which has consistently had one of the highest unemployment rates in the country. Other evidence, and casual observation, suggests that people in Bishkek were the best off in the post-Soviet economy (see Chapter 8).

agriculture and trade and catering, while employment fell by a fifth or more in industry, construction, and transport (Babetskii et al. 2003, p. 502). The trade sector continued to flourish in the early 2000s, as shuttle traders brought consumer goods from China and elsewhere not just for the domestic market but also to be shipped on to Uzbekistan, where the shuttle trade is more tightly controlled. There is also anecdotal evidence of small businesses producing for export: such as the tailors who make suits for eastern Russia at competitive prices and of better quality than suits from China and other low-wage countries. The evidence is anecdotal because the small businesses only survive by remaining unofficial and untaxed.

Despite the large decline in industrial employment, industrial output grew by nearly 50% between 1996 and 2000, which was almost entirely due to the Kumtor gold mine. The aggregate rate of economic growth remains sensitive to this single enterprise; when a landslide shut down the mine in 2002, GDP growth dropped to zero, recovering in 2003 after the mine reopened. Kumtor is one of the world's largest gold mines, with estimated deposits of around 700 tonnes. The operating agreement negotiated with Cameco of Canada after December 1992 led to sub-stantial foreign investment in 1995–97 and production began in 1997.[13] Although Kumtor is the most obvious sign of productive activity in the Kyrgyz Republic, there have been concerns about how much it has benefited the country. The returns to Cameco were front-loaded, which is not atypical of this kind of capital-intensive operation, but domestic critics assert that the country gained little benefit. A finan-cial restructuring of the joint venture in June 2004 that created a new company listed on the Toronto Stock Exchange, Canterra, was politically controversial in the Kyrgyz Republic, with accusations that high officials were personally benefiting.[14] The mine's environmental impact has also come in for criticism, with accusations of cover-ups following a truck crash spilling two tonnes of cyanide into the Barzum River in May 1998 and other hazardous materials spills in July 1998 and in January 2000.

Hydroelectricity accounts for 10–15% of exports, but other energy sources have to be imported. The fundamental arrangement is that the Kyrgyz Republic releases water when it is required for irrigation in the downstream countries, in return for which Kazakhstan and Uzbekistan guarantee energy supplies in the winter months. These arrangements were enforced by Moscow before 1992 but have become sources of dispute since the dissolution of the USSR. Ostensibly, the Kyrgyz Republic holds strong cards by virtue of its control over the flow of water, the ultimate scarce

---

[13] The decision to involve a foreign investor was technologically driven. Soviet geologists had discov-ered Kumtor in 1978, but determined that the low recovery rates made it infeasible. Cameco's December 1992 feasibility study was based on cyanide heap leaching technology, which can profitably process ores containing as little as 0.01 troy ounces per tonne. The estimated production costs at Kumtor are around $200 per ounce.

[14] The Kyrgyz Republic held a two-thirds interest in the original Kumtor joint venture. This was turned into a 27% share of Canterra. Shortly after the Canterra initial public offering the Kyrgyz government sold 7.5 million shares, reducing its holding to 16% and earning C$116.25 million.

resource in Central Asia, but its economic might is less than that of either of its neighbors, and Uzbekistan has occasionally flexed its economic muscle (e.g., in cutting off energy supplies to Kyrgyzstan in the winter of 1997–98) and threatened to wield its military power.

Geographical location has hampered the economy because of the country's land-locked position. Air transport has not been an effective option, apart from for gold exports. For much of the 1990s the country's airports were not operational for commercial flights, and the gateway airport to the northern part of the country was Almaty. Modernization of Bishkek airport was eventually completed in 2000 with the help of a $57 million Japanese loan. The national airline was corporatized in 1998 and separated from airport management in 2001, but its fleet consists of aging Soviet aircraft.

Political differences have led to frequent closures of the Uzbek border. Even the day-to-day hassle of the border crossings has become more onerous, to the extent that the Kyrgyz government has built a new road between Osh and Jalalabad to avoid transiting Uzbekistan, even though the new road is 100 km long and through difficult terrain while the Soviet road is only 55 km across the Ferghana Valley. Relations with Kazakhstan have been friendlier, but the culture of bribes at the border and along the roads meant that transiting Kazakhstan was expensive during the first decade after independence. The situation improved in the 2000s, partly because Kazakh banks with assets in the Kyrgyz Republic began to lobby in Astana for reducing the costs of exports from the Kyrgyz Republic, but more fundamental was the domestic pressure for change as Kazakhstan's economy boomed.[15] The physical connections with China remain weak, with the few roads often impassible in winter. Trade with poverty-stricken Tajikistan is largely restricted to the illicit drug trade, which uses the southern Kyrgyz city of Osh as a key transshipment point for Afghan opium en route to Europe. The situation could improve if various schemes for trans-Asian highways and rail connections are realized, and if transit trade could be facilitated by reducing border delays and other costs (see Chapter 10).

Internal transport is also poor. The Soviet system ignored republic boundaries—a much-cited example is the rail route between the two largest towns of the Kyrgyz Republic, which passes through Tajikistan, Uzbekistan, and Kazakhstan. Although rail connections between Bishkek and Kazakhstan and between southern Kyrgyzstan and the Ferghana Valley are of local importance, most domestic transport is by road (62% of freight and 86% of passenger traffic). Much interurban transport has been corporatized but the stock of lorries is aging, and many roads are in poor condition. The major project in 1999 and the early 2000s was the Bishkek–Osh road, whose importance is more than economic insofar as it links the country's two major cities, which are divided by a high mountain barrier. By 2003 the journey could be completed in 11–12 hours, but the priority given to building this expensive

---

[15] The Asian Development Bank may have provided a catalyst by making its loan for upgrading the Almaty–Bishkek road conditional on Kazakhstan curbing unofficial levies on users of the road.

road[16] plus the paucity of total public funds for transport projects meant that little money was left for maintenance of the country's roads. In the south, the tightening of border controls hampers traffic not only between Jalalabad and Osh, but also between Osh and Batken; in both cases the most direct route crosses Uzbekistan, but border delays, especially for trucks, encourage use of circuitous alternative routes. For Batken, the mountainous road round the Uzbekistan enclave of Sokh is so slow that the province is economically almost cut off from both the rest of the Kyrgyz Republic and from the wider world.[17]

The underdeveloped structure and vulnerability of the Kyrgyz economy is illustrated by the growth dip in 2002. The proximate causes of the decline were landslides that reduced gold production and climate conditions that reduced the demand for hydropower in the Kyrgyz Republic and its neighbors. More threatening to the country's long-term future is the widening north–south gap as Kazakhstan's wealth spills over to Bishkek and to the Issyk-Kul resort area in the north, while the south is stuck in the slow-growing and increasingly segmented Ferghana Valley. The north–south divide is political as well as economic.[18]

5.3   Foreign Aid and External Debt

International aid to the Kyrgyz Republic between 1992 and 2000 amounted to $1.7 billion. Assistance started to increase when the Kyrgyz Republic established itself in 1993–94 as a leading economic reformer and relatively liberal country, with an urbane and educated president. During the second half of the decade annual aid flows averaged about $50–60 per head of population, which is high by international standards. Over half of the aid came from the major multilateral agencies: the World Bank provided 23%, the Asian Development Bank 15%, the IMF 15%, and the EBRD 5%. The major bilateral donors were Japan (15% of the total), and Germany, Switzerland, and the European Union (each 4%).

Even in the Soviet era, the Kyrgyz Republic had been used to external assistance in the form of net flows from the rest of the USSR. A big difference in the post-1991 situation was that the assistance led to accumulated debt. International aid in the 1990s was provided about one-fifth in grants and four-fifths in loans. Even if World Bank, ADB, IMF, and EBRD loans were provided on better than commercial

---

[16] The Asian Development Bank and Japan provided $220.8 million funding for the road but required 20% counterpart funding from the Kyrgyz government.

[17] The bazaars in Batken, unlike in other towns in the Kyrgyz Republic, do not have many Chinese consumer goods for sale. A response to the tightening of Uzbekistan's borders was to improve air services from Batken in 2003–04; the flights' economic viability was helped by the deterioration of transport facilities from northern Tajikistan, whose residents increasingly crossed into the Kyrgyz Republic in order to make international journeys as the once-efficient routes via Uzbekistan became unavailable.

[18] The Osh–Kashgar road, which would provide a direct link from the southern Kyrgyz Republic to China and which could make Osh a significant crossroads for more than just the drug trade, as at present, is progressing slowly, and southerners allege that this is because northern politicians favor an alternative road link from Bishkek to Kashgar via Naryn.

Table 5.3. Debt indicators, Kyrgyz Republic 1993–2000
(millions of dollars and percentages).

	1993	1994	1995	1996	1997	1998	1999	2000
Public external debt stock	317	435	618	750	926	1,115	1,326	1,403
Share of GDP	30%	39%	41%	41%	52%	68%	106%	102%
Public debt service	4.5	18.6	95.8	75.9	43.4	5.8	53.4	77.6
Percent of budget revenue	3%	9%	39%	28%	16%	20%	26%	31%

Source: World Bank (2004, Volume I, p. 12).

terms, they still had to be serviced and eventually repaid. Yet, until the late 1990s, the government acted as though the foreign aid could be used to smooth out the consumption shock from transition and the dissolution of the USSR, without worrying about investing the funds in order to generate the foreign exchange earnings necessary to repay them.

Access to soft loans from multilateral institutions reduced the pressure to bring current revenues in line with expenditures, and only around the turn of the century did the government become seriously concerned about the accumulation of external debt. The infrastructure spending funded by the Public Investment Programme was a step in the direction of more productive investment of foreign aid.

In 1992 the Soviet successor states agreed to assign all the external assets and liabilities of the USSR to Russia, which meant that the other new states started life with zero external debt. A decade later the Kyrgyz Republic's public external debt ratio was over 100% of GDP (Tables 1.5 and 5.3), the highest in Central Asia. In March 2002 the government reached a Paris Club agreement reducing debt-service flows for 2002–04 from 20–24% of government revenues to 9–10%, a reduction of about $111 million in current-value terms. A further agreement in March 2005 halved the net present value of bilateral debt and restructured the balance, but the debt burden remains substantial.

Since 2000 the balance of payments has been improved by large inflows of remittances. The number of people migrating for temporary work in Russia or Kazakhstan in the early 2000s is believed to be around 200–300,000, although no reliable estimates exist. In the official BOP data the foreign-exchange inflow of remittances was $70 million in 2003, although unofficial estimates place the figure at over $100 million—offsetting the trade deficit of $76 million whatever the actual figure.

5.4 Health, Education, and Social Services

A feature of the Soviet system was the provision of social safety nets and universal access to health care and education. A major cause of the budgetary problems in the early 1990s was the government's attempt to avoid a major decline in provision of these services. By the mid-1990s it was clear that the transitional recession was more serious and more long lasting than initially thought, and the government then began to shift away from explicit safety nets. Pensions, the main direct social expenditure, were reduced after the 1998 crisis.[19] As mentioned above, this was accompanied in the second half of the 1990s by indirect assistance through mispricing of public utilities, but by the end of the 1990s it was recognized that the real level of public support would need to decline. The budgetary pressure was also felt in the health and education sectors, where the universality of the Soviet systems could only be maintained at lower quality levels. In practice, access to both health and education became less equal.

Public expenditure on health fell from 4.0% of GDP in 1995 to 1.9% in 2001. This was accompanied by a proportionate increase in private spending, so that in 2001 public financing of health spending was complemented by similar levels of private spending, about 2% of GDP (World Bank 2004, Volume I, p. viii). More recently, there may have been a gain in efficiency, as major financing reforms were adopted in four of the country's regions in 2001–02. The so-called Single Payer system allows more flexibility in provision, facilitating a movement away from the Soviet emphasis on hospitals and specialists in favor of more outpatient treatment and use of general practitioners, and requires cofinancing by the patient for inpatient care and for drugs for outpatients.

The overall health outcomes are difficult to assess. Deterioration in health indicators began before independence and continued until 1995–96, when health outcomes began a gradual recuperation. Male life expectancy declined from 65 in 1991 to 61 in 1995 and then returned to 65 in 1999, while female life expectancy fell from 73 to 70 and recovered to 73 in the same years. On the other hand, cases of communicable diseases such as tuberculosis, syphilis, and AIDS increased in the mid and late 1990s and early 2000s.

Public spending on education also fell drastically, from 7.4% of GDP in 1990 to 3.9% in 2001 (World Bank 2004, Volume II, p. 89). The government's initial moves included reducing compulsory schooling from ten to nine years and shifting costs to local authorities and parents. Due to the young population and relatively high birthrate, enrolment in grades 1–9 increased from 825,500 in 1992–93 to 945,700 in 1999–2000. In the noncompulsory grades there were dramatic changes: the number attending preschool fell from 190,100 in 1991–92 to 46,100 in 1995–96, where the number more or less stabilized; while the numbers in grades 10–11 and in higher education increased rapidly after the mid-1990s.[20]

The decline in the number of kindergartens was directly related to the transition from central planning because many kindergartens were attached to state enterprises, rather than being run by the Ministry of Education, and they were one of

---

[19] Increased retirement ages and fewer early retirement privileges also contributed to reducing the government's pensions bill. In the early 2000s pensions were just over $10 per month.

[20] Numbers in grades 10–11 fell from 114,000 in 1992–93 to 95,900 in 1995–96, but then climbed to 154,500 in 1999–2000. Numbers in higher education were stable at just below 40,000 up to 1995 but then climbed by over 10,000 per year to reach 88,924 in 1999–2000. Data are from World Bank (2004, Volume II, p. 81).

the first peripheral activities to be closed down as the budget constraints facing state enterprises hardened.[21] The consequences for the school system were important. Because of the relatively late school starting age, normally seven, children with a good preschool education are often able to read and write by the time they enter grade 1 of primary school, so that cutting the number of kindergarten places by almost three-quarters gave advantaged children, who were largely from urban rather than rural households and from better-off families, a big head start.

In the first half of the 1990s enrolment in grades 10–11, which provided specialized technical or vocational skills or academic training for the few destined to go on to university, declined by almost a sixth. The presumption appears to have been that many of the skills acquired in these grades lost their value with the end of the Soviet planned economy—a presumption backed up by *ex post* analysis of the determinants of household consumption (see Chapter 8). After the mid-1990s, however, there appears to have been an appreciation that training is the key to higher earning power in a market economy and enrolment in grades 10–11 as well as in higher education increased. These higher skills would be different to those taught before 1991, and many of the courses had substantial fees.[22] As with the decline in kindergarten availability, this development is going to be a source of increased inequality.

Although enrollments in the compulsory grades held up during the 1990s, this was at the cost of declining average educational quality. Writing in 2002 a team from the World Bank (2004, Volume I, p. x) observed:

> Although there are no time series data to track changing educational quality, there is a consensus on the part of teachers, students, and parents, that the quality of education has deteriorated seriously over the past decade in all but a few well-endowed urban schools.

This deterioration has largely been driven by budgetary neglect, leading to depleted stocks of textbooks and other materials, poorly maintained buildings, and underpaid teachers. Although the share of education in the public budget was fairly constant over the 1990s, the share of GDP spent on education fell from 7.4% in 1990 to 3.7%, of a smaller total, in 2000. A November 2000 national survey of primary education found that 80% of primary schools lacked a complete supply of textbooks, 20% had insufficient desks and chairs for the number of pupils, and 23% had no water supply. Anecdotal evidence contains many references to pupils not attending school in winter because their school had no heating.[23] Cessation of money for construction and maintenance has led to more extensive use of existing facilities: 81%

---

[21] Over a thousand kindergartens attached to state enterprises closed after 1991 (World Bank 2004, Volume II, p. 85n).

[22] Dukenbaev (2004) addresses the politics of higher-education reform in Kyrgyzstan.

[23] For example, in Howell (1996a,b). Although it is difficult to document precisely, actual attendance rates were much lower than official enrolment rates suggest; see World Bank (2004, Volume II, pp. 81–82) for a review of the evidence.

Table 5.4.   Grade 5 assessment results in numeracy, Kyrgyz Republic, November 2000.

Region	Percentage receiving lowest category scores	Percentage receiving highest category scores
Bishkek	10.2	32.1
Chui	17.0	23.3
Naryn	11.6	33.8
Issyk-Kul	21.1	33.3
Talas	26.5	27.6
Osh	20.3	26.6
Jalal-Abad	14.8	27.4
Batken	41.2	18.9

of rural schools and 71% of urban schools operate double shifts, and 9% of rural schools and 19% of urban schools operate triple shifts. Budgetary problems have led to a severe decline in teachers' real wages and frequent long delays in payment of their wages.

Parental contributions to urban schools often exceed $100 per child—in a country with a per capita income of just over $300. In rural areas parental contributions are lower, because of poverty, and the facilities are poorer. The gap between rural and urban children's achievement is reflected in grade 5 assessment results in numeracy, which are lower in rural than in urban schools in the same region, and also considerably lower in the poorest province, Batken, than in the capital city, Bishkek (Table 5.4).

One problem for the funding of social programs has been the dominance of pensions. Not only were pension payments in 1991 well above the poverty line, but they were politically difficult to touch. In 1996 pension expenditure amounted to 6–9% of GDP, and the 1990s were characterized by a continuing history of diverting health-insurance contributions to fund pensions. Pension reforms in 1997 and 1998 compressed the benefits distribution and increased retirement ages gradually (to reach 63 for men and 58 for women by 2006), but public pensions still took an unsustainable 4.7% of GDP in 2001. The government has also tried to improve the targeting of other social-assistance programs so that they reach the poor rather than universal categories such as all families with children, but social-assistance measures are dwarfed in the budget by pensions (in 2001 spending on all other social-assistance measures amounted to 1.6% of GDP, compared with 4.7% for pensions).

5.5   Conclusions

The Kyrgyz Republic is the most liberal Central Asian state, and the openness of the society is in stark contrast to that of Uzbekistan or Turkmenistan. This has also meant that better and more reliable information is available for the Kyrgyz Republic, which makes it the most analyzed of Central Asian transition economies. Some of the phenomena highlighted in this chapter, such as the resurgence of infectious diseases, are not necessarily absent from other countries, but their extent is either deliberately suppressed or simply undocumented.

The Kyrgyz Republic also has a relatively free market economy, matched only by that of much richer Kazakhstan on the wave of its oil boom. Despite the reform slow-down around the turn of the century and the institutional shortcomings emphasized in this chapter, the Kyrgyz Republic has vibrant markets. The two largest bazaars, Dordoi in Bishkek and Kara-Suu near Osh, cater not only to domestic customers but are also entrepôts where Uzbekistan's citizens come to buy imported consumer goods unavailable in their own country. Tajikistan's citizens cross the border into Batken, despite it being the poorest province in the Kyrgyz Republic with the worst-stocked markets, to do their shopping or to catch flights to the outside world.

The Kyrgyz Republic and Tajikistan started independent life with the most dif-ficult initial conditions of all Soviet successor states. They were resource-poor and landlocked, and a significant percentage of the better-educated were from ethnic groups who were likely to emigrate. Despite internal peace and generally good policies, the economic performance of the Kyrgyz Republic during the 1990s was awful, as living standards were eroded, both in terms of consumption levels and the availability of social support, education, and health services. In Central Asia only the truly desperate situation in Tajikistan is worse.

Economic weakness has led to political fragility, and the country's future is uncer-tain. Emigration has left the formerly heavily Europeanized north more Kyrgyz in ethnic composition, but economic developments have tied the north more closely to Kazakhstan. Among the DFI inflows after the recovery from the 1998 crisis were not only the Kazakhstan banks, which now dominate the banking sector, but also investors in the Issyk-Kul resort area, which increasingly caters to Kazakh tourists. The south is less changed since independence, remaining much poorer than the north and with a large Uzbek population, but the south is increasingly disaffected by what many see as neglect by the northern elite that dominates the country's politics. Poverty and a deep regional schism created a political tinderbox, even though the country's economic policies have been the best in the region.

Although political dissent was gathering force in the early 2000s, when politi-cal change came it happened remarkably rapidly. The parliamentary elections of February and March 2005 were widely perceived as unfair because leading oppo-sition candidates were barred. Even so, the first round on February 27 went less smoothly than expected for the president's candidates, and the second round runoffs were more clearly marked by dubious practices. The election of Akayev's son and daughter fueled fears that the president was planning a dynastic succession. Protests began in Jalalabad on March 10, and within a week both Jalalabad and Osh, the main cities of the south, were in opposition hands. The north was initially quiet, until on March 24 crowds converged on the White House, the seat of government, and the president fled. Despite the descent into autocratic rule during Akayev's last decade in power, he remained the least despotic Central Asian ruler. By ordering that force was not to be used against the protesters, he ensured a peaceful end to his reign. Akayev formally resigned on April 4, 2005, paving the way for the first peaceful transition of political power in Central Asia.

6

Turkmenistan: The Realm of Turkmenbashi the Great

Among all the former centrally planned economies, Turkmenistan is regularly ranked last by transition indicators measuring speed of reform or degree of economic liberalization. As far as the local leadership was concerned, however, the primary goal was not economic liberalism but economic independence, and by this criterion the transition (from communism to nationalism) was smooth and rapid. Nationhood was embodied in the leader, Saparmurat Niyazov, who, after the metamorphosis from first secretary of the Turkmen Soviet Republic to president of Turkmenistan, assumed the name "Turkmenbashi"—leader of the Turkmen.[1]

The evolution of the economic system and Turkmenistan's economic development since independence can only be understood in the context of the primary foreign-policy goal of positive neutrality and of the domestic political reality of an omnipotent leader. The pathological political conditions, described in Section 6.1, were made possible by the anticipated windfall gain from natural-resource exports; Turkmenistan was estimated to benefit by a 50% improvement in its terms of trade after switching from Soviet to world prices (Tarr 1994). President Niyazov relies on revenue from exports of natural gas, oil, and cotton to sustain an inefficient economic system. Apart from underwriting the costs of an extreme personality cult and positive neutrality, Turkmenistan embarked on an economic program of ISI reminiscent of that adopted by many new independent states of the 1950s and 1960s. Distorted prices and the lack of publicly available detailed data impede precise analysis, but the symptoms of misallocated resources, artificial exchange rate, and financial repression are clearly evident and were associated with a disappointing economic growth performance during the 1990s and increasing concerns about the sustainability of the economic system in the 2000s, although the day of reckoning was postponed by high energy and cotton prices in the early years of the new century.

---

[1] Turkmenbashi has, inter alia, a city, the main airport, yogurts, vodka, and a French perfume named after him. Posters of him are ubiquitous, and he has built a sumptuous marble-clad palace surrounded by gardens and fountains in the middle of the otherwise drab and dusty capital city.

6.1   The Political Background

The political system is characterized by a strong presidency, with centralized decision making and supported by a pervasive personality cult and security services.
The president, who is also prime minister and chairs the only political party, controls selection to the "Khalk Maslakhty" (People's Council), which has sole power
to alter the constitution and which in December 1999 unanimously extended the
president's term of office without limit. The legislature ("Majlis") and judiciary,
as well as specialized bodies, including the Central Bank, are subordinate to the
president's authority, and major decisions at all levels of government have to be
cleared by the president's office. Although the president has declared his support for
eventual transition to democracy and a multiparty system, for the immediate future
political stability is considered an essential precondition for economic growth. The
political system became more repressive after an apparent assassination attempt on
the president in November 2002.

Strict censorship makes it difficult to gauge popular sentiment. Social security
ranks highly among the government's professed goals and at least during the 1990s
this may have gained some popular support for, or at least acquiescence to, the
regime. The universal benefits from the Soviet era, such as pensions at 57 for women
and 62 for men, were supplemented by free provision of gas, electricity, water, and
salt for residential use. The drive to self-sufficiency in food has been partly justified
in terms of securing food quality for all. The social programs, as well as the ISI
projects and public investment that drive economic growth, are essentially funded out
of revenues from the major exports: natural gas and oil and cotton. As the economy
began to run into constraints, these benefits may have been cut back. Perhaps more
importantly, the megalomaniacal construction projects in the center of Ashgabat
have involved the bulldozing, with little notice or compensation, of people's houses
and the security services have arrested thousands of suspected dissidents, so that an
increasing number of people have been, or know somebody who has been, badly
treated by the authorities. Nevertheless, the threat of arrest, torture, imprisonment,
or forced labor in the uranium mines ensures that open dissent is extremely rare
within the country.

The most vocal opposition is from Turkmens abroad. The highest-profile defector,
Boris Shukhmadov, a former foreign minister and ambassador once tipped as a
possible successor to President Niyazov, joined the opposition in exile in Moscow
in November 2001. A year later, under mysterious circumstances, he returned to
Turkmenistan, where he was arrested for complicity in the assassination plot and
after confessing, apparently under torture, he was sentenced to life imprisonment.
The effectiveness of the remaining opponents in exile is reduced by personality
conflicts, although in September 2003 four opposition movements formed the Union
of Democratic Forces of Turkmenistan.

The president is adroit in stifling potential opposition. At home he regularly fires
ministers and regional governors, both to divert criticism from himself and also to

Table 6.1. World Bank lending to Turkmenistan (millions of U.S. dollars).

	To 1995	1997	1998	1999	2000	2001	2002	2003	Total
Commitments	25	65	0	0	0	0	0	0	90
Disbursements	2	2	5	0	15	6	3	0	33

Source: World Bank website, "Turkmenistan—country brief."

forestall political rivals. Senior officials are kept in line by the carrot of opportunities for corruption, but are exposed to being dismissed for corruption. In February 2003 exit visas were introduced and, although they were rescinded in 2004, exit remains difficult due to currency restrictions and the existence of a blacklist of citizens ineligible for passports. Diplomats are discouraged from defecting by a requirement that their families remain at home.

The president is suspicious of any foreign commitments that may interfere with his power. From the start, Turkmenistan viewed the CIS as a consultative grouping and nothing more.[2] It has remained outside all projected regional trade arrangements within the former USSR, and the only regional trade grouping of which it is a member is the ECO, which has been economically ineffectual, although relations with Iran, Turkey, and Pakistan provide a counterweight to Russia's still powerful influence (see Chapter 10). Turkmenistan is the only Soviet successor state not to have even initiated negotiations with the WTO.

Turkmenistan is a member of the IMF and the World Bank, but beyond provision of some technical assistance the actual operations of these institutions have been minimal in the country. Turkmenistan has not sought financial support from the IMF, but maintains a dialogue through Article IV consultations. Lack of cooperation, however, led the IMF to withdraw its resident representative in 1999, and a November 2000 IMF mission was denied access to information needed for an Article IV consultation. World Bank loans approved between 1994 and 1997 were frozen between 1997 and 1999 due to misprocurement, and in 2000 new loans were frozen until specific transparency and collateral issues were resolved (Table 6.1). Like the other Central Asian countries, Turkmenistan is a member of the EBRD and the ADB, but the operations of both regional development banks have been limited.[3] The EBRD halted public-sector loans in 2001, and the minuscule size of the private sector in Turkmenistan leaves little scope for other loans.

Turkmenistan has a positive attitude towards the United Nations, as an institution which imposes no constraints on domestic policy-making and is viewed as the guarantor of the country's neutrality. The UN General Assembly formally

---

[2] Turkmenistan refuses even to supply statistical data to CIS agencies. It carefully avoided siding with the Eurasian Union or the GUUAM group, each of which contained five of the twelve non-Baltic Soviet successor states. In 1999 Turkmenistan withdrew from the CIS visa-free zone.

[3] Turkmenistan was the last Central Asian country to join the ADB, in 2000.

recognized Turkmenistan's neutrality in a resolution of December 12, 1995 (Freitag-Wirminghaus 1998; Werner 2001). In 1999 the Arch of Neutrality was erected in Ashgabat as a national symbol. The Arch is topped by a 13-meter-high gold statue of Turkmenbashi, which rotates so that the ruler always faces the Sun.

As international criticism of the regime's human-rights record mounted, and especially after the invasions of Afghanistan in 2001 and Iraq in 2003 to overturn nearby tyrannical regimes, Turkmenbashi started to show less confidence in the adequacy of the UN guarantee of the country's neutrality. Some observers saw the revocation of exit visas in 2004 as a preemptive move to forestall sanctions by either the United States (under the Jackson–Vanik Act) or more worryingly by the United Nations. The April 2003 summit with President Putin in Ashgabat, where long-term agreements for gas supply and for Russian investment in Turkmenistan were announced, signalled a reversion to the old alliance with Russia. The November 2004 Bukhara summit with President Karimov could also be seen as an attempt to build bridges with a neighbor who, although personally disliked, shared Turkmenbashi's disadain for human rights.

6.2   Initial Conditions and Economic Strategy

At independence Turkmenistan was one of the less populous and poorer Soviet republics, with an economy dominated by cotton and energy. The Karakum Canal, begun in 1954, allowed an increase in the total sown area from 368,000 hectares in 1950 to over 1.3 million hectares in 1990, when over half of the arable land was devoted to cotton. In the 1980s, agriculture's share of GDP fell as natural gas came to dominate the economy; proven recoverable natural-gas reserves are the fourth largest in the world. Turkmenistan is also an oil producer, although output was declining in the years before independence. In the early 1990s, Turkmenistan's newly nationalistic leadership blamed the USSR for not having invested in oil and for creating the cotton monoculture. The industrial sector was very small, apart from two oil refineries and the cotton gins. The transport and pipeline network was adequate for connecting Turkmenistan to other parts of the USSR, but did not provide links to other countries, nor was there a dense internal network.

In 1992–93 Turkmenistan moved cautiously through the early stages of nation building and replacing the planned economy. Turkmenistan, still using the ruble, had to follow Russia's January 1992 price liberalization, but many price controls were retained and the president decided very early on that gas, electricity, and water should be free to households. Housing was not privatized, and housing costs were kept low. The national currency, the manat, was introduced in November 1993, apparently as a planned step towards economic independence rather than as a first step in establishing monetary control. Annual inflation remained around 1,000% in 1995 and 1996, when it was falling in other transition economies. The currency depreciated rapidly.

The first stage of privatization was completed in 1994–96 when 1,698 enterprises were privatized, 27% by auction and 73% by sale to employees. After some attempts to convert former all-Union enterprises into joint stock companies, the second stage of larger-scale privatization was put on hold. By November 2000 a total of 2,053, overwhelmingly small, entities had been privatized of which 1,942 were in consumer services and retail trade. Although the liberalization has been gradual, retail trade, cafes, and so forth now operate in a market setting with unregulated prices, although not a single one of the privatized enterprises has gone bankrupt.

Turkmenistan appeared to take the lead in Central Asia in reforming land tenure with the 1997 decree on land privatization. The state and collective farms were divided into individual plots, leased out to farmers who could obtain ownership rights subject to satisfactory output performance (Lerman and Brooks 2001). In practice, however, farmers remain subject to severe restrictions because to obtain a lease they need to enter into a contract to fulfil specified state orders. Government control over essential inputs, notably water and fertilizer, locks farmers into such arrangements, which are administered by the single bank dealing with farmers (the Dayhan Bank).

For a brief period in 1996–99 the Central Bank was permitted some independence, and it succeeded in using a tight monetary policy to bring inflation down from almost 1,000% to 17% (Table 1.2). The inflation rate mattered little, however, because outside the petty trading of the bazaar relative prices did not determine resource allocation. After 1999 the president reestablished control over the Central Bank, which henceforth passively monetized budget deficits. Public finances in Turkmenistan are extremely nontransparent, with a large proportion not recorded in the state budget but passing through a number of funds, some of which are directly controlled by the president. Thus, official data on the budget provide no real guide to the overall position or the financing requirements, which have to be guessed at from signs such as movements in the black-market premium on foreign exchange.

The state retained control over the gas and oil sectors. Foreign firms were brought in for their expertise, but in production-sharing arrangements which left the state in control. The two main crops, cotton and wheat, remain subject to state orders at prices well below world prices, which provides substantial earnings to the government from cotton exports (Pastor and van Rooden 2000). Export earnings were subject to surrender requirements and foreign exchange controls were universal and restrictive after December 1998, when the official exchange rate started to become increasingly artificial. Key inputs such as water and fertilizer are subsidized, but because access to them is tied to fulfilment of state orders, farmers are constrained in their choice of output mix. During the 1990s the state pushed for self-sufficiency in wheat—this appears to have been achieved, although yields in both major crops are low.

During the second half of the 1990s Turkmenistan pursued a statist development strategy in which growth was led by construction of infrastructure and monuments and by ISI. Starting in 1995 the government financed development of a modern textile industry processing domestic cotton and silk, which became the centerpiece of ISI. The process was directed and implemented by the government, with the private sector playing a passive role, more or less restricted to contract work by foreign firms. The financial sector remained heavily repressed, doing little more than allocate government-directed credits.

The development strategy in 1995–99 centered on maintaining a high investment to GDP ratio: 34% in 1995, and 45%, 49%, 51%, and 49% over the remaining years in the decade. The investment has been directed to three types of projects: unproductive, infrastructure, and industrial.

The most striking construction works are in the national capital, with its grand statues and new public buildings. These are financed off-budget through funds whose details are not publicly available. Some of these projects were intended to be productive, such as the row of theme hotels south of the capital constructed in the mid-1990s for a flood of businesspeople and tourists who never came. Others, such as the huge statues of the president and of his mother, have no value beyond feeding the personality cult. The state also financed construction of a large mosque in Kipchak, the president's birthplace, and a mosque at Gök Tepe to commemorate the 1881 battle in which a Russian army killed 14,500 Turkmen, mainly from the president's clan.

The government has tried to diversify external transport links and improve the domestic network. The national airport and pipeline to Iran have already been mentioned. In May 1996 a rail link was completed, the first line south from former Soviet Central Asia. In the late 1990s the government embarked on an ambitious road-building program, connecting all the nation's major towns by divided highways and, in the case of the recently begun north–south highway from Dashoguz to Ashgabat, accompanied by a parallel rail link. Another rail project connects Kerkishi directly to Turkmenistan's rail network rather than via Uzbekistan. The Caspian Sea port of Turkmenbashi (formerly Krasnavodsk) has been upgraded. All of these projects yield social benefits, but the railway to Iran, the Ashgabat airport, and the new roads are all operating far below capacity.

The industrial investments have focused on a $1.5 billion upgrade of the Turkmenbashi oil refinery and development of petrochemicals there, and the creation of a cotton textile industry. Industries such as petrochemicals and capital-intensive textile factories do not accord with the comparative advantage of a country with abundant labor where average rural incomes in 1998 were around $200 per year.[4] Between 1995 and 2000 the share of cotton processed domestically rose from 3% to 35%. The mills are typically joint ventures with Turkish partners, using Italian equipment. Their operations are not transparent but the state appears to have financed

---

[4] Based on the 1998 household survey conducted under World Bank auspices, in which the average rural household of six had an annual income of $1,200. The government's own figures report a nominal monthly wage of 330,700 manat for 1999, which is $63 at the official exchange rate and between a third and a quarter of that at the curb rate.

Table 6.2. Sectoral composition of investment, Turkmenistan 1992–99
(in billions of manat, current prices).

	1992	1993	1994	1995	1996	1997	1998	1999
Oil and gas (including refinery and pipeline)	—	—	1.9	22.3	486	1,390	3,242	3,838
Light industry	—	—	4.0	23.8	386	404	269	756
Electricity	—	—	0.2	6.3	39	231	238	44
Agriculture	—	—	3.1	15.6	144	142	798	171
Transport and communications	—	—	0.6	7.9	960	412	378	643
Total	**0.1**	**2.3**	**21.5**	**143**	**3,112**	**4,297**	**6,367**	**7,955**

Source: Government of Turkmenistan figures.

most of the equipment purchased and provides cotton at below world prices; yet, despite generous treatment of depreciation, the mills are not making high profits. As well as displacing imports, the textile industry is supposed to generate exports, but in 1999 these amounted to $21 million, mostly to Turkey, Russia, and Iran, and less than half of the export earnings that could be generated by exporting a third of the cotton crop as fibre. The government's response to these problems was to use export credits from Japan and an EBRD loan to fund what is claimed to be the world's largest textile complex, the Turkmenbashi Jeans Factory, which is equipped with state of the art equipment. Although their accounts are not in the public domain, it is likely that many of the textile factories have negative value-added.

Regardless of the social desirability of individual projects, the degree of centralization and lack of tendering suggest that resources may be extravagantly used. Much construction is based on simple cash contracts negotiated with a single firm. Some projects have been financed by directly assigning part of the cotton crop to a foreign contractor. Some large contractors have undertaken social projects without payment, in return for being granted a large construction deal or other privilege.[5] In a nontransparent society much of the evidence is hearsay, but the projects are real and the payments are large. Most grandiose of all is the construction of the Golden Lake in the Karakum Desert during the first decade of the 2000s as a drainage-cum-irrigation project, despite its $4.5–6 billion cost and almost universal condemnation by external observers as unable to achieve the stated impact on agricultural output and as being an environmental disaster.[6]

---

[5] Wehner (2001, p. 128) describes the $40 million heart clinic and $27 million kidney clinic built by Siemens primarily for the president's own use. Siemens had earlier arranged the president's heart bypass operation in Munich in 1997.

[6] Kalyuzhnova and Kaser (2006) observe that, although the 2,092 km^2 reservoir is intended to increase and stabilize water availability for the cotton sector, it may eventually lose much of its water by evaporation, induce widespread salinization of arable land, and accelerate desiccation of the Aral Sea.

Table 6.2 provides the official statistics on the composition of investment in the 1990s. The large unaccounted-for component is presumably the prestige and other unproductive projects. Of the remainder the capital-intensive oil and gas sector dominates. Another striking feature is the small and declining share of the agricultural sector (from 15% in 1994 to 2% in 1999), in which half the population works.

6.3 Economic Performance

Tracking Turkmenistan's output performance is complicated by poor data, but the general pattern is clear. According to IMF figures, real GDP dropped steadily during the first half of the 1990s and in 1996 stood at 58.4% of its 1991 level, and then real GDP fell by a quarter in 1997.[7] The big decline in 1997 reflected falling cotton prices and a poor cotton harvest, with cotton export earnings down to $84 million from $791 million in 1995 and $332 million in 1996, and the cessation of gas exports in March 1997, which left annual export earnings from gas at $70 million, compared with around a billion dollars in the two previous years (and $1,454 million in 1994). This was the backdrop to the tightening of foreign-exchange controls in 1998.

The problems with gas exports arise from the inherited pipeline network, which only led to Soviet markets. After independence, the Russian pipeline monopolist Gazprom refused to export Turkmenistan's gas to Western European markets, and Turkmenistan remained dependent on CIS markets. Several countries fell behind in payments, but Turkmenistan's export data record the contract value of gas exports, whether paid for or not, while arrears enter into the balance of payments as increased foreign assets. In March 1997 Turkmenistan cut off gas supplies to its main debtor, Ukraine. After protracted negotiations with Russia and other gas importers over debt rescheduling and future payment arrangements, large-scale gas exports were only resumed in January 1999 (Sagers 1999).

A solution to Turkmenistan's problems with gas and oil exports must include construction of new pipelines to reduce dependence on the Russian network and the destinations to which this leads. The problem, however, lies in organizing pipeline construction to new markets. A small gas pipeline to Iran became operational in December 1997,[8] but more substantial projects through Iran are stymied by the nonparticipation of U.S. companies. Perhaps even more fundamental is that neither Iran nor Russia has an interest in providing pipeline facilities for Turkmenistan's natural gas to become a competitor to their own natural-gas supplies to Turkish or European markets. Thus, Russia is happy to continue shipping Turkmenistan's

---

[7] IMF staff estimates, reported in Mercer-Blackman and Unigovskaya (2000, p. 4). Several international agencies stopped publishing GDP estimates in the mid-1990s. The EBRD reported a 26% decline in Turkmenistan's real GDP in EBRD Transition Report 1999, p. 277, but six months later in the May 2000 EBRD Transition Update, p. 83, the decline was revised to 11.3% (as in Table 1.3).

[8] The 200 km Korpedeke–Kurt–Kui gas pipeline, built by an Iranian company, has a projected annual capacity of eight billion cubic meters, although it only carried five billion in 1999. The main attraction for Iran is that the pipeline reduces the cost of supplying the domestic demand in northern Iran while freeing Iran's own natural-gas supplies for export.

Table 6.3. Cotton and grain in Turkmenistan: output (thousands of tonnes) and cultivated area (thousands of hectares), 1999–2004.

	1999	2000	2001	2002	2003	2004
Cotton						
Output	1,304	1,630	1,140	489	714	N/A
Area	550	573	770	640	640	650
Grain						
Output	1,632	1,700	1,500	2,300	2,535	2,844
Area	570	680	775	850	760	760

gas to CIS markets, including Russia itself, where it is bartered or collecting payment is difficult, while Russia's own natural-gas supplies can be exported to hard-currency destinations. A route across the Caucasus is less attractive for gas than for oil because Azerbaijan is mainly an oil producer.[9] Negotiations that began in 1995 with Unocal of California to construct a pipeline through Afghanistan to the energy markets of South Asia collapsed in 1998 (see Section 9.2), but this route is still on Turkmenistan's agenda, assuming the post-Taliban government will become a more acceptable counterpart for the major energy companies and their governments.

The agricultural sector has absorbed most of the increase in the rapidly growing labor force, and by the late 1990s employed about half of the economically active population. Low state prices for the major crops, even allowing for subsidized inputs, provide little incentive for farmers. The limited information on rural living standards, and casual observation, suggest that rural households are significantly poorer than urban households and that public services, such as water supply, have been declining more in rural areas. There appears to be little incentive for farmers to experiment with new methods to increase yields and they are discouraged from shifting their output mix beyond cotton or wheat. The agricultural stagnation augurs poorly for the first decade of the twenty-first century, during which population is expected to increase from 5.3 to 8.6 million. Agriculture is expected to absorb much of the increased labor force, maintain food self-sufficiency, and double raw-cotton production.

The first decade of Turkmenistan's existence saw the country sustain its political and economic independence, and the president consolidate his personal position. Economic independence is incomplete; the country still depends on the Russian-controlled pipeline system for much of its gas exports, and oil and cotton exports are subject to large fluctuations in world prices. Self-sufficiency in grain and textiles has involved substantial resource costs. Increases in the acreage under grain, combined with loss of land to salinization as a result of poor irrigation practices, have reduced the area under cotton in the early 2000s to less than half what it was in

---

[9] In any case, because jurisdictional disputes over the delimitation of the Caspian Sea have been particularly bitter between Turkmenistan and Azerbaijan, Azerbaijan is unlikely to agree to any kind of pipeline across the southern Caspian.

1990 (Table 6.3). The volatile but substantially reduced cotton harvest reduces the second pillar, after gas, on which the government's economic strategy is based.

The living standards and social well-being of the population are harder to assess. As in other Soviet successor states, real per capita GDP was lower at the end of the 1990s than at the beginning. In the comparative estimates of poverty rates by Milanovic (1998), Turkmenistan experienced a substantial increase in poverty after the dissolution of the USSR, but it was not the extreme case. Both of these results are based on dubious data. The World Bank's poverty assessment based on the 1998 LSMS survey is more cautious, concluding that poverty was not as serious in Turkmenistan as elsewhere in Central Asia, but a large segment of the population is living not much above the poverty line.[10]

The free provision of gas, water, electricity, and salt to households, plus public housing at low cost, and other subsidized basic goods and services, undoubtedly protected poorer members of society. Such untargeted social assistance is, however, costly and may be regressive; richer households have more electrical appliances and are most likely to have indoor toilets, benefiting more than poor households from free electricity and water. The lack of basic political and social rights seems universal.[11]

Officially Turkmenistan allocates 10% of GDP to health and education, but evidence on outcomes is mixed. Official statistics are positive but unreliable, whereas external sources report anecdotal evidence which can diverge widely. UNICEF statistics record an infant mortality rate of 20.1 per thousand live births, down from 54.7 in 1989. The CIA Factbook (www.cia.gov/cia/publications/factbook/) reports a life expectancy for men of 58 years and for women of 65 years in 2003. There is evidence of high morbidity, but the official response is always to deny a problem. Thus, reported cases of HIV infection in Turkmenistan before 2000 were zero. In March 2004 the government laid off about 15,000 health workers, and in May 2004 banned those remaining from diagnosing infectious diseases such as tuberculosis, cholera, or dysentery.[12] When typhoid broke out in Dashkoguz, the response of the senior local official (*hakim*) was to build a wall around the hospital containing the infected people. Visiting epidemiologists report hepatitis A to be endemic and hepatitis B widespread, largely due to poor upkeep of water and sanitation services.

---

[10] The LSMS data are not in the public domain so independent assessment of the result is not possible, and comments on the survey's findings are based on reports in World Bank and IMF publications which refer to 7% of the population living below $2.15 at PPP. The UN statement that "poverty incidence in Turkmenistan is perhaps the lowest among the transition economies" is not credible in terms of absolute poverty (cf. Slovenia or east Germany), and is undermined a paragraph later by the statement that "the country does not have overall precise or updated figures on poverty" (The United Nations System in Turkmenistan, "Common country assessment, February 2004," p. 11).

[11] Anecdotal accounts of summary expropriation or arrest are widespread but hard to document. Many of the construction projects, especially in the capital city, involved bulldozing houses with little warning or compensation.

[12] They are usually diagnosed as simple viruses; see "Reported plague outbreak renews concerns about Turkmenistan's health care system," *Eurasia Insight*, posted at www.eurasia.org on July 21, 2004.

Reports on education point to deteriorating facilities, lack of textbooks, and curricula heavily focused on the presidential personality cult.[13] The government increasingly encourages schools to focus on teaching "native traditions" and "natural spiritual values," while abandoning "subjects of minor importance" such as algebra or physics. Textbooks are strictly censored, and closure of the State Library in 2000 and almost total censorship of foreign media limit access to information and ideas. The government is clearly placing social control above human-capital formation, fearing educational institutions as potential centers of dissent. Meanwhile, the number of years required to complete school has been reduced from ten to nine, and some university degrees now require two years' study instead of four, with admissions, grades, and degrees reported to be for sale. The inevitable conclusion is that standards in previously mainstream subject areas have fallen drastically since independence. From September to November most students above grade 5 are forced to harvest cotton. The number of students in higher education fell from 40,000 in 1991 to less than 10,000 by 2004, as those who could afford it studied outside the country, most commonly in Moscow.[14] In the 2000s, however, declining high-school standards led a growing number of universities in other CIS countries to turn down students from Turkmenistan. The government's response to the exodus of students was to declare that after June 2004 degrees obtained abroad since July 1993 would not be recognized.[15]

6.4 Sustainability

The economic crisis in spring 1997 fostered recognition that Turkmenistan's initial economic strategy was not sustainable. The Thousand Days Economic Program announced in April 1997 acknowledged the need for policy reform, even though subsequent performance fell far short of the targeted 60% increase in GDP by 2000. The lack of will to reform is reflected in the president's official view that the economic achievements of the 1990s would be a springboard for greater progress by 2010. A revival of economic growth (Table 1.4), as a rebound from the artificially low levels of 1997–98 and then driven by buoyant oil and cotton prices in 2001–04, removed some of the pressure for change.

The Economic Program released in December 1999 provided a detailed and ambitious agenda for the years up to 2010. Growth in GDP will be 18% per annum over the decade, led by a 330% increase in gas exports, a 270% increase in oil exports, and a doubling of cotton exports. Real GDP per capita is projected to be three and a

---

[13] In 2001, 12,000 teachers were dismissed and the Academy of Sciences closed, reportedly for failure to teach or follow the president's thoughts. Knowledge of "Rukhnama" is required for an increasing number of jobs, and in 2004 was introduced as part of the driving test.

[14] The figure of 10,000 is the official enrolment in higher education. Other sources report estimated enrolment in 2004 as low as 3,500 students (see, for example, "Turkmenistan wrestles with child labor issue as cotton harvest approaches," posted at www.eurasianet.org on September 1, 2004).

[15] This led to many now-"unqualified" teachers and academics losing their jobs in the educational system. See the article "Brain dead" published in *The Economist*, July 24, 2004.

half times its 2000 level by 2010. The EBRD (in Transition Report 2003) described the president's program for the socioeconomic development of Turkmenistan up to 2010 as a "Soviet-style ten-year plan." A new long-term development plan published in mid-2003 provided a similar recipe for similarly stellar progress up to 2020.

How sustainable is Turkmenistan's economic progress? One warning sign was the external debt situation, which deteriorated in 1997–98, after which data ceased to be available.[16] As of September 2000 Turkmenistan had external assets of $1.3 billion in arrears owed by Ukraine, Georgia, Armenia, Azerbaijan, Iran, Kazakhstan, Uzbekistan, and Itera (a Russian-owned U.S.-registered gas distribution company), which the government was trying to sell at a discount rather than waiting for eventual settlement.[17] External debt was generally assumed to exceed the nominal value of assets, and the seriousness of the problem in 2000 was reflected in failure for the first time to meet payment deadlines on construction projects and other expenditures. According to EBRD data, the debt/GDP ratio exceeded 100% in 1999. In 2001 the rating agency Fitch–IBCA downgraded Turkmenistan's long-term debt from B– to CCC– and its short-term debt from B to C.

A second, more opaque, danger signal was the end of a surplus in the state budget in 1999 and 2000, and a deficit in 2002 equal to 2.7% of GDP. This measure is opaque because a large proportion of state transactions are through off-budget funds whose contents are secret. Clearly, in most years the consolidated state budget required some financing by money creation, because the inflation rate has been substantial. Inflationary pressures are inadequately reflected in the official consumer price index figures. A better guide is the value of the currency in foreign exchange markets, where it started at two manats to the dollar in November 1993.

The foreign exchange regime is a deeper symptom of economic problems. The depreciation of the manat in the mid-1990s reflected the hyperinflation, but by 1997–98 the worst was over and, when the currency was pegged at 5,200 per dollar in April 1998, this was close to the market rate. Since then, however, the government has maintained the official rate despite strong excess demand for foreign currency. In December 1998, surrender rates for foreign currency earnings were raised and access to foreign currency at the official exchange rate tightly controlled. The parallel exchange rate fell precipitously to over three times the official rate by mid-1999

---

[16] Even when data were released there is doubt about its comprehensiveness, because ministries or other agencies contracted foreign debts without central coordination. The World Bank is unable to provide new loans to Turkmenistan because its failure to report external debt violates the Bank's negative-pledge clause.

[17] In November 2000 the Turkmenistan government announced plans to sell $115 million in debt owed by Azerbaijan and Kazakhstan because "it had not seen any effort by these countries to pay their debts" (*Times of Central Asia*, November 30, 2000)—presumably not a statement likely to encourage high bids. Azerbaijan's $59 million principal is for gas deliveries from 1993–94, which was restructured in 1995 but on which there were no payments in 1998 or 1999. Kazakhstan owed $56 million for electricity. Some outstanding debt repayments have been renegotiated as barter deals, e.g., Georgia has repaired fighter aircraft and railway carriages, delivered patrol boats and dredging equipment, and promised to build a special presidential train.

and to four times the official rate by late 2000. The black-market exchange rate stabilized during the first half of the 2000s, standing at around 21,000 manat to the dollar in 2003. The black-market rate is not an ideal guide to macroeconomic pressures because the black market is thin because few people have money to trade. Nevertheless, the apparent worsening of the overall public deficit in 2003–04 and the need to monetize it were reflected in a widening premium, and the manat was trading at around 24,500 per dollar at the end of 2004. The substantial black-market premium has rapidly introduced many counterproductive practices into the economy as people seek ways to benefit from the spread rather than pursuing directly productive activities.

The lack of financial reform is also a symptom of economic malaise. Although two-tier banking was quickly introduced after independence, the financial system is still in many respects the old monobank system, with the central bank's functions not clearly separated from those of the state banks which control most of the deposits. All of these entities act as agents of the government's directed credit policies. The main quasi-independent bank is the Vneshekonombank, which has a monopoly over foreign economic transactions and which operates on its own account as a separate arm of government reporting to the president, rather than to the Central Bank or to the Ministry of Economics and Finance. There is no entrepreneurial commercial banking using loan analysts to identify the best borrower at a market-driven interest rate.

Both of these symptoms reflect the fact that Turkmenistan is far from a market-driven economy, with the two key prices in such an economy (exchange and interest rates) having no economic function in the country. More fundamentally, the economy remains tightly controlled through a single person, which often leads to nondecision and makes real coordination difficult. Such a system is likely to have the stultifying negative consequences of the centrally planned economy without achieving the degree of organization that allowed the planned economies to survive so long. Turkmenistan has a relatively simple production structure, so the disorganization may be limited on that side, but it is unlikely that the present system could supply the range of goods and services appropriate to the more diversified economy envisioned by 2010 in the presidential program for socioeconomic development.

The recidivist influences are reflected in the official suspicion of the private sector, which is only really permitted in petty retailing. This too is likely to stifle economic dynamism. Yet there are signs of entrepreneurship in the shuttle trade, believed to be equal in value to 10–20% of official trade in 1999 and 2000,[18] and in Ashgabat's huge outdoor Sunday market. Beyond that, however, private activity is quickly discouraged by excessive red tape and a widely held belief than any successful business will be heavily taxed or nationalized. Freedom of movement of individuals and

---

[18] The shuttle trade, involving small traders flying abroad, especially to Istanbul, quickly developed specializations. Carpet sellers and clothing buyers trade their baggage rights on outward and return flights, and appear to have quasi-formal arrangements with customs officials.

travel outside the country are limited. All media outlets are censored, and access to the internet is heavily controlled.

There are also environmental constraints on sustainability. Over-irrigation of land where the natural salt level is high has led to severe salinization problems, especially in the Dashoguz and Lebap regions, which are major agricultural producers (O'Hara and Hannan 1999). The desiccation of the Aral Sea has also had dramatic consequences for Dashoguz, where, according to the government's own National Environmental Action Plan of 2002, between 70 and 85% of the population do not have access to safe water.[19]

6.5 Conclusions

Turkmenistan's economic performance during the first decade after independence is interesting because it was an extreme case. The government gave a low priority to economic reform, while emphasizing the country's neutrality and minimizing internal political change. The country's abundant resource endowment provided favorable initial conditions for pursuing this agenda. Nevertheless, in 1997 the unreformed economy suffered a deep decline and, although it has enjoyed some recovery since 1999, the overall performance of GDP since independence is poor given the country's potential. Although the government had achieved its external and internal political goals, the economic strategy appeared to be unsustainable.

In the early 2000s the economy was subject to serious imbalances associated with rising external debt and budget deficits. Economic disaster was averted by a sustained increase in world energy prices. Although the use of oil revenues is nontransparent, it seems clear that some of the oil revenues deposited in the Oil Fund were used to reduce the external debt. Similarly, the budget situation has been improved by increased oil prices, but the precise situation is obscured by the dubious economic data.

In April 2003 Turkmenistan appeared to seriously compromise its much-vaunted neutrality by signing a pact with Russia. The political background was the U.S. invasion of Iraq in the previous month, which made the authoritarian regime of Turkmenbashi wary of whether its UN guarantee of neutrality would count for much if the U.S. asserted its objections to human-rights abuse in Turkmenistan. Apart from the military security aspects, the centerpiece of the accords with Russia was a twenty-five-year agreement for sale of natural gas, which offers Turkmenistan some measure of economic security in return for being drawn tightly into the Russian sphere of influence. An apparent "gas war" in the early part of 2005, which was resolved by agreement on a new payments regime, suggested that Turkmenbashi

---

[19] Reported in the United Nations System in Turkmenistan, "Common country assessment, February 2004," p. 21.

was still capable of independent gestures.[20] A year later, however, when Russia was involved in a similar gas war with Ukraine, the Russian authorities had no compunction in ordering and enforcing cessation of Turkmenistan's gas supply to Ukraine until the conflict was over.[21]

---

[20] The dispute was in the context of the rapid rise in energy prices in the early years of the twenty-first century. In January 2005 Turkmenistan raised its gas export price from $44 to $58 per thousand cubic meters. Russia refused to pay the higher price but after high-level meetings and threats, Gazprom agreed to pay the old price in hard currency instead of in the preexisting cash–barter mix, which has been estimated at being worth only $36–37 in hard currency (Sergei Blagov, "Russia outmaneuvers Ukraine for Turkmen Gas—for now," posted at www.eurasianet.org on April 21, 2005).

[21] The Russia–Ukraine conflict was similar to the earlier Russia–Turkmenistan dispute in that both had their origin in inherited underpricing of gas. In the Ukraine conflict, however, Russia's role was reversed as it replaced a long-term contract to supply gas to Ukraine at $50 per thousand cubic meters until 2009 with a demand that Ukraine pay the market price (potentially the EU price of $240 for Russian gas). Russia supported its demands by cutting off gas supplies to Ukraine on 1 January 2006 and by stopping transhipment of gas from Turkmenistan and Kazakhstan to Ukraine. Amid protests from Russia's western European customers whose gas pressure had suffered, the dispute was settled within a week by Russia and Ukraine agreeing on a temporary price of $90 for six months, and gas supplies were resumed. In all of this, Turkmenistan was never consulted by Russia although its major source of export earnings was put at risk.

Part II

Economic Performance

7

Measuring Economic Performance

How should we assess the economic performance of the five Central Asian countries since they abandoned central planning and became independent in 1991? By the usual measure, real GDP, they were to varying degrees worse off during the decade after 1989, with the poorest experiencing a decline of over 50% (Table 7.1). These dramatic numbers do not, however, fit readily with casual empiricism. Especially in the main cities of Kazakhstan, the Kyrgyz Republic, and Uzbekistan, the quality of life seemed much improved a decade after independence. Is this a symptom of distributional inequities, or do the macroeconomic data fail to capture even the aggregate picture?

National-accounts data are known to be especially flawed in economies in transition from central planning. They are also inadequate measures of material well-being. The first two sections of this chapter analyze the most important biases in the Central Asian countries' macroeconomic data. The conceptual issues mainly concern the era of transition from central planning and became less acute as market-based economies were established. Although other, more universal, issues of data reliability remain, these are less severe for the region as a whole.

Household surveys provide an alternative data source—one which is essential to address distributional questions and which can also provide a cross-check on national-accounts data. The survey evidence from Central Asia is presented in Section 7.3. Household surveys can shed light on aspects of performance such as the significance of nonmarketed output or of small enterprises, which may be inadequately covered by national-accounts statisticians. They can also be used to analyze characteristics of the winners and losers, whether identified by location or gender or education, and Chapter 8 addresses these issues in greater detail. The final section of the present chapter provides an overview of how the macro and micro evidence fits together in providing an answer to the opening question.

7.1 National-Accounts Measures of Output

National-accounts measures in economies in transition from central planning contain several substantial biases and there is no reason to expect that these will balance out. Bloem et al. (1998), reviewing the evidence for all transition economies, conclude that in the 1990s the underestimation caused by under-coverage outweighed the other biases. This is probably also true for the Central Asian countries, but there

Table 7.1. Real GDP (as a percentage of that in 1989).

	1996	1999	2001	2003
Kazakhstan	45	59	84	101
Kyrgyz Republic	52	62	71	78
Tajikistan	37	43	56	66
Turkmenistan	57	53	96	110
Uzbekistan	84	89	105	110

Sources: EBRD Transition Report Update, April 1997, pp. 7, 9; EBRD Transition Report 1999, Table 1.1; EBRD Transition Report 2002, Table A.3.1; and EBRD Transition Report Update, April 2004, p. 16.

are specific features. Before looking at the transition era, let us look briefly at the pre-independence situation.

In Soviet statistics, output was measured by material product. In order to be comparable with other countries' output measures, the official data need to be reworked, in particular to include services. The World Bank estimates reported in Table 1.1 are the best we have, but comparison with countries at similar levels of GNP per capita in 1990 gives the impression that the Central Asian figures are too high. Valuation of Soviet services, often based on proxy valuations from market-based economies, was probably too high, because the services in a planned economy were not necessarily oriented towards recipients' needs. Similarly, some manufacturing output was overvalued, because goods were produced that were not used.[1] The Soviet data also contained a bias towards overestimation because producers were oriented towards plan fulfilment and they overstated output rather than admitting under-fulfilment. Although the direction is clear, it is difficult to assess the extent of these biases. There is also a problem of which exchange rate to use to convert ruble amounts into dollars (Pomfret 1995, pp. 171–72).

Measuring changes in real output in 1991–93 is very difficult. Nominal GDP increased rapidly due to hyperinflation, but real GDP estimates are highly sensitive to the choice of deflator (and exactly when production is deemed to have taken place) and international comparisons are sensitive to the choice of exchange rate. Moreover, the huge changes in relative prices create an index number problem, similar to that well known for the Soviet economy in the 1930s.[2] This was exacerbated by the

---

[1] I do not know of any reliable measures of undelivered inventories. Some goods were shipped but were of little value to the consumer or user. Pomfret (2002a) estimates that around a billion U.S. dollars worth (at 1960s prices) of cotton harvesters were produced in Central Asia between 1958 and 1991, whose real value to the farms receiving them was close to zero because handpicking was the most efficient technique in Central Asian conditions.

[2] The rapid change in the output mix during the 1930s created an insuperable index number problem, sometimes known as the Gerschenkron effect. Bergson (1961, pp. 128, 153) shows that using base-year prices GNP was 171% higher in 1937 than in 1928, but only 62% higher when 1937 relative prices are used, because the relative prices of items in the rapidly growing machine-building sector dropped (Pomfret 2002b, pp. 11–13). Koen (1995) analyzes problems associated with Central Asian price indices for the hyperinflation period 1991–93. On the 1990s, see also Pomfret (1999a).

introduction of new goods and services that did not exist in the Soviet economy; even the decision of whether to record a higher-quality item as a new good or not is arbitrary.[3]

National-accounts measures of output are complicated by the large-scale migration from Central Asia and unmonitored capital flight. During the first half of the 1990s, both the Kyrgyz Republic and Kazakhstan experienced large net emigration, predominantly of ethnic Germans and Slavs.[4] Emigration from Tajikistan has also been substantial, and especially in recent years included hundreds of thousands of ethnic Tajiks, reflecting the dearth of economic opportunities; many of these emigrants view their move as temporary and they send remittances to their families, at least for a while. There are also substantial numbers of refugees, especially from Afghanistan, in the southern parts of Central Asia, but their economic significance is not large. Output measures for the 1990s capture gross domestic product (GDP), which is almost certainly less than gross national product (GNP) due to the omission of remittances and returns on assets held outside the country.[5]

Apart from these peculiar problems of transitional economies, the national-accounts aggregates are subject to the usual omissions of illegal, unreported, and nonmarketed activities. Opium from Afghanistan, the world's largest producer, passes through Tajikistan, and the southern Kyrgyz city of Osh is believed to be a major transshipment point. Other activities are in a gray area. The rapid expansion of prostitution in the early 1990s, for example, while not necessarily illegal went almost universally unreported. More generally, the reporting bias shifted suddenly and markedly from claiming plan fulfilment to sheltering income from suspected tax collectors. This was especially true of small-scale service activities, which may have been relatively highly remunerative.[6]

---

[3] If a good unavailable in period t is valued at its reservation price (i.e., the price at which demand equals zero), then introduction of a new good reduces its price in period $t + 1$. Omitting this phenomenon will overstate the aggregate price increase between t and $t + 1$, and therefore understate real output growth. Feenstra (1994) estimates this effect on price indices for six imported products into the United States, with large variation from product to product, but the overall effect of adjustment for new goods was sufficient to impact significantly on estimated aggregate U.S. import demand in the period 1973–87. Åslund (2001) argues that the universal post-Soviet "output collapse" is a myth.

[4] Heleniak (1997, p. 16) estimates net migration between 1989 and 1996 from Kazakhstan to have been 1.3 million, from the Kyrgyz Republic 370,000, and from Tajikistan 268,000—representing 7.9%, 8.6%, and 5.2% of the respective 1989 populations. German emigration was mainly from Kazakhstan, which had 958,000 Germans in the 1989 census, and Kyrgyzstan, which had 102,000. Olcott (1996b) reports data from the Russian Academy of Sciences of 1,142,400 Russians having emigrated from Central Asia between 1990 and 1994. The much smaller number of Jews emigrating to Israel or the United States (12,336 in 1993 according to Olcott (1996b, p. 551)) came primarily from Uzbekistan. Over 120,000 ethnic Kazakhs immigrated to Kazakhstan 1991–94, about half from the CIS and most of the rest from Mongolia.

[5] GDP is a measure of the value of goods and services produced within a country. GNP measures the output of goods and services by a country's residents.

[6] Evidence from Mongolia indicates that taxi drivers in the capital city could earn more than the president's official salary (Pomfret 2000a). Other remunerative service-sector jobs included translation, or anything else that tapped into the dollar rather than the local-currency economy.

The extent of these reporting biases is by its nature difficult to assess, but it is large and it is uneven across time and between countries. Filer and Hanousek (2002) emphasize the importance of improved capabilities of national statistical offices. Such retooling and upgrading has now taken place in almost all transition economies, but at varying speeds and to varying degrees, so that both comparisons over time and cross-country comparisons at a single point in time are subject to measurement problems.

One part of the economy which has flourished in every Central Asian economy has been the shuttle trade, involving small-scale traders. During the 1990s such traders, traveling often by air and trading as much as they could carry, took advantage of the gap between prices in places such as Istanbul, Dubai, Bangkok, or Beijing and the Central Asian cities, and the latent demand for consumer goods that had been unavailable in the Soviet era. Shuttle trading continues, but since 2000 new niches have arisen for informal cross-border trade to take advantage of price differences within Central Asia, e.g., between the less regulated Kyrgyz Republic and the more repressed market economy of Uzbekistan. In dealing with customs officials the shuttle traders have a strong incentive to underreport the value of their imports (or, if the officials accept a bribe in return for not levying taxes, then the reported trade will again be low). Estimates, usually based on multiplying the number of traders by a guess at the turnover of a representative trader, have placed the size of this trade at between a tenth and a half of recorded trade (see Section 10.1). It is larger in the more open economies of Kazakhstan and the Kyrgyz Republic, but a visit to the bazaars indicates that it is active in all of the region's economies.[7] The shuttle trade represents a large omission from the balance of payments. Although the value-added (and hence its impact on GDP) may be less important, the shuttle trade, as pointed out in the next section, contributes positively to economic welfare.

Another underreported activity is household production, and especially agricultural production on household plots. Here again the significance is not uniform across countries. In Tajikistan, where aggregate output has fallen drastically, as much as half of household consumption might have been coming from household plots in 1999.[8] In the Kyrgyz Republic too a response to coping with the hardships of transition has been a return to the land and greater self-sufficiency. Changes in gender roles may have contributed to greater household production, as some women withdrew from the formal labor force and produced services within the household

---

[7] The shuttle trade is least active in Tajikistan, with its poor transport links and lack of domestic purchasing power, but Chinese consumer goods are readily available in the bazaars. Even in tightly controlled Turkmenistan there has been an active and well-organized shuttle trade, with carpet exporters to Turkey and consumer-goods importers exchanging luggage allowances on outbound and return flights. In Uzbekistan the shuttle trade flourished in the 1990s because Tashkent had the best air services, but it became more difficult after the introduction of currency controls in 1996, and was forced even more underground after the clampdowns in 2002.

[8] This is based on a figure of 45% reported from the 1999 LSMS survey, which is likely to be an underestimate because the survey was conducted in the spring and because even in a household survey people may have underreported for fear of tax or other implications of revealing output.

that were not included in GDP. This was more prevalent in the poorer and more traditional areas, and less so in Kazakhstan. The light shed on the magnitude of these phenomena by survey data will be discussed in Section 7.3.[9]

7.2 National-Accounts Measures and Material Well-Being

A recurring aspect of the discussion of performance in transition economies is the use of aggregate output measures from the national accounts as primary performance indicators.[10] There is, of course, a basis for this, insofar as long-term well-being will be related to output performance, but in the short and medium term it is misleading. In particular, the decline in material well-being may be overstated.

I have already mentioned the problem of shifting from GNP measures for 1990 to GDP measures for post-1992, which understates the increase in output by Central Asians. A better welfare measure would be to use gross national expenditure (GNE = GNP + net imports), but this opens up a debate about the extent of unrequited imports into Central Asia before 1991. The conventional wisdom is that the Central Asian republics benefited from large net inflows from the rest of the USSR, and when these were cut off in 1991 the new independent states suffered a large one-off drop in GNE (e.g., Pomfret 1995, p. 72; Griffin 1996, p. 19). This interpretation, based on reported interrepublic trade flows, has been challenged by Central Asian economists, who point to other offsetting drains on resources out of the region (Islamov 2001). The debate is unlikely to be resolved, because many transactions occurred within all-Union enterprises; the net impact on individual republics was not a concern, and was not recorded.

These major conceptual problems apply especially to the early years of independence and transition. Even if the relationship between GDP, GNP, and GNE had stabilized by the mid-1990s problems of interpreting the output measures in welfare terms remain. Two major benefits of creating a market economy are to reduce time spent queuing and to open up the potential for gains from exchange. A commonly cited example of gains from exchange without any increase in output is housing reform, which allowed people to change their housing arrangements as their occupational or family situation evolved. This could leave both parties to an exchange better off even without any change in the housing stock. In practice, in Central Asia

---

[9] Attempts to adjust GDP estimates to include the shadow economy, usually relying on assumptions about electricity intensity as guides to aggregate economic activity, are not convincing for Central Asia. Eilat and Zinnes (2002), for example, estimate the shadow economy in the Kyrgyz Republic in the mid-1990s to have been twice as large as official GDP.

[10] The GDP estimates reported in Tables 1.3 and 7.1 have been assembled by the IMF and the EBRD from national sources, and care has been taken to ensure conceptual consistency. Even a cursory glance, however, reveals inconsistencies between the different data sources. The growth rates in Table 1.3 are especially sensitive to the measurement and deflator problems. The World Bank's estimates of gross national income per capita for 2000 in U.S. dollars were $1,190 for Kazakhstan, $270 for the Kyrgyz Republic, $170 for Tajikistan, $840 for Turkmenistan, and $610 for Uzbekistan. These data should be comparable to the GNP per capita data in Table 1.1, but obviously do not track the real GDP patterns in Table 1.3 or Table 7.1.

the housing market has been slow to develop, which complicates the assessment because it cannot be treated as a one-off outward shift in the consumption possibility frontier.[11]

In other markets, expansion of the choice set and of opportunities for mutually beneficial exchange has been more dramatic. The shuttle traders, typically seen as a problem for calculating trade balances, have contributed significantly to material welfare by allowing domestic consumers the opportunity to buy imported consumer goods, which clearly dominate the previously available goods. If consumption weights were used to calculate the price index, then apparent real income would register much higher growth than the conventional real GDP determined by production weights and reported in Table 1.3.[12]

The nontradables sector has expanded rapidly since independence. Facilities such as tea houses, restaurants, and mosques appeal to cultural preferences that were repressed during the Soviet era. Their flourishing in the 1990s contributed little to measured GDP, but yielded large consumer surplus.

The expansion of markets increases utility, for given output levels, by reducing queuing and increasing opportunities for exchange, but it also increases economic uncertainty, which for most people reduces utility. Increased economic uncertainty is especially likely if the labor market is not clearing, but in times of rapid change it can also reflect changing market valuations to different human-capital attributes. In the Central Asian context, the benefits of marketization are likely to be strongest in the more liberal economies. During the 1990s, however, Uzbekistan did better at maintaining government revenues and hence the resources to provide a safety net, and is also credited with innovative and reasonably successful targeting of delivery of social assistance through the *mahallah* system. One indicator of increased stress from economic uncertainty in Kazakhstan during the 1990s was the higher male mortality rate.[13] Uncertainty has been greatest in Tajikistan due to the tense security situation, and probably also in Turkmenistan due to arbitrary rule.[14]

In general, the national accounts have become better guides to economic performance and material well-being as market economies are more firmly established. There is little doubt that economic conditions have been improving since 1999,

---

[11] There were some immediate gains as people who acquired apartments in the capital cities were able to rent them out to foreigners. The reduction in time spent in queues did happen rapidly. Alexeev and Leitzel (2001) have argued that fixed prices plus queuing is superior to poorly targeted subsidies as a way of providing a safety net, but this is very much a second-best argument. The end of ubiquitous queues appears to be an indisputably good thing, especially for women.

[12] Bailey (1991) has emphasized the exclusion of the value of increased imports of consumer goods, which arises from using production-weighted rather than consumption-weighted deflators. See also Pomfret (1995, pp. 174–76).

[13] Male life expectancy had fallen to 59 years in 1998, compared with 66 in neighboring Uzbekistan (World Bank, World Development Report 2000/2001, pp. 274–79).

[14] The lack of reliable information about Turkmenistan makes this difficult to document, but in the capital city stories abound of streets of houses being demolished at very short notice to make way for new monumental structures. In all five countries there is a bias insofar as information about conditions in the capital cities is much more abundant than information about conditions in rural areas.

although questions are being raised about the accuracy of the raw data reported by Turkmenistan and perhaps Uzbekistan, whose governments are thought to doctor politically unpalatable data. Although the international agencies publish GDP data based on official statistics, they regularly issue warnings, e.g., the EBRD's Transition Report 2003 states baldly: "There are no reliable statistics on GDP growth in Turkmenistan."

7.3 Survey Evidence

In light of the weaknesses of the national-accounts aggregates, it is tempting to use household-survey data as an alternative measure of aggregate welfare. For questions of poverty and distribution there is no alternative. Substantial job losses in the formal economy were a prime reason for growing inequality and poverty, but the extent of unemployment is difficult to assess. Registered unemployment remains low (3–4% in Kazakhstan, the Kyrgyz Republic, and Tajikistan in 2000) because people do not register. Widespread coping mechanisms included turning to subsistence agriculture or the informal sector, in which many people are underemployed with very low incomes.

Milanovic (1998) has made the most thorough attempt to collate comparable survey data for transition economies, and his estimates of poverty headcount rates and Gini coefficients for Central Asia before and after independence are presented in Table 7.2. They show a slight increase in Gini values between 1987–88 and 1993–95 in Kazakhstan, Turkmenistan, and Uzbekistan, and a huge increase in the Kyrgyz Republic. Tajikistan was not included, presumably due to the civil war. Combined with falling average income the increased inequality translated into high poverty rates, between 61% and 65% in the first three countries and 88% in the Kyrgyz Republic—the highest in any transition economy. Although the cross-country comparison is useful, less attention should be given to the absolute poverty rates, which are susceptible to arbitrary decisions about poverty lines as well as data problems (Deaton 2001).

Although Milanovic's estimates represent an impressive job of reconciling data and are widely quoted, there are some fundamental problems. For the most part, he relies on the Soviet household budget survey (HBS) as his data source. These were initiated in the 1950s and continued through the 1990s with essentially the same samples, changed only through attrition. The original intention was to survey living standards of households whose head worked in state enterprises or on collective farms, and both tails of the income distribution are underrepresented.[15] The HBS has been characterized as "a survey with a long history and terrible reputation" (Falkingham et al. 1997, p. 48). Before 1991 the HBS is the only real source and at

---

[15] Certain occupations (e.g., party officials, high-level bureaucrats, KGB and military officers) and people in the private sector were excluded. Atkinson and Micklewright (1992) and Marnie and Micklewright (1994) describe and criticize the HBS.

Table 7.2. Inequality and poverty in Central Asia:
Milanovic data for 1987–88 and 1993–95.

	Poverty headcount (%)		Gini coefficient (income)	
	1987–88	1993–95	1987–88	1993–95
Kazakhstan	5	65 (62)	26	33
Kyrgyz Republic	12	88 (86)	26	55
Turkmenistan	12	61 (57)	26	36
Uzbekistan	24	63 (39)	28	33

Source: Milanovic (1998, pp. 41, 68, 69, 75).

Notes: data are household income taken from HBS, apart from those for the Kyrgyz Republic in 1993 (KPMS); the poverty line is $120 per month in "international" (PPP) dollars at 1990 prices, which was equal to 54 rubles in 1987–88; figures in brackets are adjusted to allow for differences between HBS income levels and income levels from macroeconomic data sources; Turkmenistan's Gini coefficient is from 1989 not 1987–88.

least it is roughly comparable across republics, although underrepresentation of rural households is a problem for the Central Asian republics with their large, but differing, rural sectors.[16] Milanovic also had available a 1993 survey for the Kyrgyz Republic conducted under the aegis of the World Bank Living Standards Measurement Study (LSMS), which is superior in its sampling methods, but including it in the cross-country comparison begs the, unanswerable, question of comparability.

Later in the 1990s, LSMS surveys were conducted in Kazakhstan (1996), Turkmenistan (1998), and Tajikistan (1999), as well as annually in the Kyrgyz Republic from 1996.[17] Poverty headcounts from these sources provide a less bleak picture than Milanovic's poverty rates for 1993–95. With the commonly used $2.15 per day poverty line, both Kazakhstan and Turkmenistan had poverty headcounts of less than 10%, well below Russia, for example (see Table 7.3). The Kyrgyz Republic's headcount was higher, at 49%, while two-thirds of Tajikistan's population lived below the poverty line. Using the World Bank's headline dollar-a-day measure the poverty rates would be still lower (Table 7.4).[18]

---

[16] After 1991 the advantage of comparability diminishes as some successor states continued to devote resources to the HBS and treated them seriously (e.g., Uzbekistan) while others paid less attention to statistical services (Tajikistan) or redirected their energies to LSMS surveys (the Kyrgyz Republic).

[17] An LSMS survey conducted in Uzbekistan was aborted amid disagreement over financial conditions. Grosh and Glewwe (1998) describe the LSMS methodology, and further information on the LSMS project is contained in the references cited by Atkinson and Brandolini (2001, p. 772). Falkingham (1999) and Kandiyoti (1999) discuss the LSMS surveys in Central Asia. Kandiyoti emphasizes conceptual problems arising from the differing understanding by Central Asian respondents and western analysts of terms such as "household" or "employment." Although these are relatively high-quality household surveys, they still suffer from inevitable weaknesses, such as the exclusion of homeless people.

[18] The $2.15 and $1 per day criteria are useful for international comparisons, but the PPP exchange rates are opaque (Deaton 2001, pp. 127–30) and may be especially so for Central Asia. Some studies have used a nutrition-based poverty line, but this is controversial in a region where obesity is a health problem (Falkingham et al. 1997, pp. 61–77).

Table 7.3. Inequality and poverty in Central Asia:
poverty headcount from LSMS data ($2.15 PPP per day).

	Headcount
Tajikistan (1999)	65.4%
Turkmenistan (1998)	7.0%
Kyrgyz Republic (1996)	49.1%
Kazakhstan (1996)	5.7%
Azerbaijan (1995)	23.5%
Russia (1996)	18.9%

Source: calculated from LSMS survey data.

Table 7.4. Inequality and poverty in Central Asia: share of
population living on less than $1 per day, 1993.

	Poverty share
Kazakhstan	< 2%
Kyrgyz Republic	18.9%
Turkmenistan	4.9%

Source: "World development indicators 1998," World Bank, Washington, DC, 1998, pp. 65–66.
Notes: the poverty line is $1 per day at PPP prices; figures for Tajikistan and Uzbekistan are not
reported in the source.

How to interpret these various poverty measures? Clearly the incidence of poverty
increased after independence, but not as drastically as Milanovic's much-cited
poverty rates imply. The poverty rates in Table 7.2 are based on a fairly high poverty
line (the $120 per month was meant to be roughly comparable to the Soviet poverty
line used in Table 1.1) and low-quality data. The LSMS data from the second half
of the 1990s paint a picture of fairly high poverty in the Kyrgyz Republic and very
high poverty in Tajikistan, but not so bad a picture in the other countries. Other
evidence lends some support to this ranking. Average monthly wages reported by
the IMF, for example, indicate a much better situation in Kazakhstan and a much
worse situation in Tajikistan than in the other three countries in 1997 (Table 7.5).
There can be no doubt that Tajikistan and the Kyrgyz Republic experienced massive
increases in poverty, while the other Central Asian countries also experienced widespread poverty for the first time in living memory. The qualitative studies of poverty
in Dudwick et al. (2003) repeatedly illustrate the novelty aspect. In the early post-
Soviet years, poverty was seen as an aberration, and it bore a stigma because only
slackers or moral reprobates could be poor. By the second half of the 1990s, however, it was becoming an accepted state for many people who were, with difficulty,
coming to terms with long-term poverty.

Table 7.5.   Inequality and poverty in Central Asia:
average monthly wage in U.S. dollars, 1997.

	Average wage
Kazakhstan	$120
Kyrgyz Republic	$40
Tajikistan	$6
Turkmenistan	$35
Uzbekistan	$53

Source: "Turkmenistan: recent economic developments," IMF Staff Country Report No. 98/81, August 1998, p. 19; "Republic of Tajikistan: recent economic developments," IMF Staff Country Report No. 98/16, February 1998, p. 21.

Table 7.6.   Inequality and poverty in Central Asia: Gini coefficients from LSMS data.

	Gini coefficient
Kyrgyz Republic (1993)	0.54
Kyrgyz Republic (1996)	0.46
Azerbaijan (1995)	0.35
Kazakhstan (1996)	0.35
Turkmenistan (1998)	0.41
Tajikistan (1999)	0.47

Source: World Bank (2000, p. 19), based on per capita expenditure.

Gini coefficients calculated from the LSMS surveys (Table 7.6) corroborate Milanovic's estimates, but provide a subtler picture. In particular, the Kyrgyz Republic's Gini coefficient in 1993 was a spike. In the first years after independence, after the ending of central planning and dissolution of the USSR but before the creation of a market economy had really begun, inequality shot up, but by 1996 it had fallen again (although it was still high with a Gini of 0.46). The Gini for Kazakhstan does not differ much in Table 7.2 and 7.6, but those for Turkmenistan and Tajikistan appear to have risen during the decade, which is consistent with other evidence of deteriorating economic conditions and widening inequality in these two countries.

The Gini coefficients reported in Table 7.6 are calculated from the distribution of per capita expenditure rather than income. One reason not to use income was the ubiquity of payment arrears. During the 1990s many workers received no wages for weeks or months and then one large back payment, reflected in an income distribution over the two-week LSMS survey periods in which many workers report zero income and others have income far in excess of expenditure. Thus, expenditure is a more reliable guide to expected permanent income. It is also probably less subject to downward reporting for tax reasons.

The superiority of expenditure over income in survey data is widely recognized, and appears to track the national-accounts concept of consumption.[19] Roberts (1997) has analyzed the Kyrgyz HBS data, and estimates that private household consumption fell by 33% during 1990–93 and rose by 7% in 1995.[20] This is substantially smaller than either the fall in consumption implied by GDP estimates,[21] or official estimates of a 44% decline in 1990–93 followed by a further 5% drop in 1995. The main reason for the discrepancy is the rapid growth of the private sector, especially in 1991, to the extent that by 1995 the shadow economy was supplying between a quarter and a half of household consumption. Although Roberts presents a less gloomy picture than official figures, his estimates still represent a large drop in consumption during the first half of the 1990s. The corner was turned in the mid-1990s. Comparison of per capita household expenditure in the 1993 and 1997 LSMS surveys shows, for given household characteristics, a significantly higher level in the latter year (Anderson and Pomfret 2002). The implication is that the magnitude of the economic decline in the Kyrgyz Republic during 1993–95 is overstated by the GDP estimates in Table 1.3.

The LSMS household expenditure figures include estimates of the value of consumption of home-produced items. In the 1999 Tajikistan LSMS survey, 45% of rural households' consumption came from household plots, and this may be an underestimate because the survey was conducted in the spring, before the main harvest seasons, and because some output may have gone unreported. This provides an indication of likely understatements of national accounts from this source.

Another likely source of underreporting in both national accounts and surveys is small private enterprises. In some surveys, e.g., Tajikistan in 1999, no questions were asked about nonfarm household businesses, because they did not legally exist. The Kyrgyz Republic's LSMS surveys of 1993 and 1996–98 contain abundant information about the characteristics of such enterprises, but almost all of the household nonfarm enterprises reported low revenues and big losses (Anderson and Pomfret 2001); fear of taxation or expropriation of profits in some other way clearly played a role.

---

[19] Ravallion (2001) documents this relationship for a large set of countries, but finds that it does not apply to Eastern Europe and Central Asia, where his twenty-seven observations show no correlation between the growth of expenditure in survey data and the growth in the consumption component of the national accounts. He ascribes this anomaly to the region's severe data problems, and appears to question the magnitude of the economic contraction of the 1990s as measured by the national accounts.

[20] According to Roberts, a substantial change in the Kyrgyz Republic's HBS methodology in 1994 invalidates comparisons between before and after 1994.

[21] The micro–macro comparison is complicated by changes in the consumption share of GDP. According to the official CIS statistical yearbook between 1991 and 1999 fixed investment fell by 21% in Kazakhstan, by 52% in the Kyrgyz Republic, and by 77% in Uzbekistan (no data are given for Tajikistan or Turkmenistan). Assuming that a decline in the investment–GDP ratio implies an increase in the consumption–GDP ratio, the decline in GDP during the 1990s exceeded the decline in aggregate consumption, but the magnitude is uncertain.

7.4   Other Considerations

The survey data shed additional light on some other issues. Distribution concerns may involve regional or gender dimensions.

Spatial variations in living standards existed in the Soviet era, but have widened during the 1990s. National-accounts data reveal the existence of spatial variations, but may not capture their magnitude. Regional GDP estimates are misleading guides to living standards when there are differences between where production occurs and where income accrues; oil and mineral revenues, for example, appear to accrue in the political and financial centers (Pomfret 2005c). Other problems with national-accounts data, such as failure to include nonmarketed output, have a regional dimension in that they may disproportionately understate rural living standards. The survey data can help to overcome some of these problems by focusing on household expenditure and by including imputed values of nonmarketed output.

The general pattern is of the capital cities doing relatively well, and in Kazakhstan and the Kyrgyz Republic there is also a tendency for northern regions to do better than southern regions. The survey data permit us to identify whether these patterns are due to the fact that households in the relatively well-performing regions had higher human-capital endowments or whether they are due to other factors that could account for higher living standards. Econometric analysis of the survey data using a human-capital model, with variables for demographic and other household characteristics, finds significant regional effects on household expenditure; households with identical characteristics have substantially different per capita expenditure depending upon regional location (see Chapter 8).

In Central Asia, although international migration took place on a large scale, internal migration was much less common. The LSMS evidence establishes that, even in what are the three least-regulated economies (Kazakhstan, the Kyrgyz Republic, and Tajikistan) there is not a national labor market. Given the tighter control over the economy and over internal mobility in Uzbekistan and Turkmenistan, it is safe to conclude that labor mobility is not reducing spatial inequality to any great extent in the Central Asian countries. Two main sets of explanations can be offered for why the move to a market economy has not been followed by establishment of national labor markets with people relocating in response to economic incentives: the economies are not physically integrated, and social factors discourage mobility.

The infrastructure prevents a national economy being established. The Soviet transport network ignored republic boundaries and many regions were better connected to the Tashkent rail hub or, in the case of northern Kazakhstan, to Russian cities than to other parts of their own republic. In the southeast of Central Asia, physical boundaries are formidable, with the Ferghana Valley blocked from the rest of Uzbekistan, northern and southern Kyrgyz Republic separated, and many parts of Tajikistan cut off by snow in winter. Since independence all five countries have aimed to create national transport networks, with Turkmenistan devoting most resources to the specific task and impoverished Tajikistan and the Kyrgyz Republic suffering from acute resource constraints.

The extended family is very strong in Central Asia. Buckley (1998, p. 72) has argued that these ties are so strong that people will prefer to remain in their place of birth within the family than to move elsewhere for higher economic returns. The international migration has largely involved non-Central Asian groups such as Germans and Slavs, while Central Asian groups have not relocated. Central Asian groups have not tended to migrate across borders; in particular there have not been cross-migrations of people to their "ethnic homeland" (e.g., Turkmen to Turkmenistan and Uzbeks to Uzbekistan in the Khorezm/Dashoguz region), as happened between Azerbaijan and Armenia in the early 1990s.

There are limits to nonmobility. In the dire economic conditions of Tajikistan in the late 1990s migration did increase, although this consisted mainly of males moving to Russia in search of work (and sending remittances to their families), rather than internal migration. Tajiks and Uzbeks (and others) have fled from Afghanistan and live as refugees in border areas of Tajikistan and Uzbekistan, although the economic impact of these movements is secondary. Yet, under nonwar conditions the resistance to relocating within Central Asia is striking.

The household survey data suggest a need to temper the belief that centrally planned economies were abundant in physical and human capital. Much of the physical capital turned out to have little value in a market setting. Hence the difficulty in privatizing state enterprises by sale (nobody wanted to pay for their assets) and the importance of de novo enterprises in the success stories. The high education levels also turned out to be a mixed blessing. Literacy was universal and therefore it is difficult to measure its marginal benefit, but secondary education and vocational post-secondary training appear to have provided skills with little economic value in the market economy. On the other hand, the higher-level general-purpose skills acquired through university education are associated with higher living standards in Central Asia during the second half of the 1990s (Anderson and Pomfret 2002).

These results have important implications. Loss of economic status has been pronounced among those with vocational training, who tend to be male. This has been especially evident in the company towns of Kazakhstan, where a single enterprise dominated the local economy in the Soviet era, and where the specialized workers have found difficulty in adjusting to the market economy. Another side of the gender issue is that females were at least as well represented as males in Soviet universities. While newspaper headlines have highlighted the difficult position of some women in Central Asia, the overall situation is more nuanced, and college-educated women have been among the biggest winners from the end of central planning (Anderson and Pomfret 2003, Chapter 6).[22] The survey data also shed light on whether

---

[22] The more lurid headlines report on the trafficking in women, especially from the Kyrgyz Republic to the Gulf states, but even more sober analyses—such as Falkingham (2000a) on Tajikistan, Bauer et al. (1997a) on Kazakhstan, or Bauer et al. (1997b) on the Kyrgyz Republic—focus on specific problems

women have left the workforce voluntarily to specialize in household production and child raising or whether they are involuntarily unemployed.[23] Household-survey data could also be used to analyze intra-household distribution, which may be key to understanding changes in the status of women, but such analysis has yet to be done with the Central Asian data.

Neither national-accounts nor household-survey data reveal much about the serious and probably growing environmental problems in Central Asia.

7.5 Conclusions: Putting It All Together

The generally accepted picture of the Central Asian countries' economic performance during their first decade of independence is negative. While they all suffered severe economic hardships in the 1990s, the picture is more nuanced than such a blanket statement implies. The claim by Fischer and Sahay (2000, p. 5) that "measured GDP is the single most useful summary statistic of economic performance" may be literally true, but relying only on that measure as a cardinal indicator of economic performance in Central Asia since independence is inadequate.

The large declines in real GDP in Tables 1.3 and 7.1 overstate the situation for two major reasons. First, the reporting bias shifted from overreporting in the centrally planned economy to underreporting in the market economy, and the downward bias after the transition was exacerbated by far-from-complete coverage of household production and new private enterprises.[24] Second, the changing composition of output and the pervasive phenomenon of new and higher-quality goods and services meant that the output changes in the early transition years (roughly 1991–94) are over-deflated. The divergence between output measures and economic welfare exacerbates the underrepresentation of transition benefits. By their nature these sources of bias are difficult to quantify, and there is no reason to expect them to be evenly distributed over time or across countries.

Although the early 1990s are especially problematic, focusing only on subsequent years raises ligation questions, i.e., in disequilibrium situations separating growth

---

facing women in post-independence Central Asia, rather than attempting an overall assessment of changes in the economic status of women. By contrast, Paci (2002) in her review of all transition economies finds evidence of declining economic status of women only in Tajikistan, although compared with Eastern Europe or the western CIS the evidence from Central Asia is limited. Paci concludes that there is no overall pattern but that some groups of women and of men have been big losers, and the pattern is country specific. The most shocking statistic, the huge decline in male life expectancy in Russia and Ukraine, is also evident in Kazakhstan, where in 1998 male life expectancy had fallen to 59 years compared with 66 in neighboring Uzbekistan (World Bank, World Development Report 2000/2001, pp. 274–79).

[23] Preliminary results reported by Anderson and Pomfret (2003, p. 108) suggest some, but not many, voluntary quits.

[24] An opposing bias is the omission of public services from LSMS measures (Kanbur 2001). To the extent that public provision of local transport, health, or education deteriorated, the decline in household well-being is understated. Such services are also undervalued in national-accounts data, where they are estimated at factor cost, but at least some measure is included in GDP. Imputed housing rents and consumption by nonprofit organizations are also omitted from household-survey data (Deaton 2001, p. 133), but in Central Asia they have probably not been captured in the national accounts either.

rates from the history of the preceding years can be misleading. Wiping the slate in 1997, for example, suggests that both Tajikistan and Turkmenistan did well in the late 1990s, but their relatively high growth rates in 1998–2001 have a large element of recovery from the deep troughs of 1996–97.[25] The less spectacular 1998–2001 growth rates for the other three countries are more representative of good performance because they continue positive growth dating back to 1996. Even a decade after independence, long-term indices as in Table 7.1 have advantages over annual growth rates as in Table 1.3.

Although the cardinal measures need to be treated skeptically, the rankings in Table 7.1 appear to be reasonable guides for the 1990s. Uzbekistan was relatively successful in maintaining output levels. Although the heavy hand of the government may have reduced the positive effects of increased exchange possibilities, the government did relatively well on distribution and in providing an economic safety net. Underestimation of 1999 real GDP is greatest in Kazakhstan and the Kyrgyz Republic, because of incomplete coverage of new enterprises and nonmarketed output, and the potential gains from exchange are greatest in these less regulated economies. Tajikistan and Turkmenistan have the fewest offsetting factors, and the gap between output, and *a fortiori* consumption, performance between these two laggards and the other three countries is probably larger than Table 7.1 implies.

In the 2000s the GDP data are conceptually less problematic. There are issues of reliability with respect to the Turkmenistan data, and perhaps with respect to the Uzbekistan data, as the economy's underperformance encourages the autocratic governments to inflate the output data. The rapid growth in Kazakhstan and slower growth elsewhere is indisputable post-2000.

In all five countries the move to a market economy was, unsurprisingly, accompanied by increased inequality. This translated into high poverty rates in the relatively poor and unregulated Kyrgyz economy, although the situation appears to have improved after the mid-1990s as the market economy's operation improved. Poverty rates are even higher in Tajikistan, which was the poorest republic before independence and has suffered from a half decade of civil war and continuingly ineffective economic management. The more regulated economic systems of Uzbekistan and Turkmenistan have been more successful in containing increases in inequality and poverty, although the Turkmenistan data are opaque.[26] Kazakhstan, with its relatively high initial income, has the least absolute poverty.

---

[25] The most spectacular example is Bosnia and Herzegovina's 1996 GDP growth rate of 86% (EBRD Transition Report Update, April 2001, p. 53), which must be one of the highest ever but, although it signalled something positive (recovery from a deep trough), it did not necessarily indicate robust economic health. The Turkmenistan data are especially problematic, and the huge adjustment between the last two columns of Table 7.1 is not consistent even with the high 1999–2001 growth rates in Table 1.3.

[26] Anecdotal evidence for areas away from the capital is less positive. Especially in the Dashoguz district of Turkmenistan, near the Aral Sea, environmental problems have contributed to deteriorating living standards. This is also true of Karakalpakstan and Khorezm in Uzbekistan, but countervailing public actions are more visible in Uzbekistan than in Turkmenistan.

Inequality has increased, as one would expect following the move to a system based on economic rewards, but there has also been substantial movement within the income distribution as different skills and other characteristics are rewarded in the market economy than in the planned economy. The identities of winners and losers will be analyzed in the next chapter. In this chapter I have mentioned the increase in spatial inequality, which may have implications for political stability, especially when regions have ethnic characteristics. Thus, the Russian population in the relatively well-performing northern regions of Kazakhstan may be tempted to secede rather than allow redistribution of their income to other regions. In the Kyrgyz Republic the poor south has become a more fertile ground for political activism and, in general, areas away from the capital cities may resent the contrast between the ostentatious wealth of the elite and their own impoverished situation.

8
Winners and Losers

Who have been the winners and who has lost from the twin changes of the end of central planning and the dissolution of the Soviet Union? Those in power have become wealthy, converting the privileges of the Soviet era into material wealth, and in some cases a new class of rich businesspeople arose from inegalitarian privatization of state assets (or access to their use) or from illegal activities. This phenomenon is most obvious in energy-rich Kazakhstan and Turkmenistan, but throughout the region the *nouveaux riches* could be seen in their BMWs and Mercedes even during the depths of the transitional recession. Apart from this class, there have been other systematic movements in the income distribution. In Eastern Europe and Russia, although inequality and poverty increased, considerable mobility occurred within the income distribution (Jovanovic 2001; Rutkowski 2001). This chapter examines the evidence of such mobility in Central Asia, identifying general patterns and country variations.

8.1 Household Survey Data from the 1990s

In this chapter, household-survey data from Central Asia are used to address the question of who were the winners and who were the losers from the establishment of market-based economies?[1] Chapter 7 described the weaknesses of the household budget survey (HBS) inherited from the Soviet era, and the far superior surveys conducted under the aegis of the World Bank's Living Standards Measurement Study (LSMS). Within Central Asia this dataset is especially rich because we have for the Kyrgyz Republic what is arguably the only before and after transition LSMS surveys (for 1993 as well as for 1996 and later years).

The data for the analysis in this chapter are obtained from five household surveys. Four of these are LSMS household surveys: the 1993 and 1997 Kyrgyzstan LSMS surveys; the 1996 Kazakhstan LSMS; and the 1999 Tajikistan LSMS. For Uzbekistan, the data were collected in the Fergana oblast in 1999 as a pilot study for redesign of the national HBS; although technically not an LSMS survey, the Fergana pilot study followed LSMS methodology. Turkmenistan is not

---

[1] The research on which this chapter is based was conducted jointly with Kathryn Anderson of Vanderbilt University. For more detailed information on the data sources and methods see Anderson and Pomfret (2003).

considered because, although an LSMS survey was conducted in 1998, the results have not been publicized and the data are not available for analysis. The sample sizes are as follows: 1,926 households in 1993 and 2,618 in 1997 for the Kyrgyz Republic;[2] 1,890 for Kazakhstan; 1,983 for Tajikistan; and 542 households for Uzbekistan.

Differences in the samples reflect the higher incomes and more European culture of Kazakhstan, and the more traditionally Central Asian society in Tajikistan and the Fergana oblast of Uzbekistan. Table 8.1 provides summary statistics. The Kazakhstan sample is the most urban, with 44% of households living in rural communities, which is fewer than in the Kyrgyz Republic (57% in 1993 and 62% in 1997), the Fergana oblast of Uzbekistan (72%), or Tajikistan (73%). Households in Kazakhstan are less likely to be headed by a man, and the head is less likely to be married than in households in the Kyrgyz Republic, Tajikistan, or the Fergana oblast of Uzbekistan. Household heads in Kazakhstan are older on average (46 years), than heads in the Kyrgyz Republic (40–41 years), Tajikistan (40 years), and Uzbekistan (39 years). Households are smaller in Kazakhstan than in Tajikistan, Uzbekistan, or the Kyrgyz Republic. The average number of children in a household in Kazakhstan is 1.3, which is less than in the Kyrgyz Republic (1.8 in 1993 and 2.2 in 1997), Uzbekistan (2.7), or Tajikistan (3.5), while the average number of elderly household members is similar in each country (0.4–0.5).[3] The number of children is substantially higher than in European transition economies or elsewhere in the CIS.

The education variables indicate the high education level, relative to income levels, of these countries. Over two-fifths of household heads in each country have post-secondary education. In Kazakhstan the proportion with university education is slightly higher than in the Kyrgyz Republic, Tajikistan, or the Fergana oblast of Uzbekistan.[4] The other human-capital variable, self-reported health of the household head, has some implausible variations, with much worse health reported in Kazakhstan and much better in the Kyrgyz Republic.

The LSMS data have provided the basis for poverty analyses by the World Bank and other researchers. The picture of poverty presented by descriptive analysis is that poverty is higher in rural areas, varies across regions, and is related to ethnicity,

---

[2] The Kyrgyz surveys are not a panel. The sampled households differ, although the technique of random sampling, stratified by community, is constant. Updating of the national household registration files in 1996 led to more households from the mountain region being included in the 1997 sample than in 1993, but the impact of this change is unclear.

[3] An adult is defined as elderly if he or she is eligible for a state pension, normally at age 60 for a man and age 55 for a woman.

[4] The Kyrgyz surveys report a large drop between 1993 and 1997 in the proportion of household heads with vocational education and a consequent increase in the proportion of heads classified with completed secondary education and no additional training. In the Soviet system, vocational-technical programs were often linked to state enterprises, which provided the training to employees who were still completing their secondary education. The precipitous decline in state-enterprise employment during the mid-1990s was associated with the collapse of many of these programs, and people were reclassified as secondary school graduates rather than having vocational training.

Table 8.1.   Summary statistics from Central Asian LSMS surveys.

Variables	Kazakhstan (1996)	Kyrgyz Republic (1993)	Kyrgyz Republic (1997)	Tajikistan (1999)	Fergana (Uzbekistan)
Per capita expenditure	4,963.76	144.61	641.16	15,636	4,115.55
	(3,515.27)	(140.26)	(752.00)	(13,095)	(3,888.75)
Demographic traits					
Male head (%)	61.6	81.8	86.8	91.3	93.9
Head is married (%)	72.1	77.5	77.3	85.5	90.8
Age of head (years)	46.326	41.337	39.713	39.850	38.760
	(14.218)	(13.722)	(12.668)	(11.047)	(10.444)
Health of head of family					
Head in good health (%)	28.9	90.7	90.5	69.3	—
Education of head of family					
College graduate (%)	18.2	16.3	15.8	14.8	14.4
Tecnikum (%)	23.2	18.5	16.9	12.0	14.6
Vocational-technical (%)	32.2	38.0	10.7	22.6	14.8
Completed secondary (%)	11.5	16.9	44.4	35.6	45.3
Incomplete secondary (%)	14.9	10.3	12.2	15.0	10.9
Location of household					
Rural community (%)	43.6	57.1	62.4	72.8	71.5
Capital city (%)	9.4	16.5	15.2	8.9	—
Region 1 (%)	20.7	24.6	13.8	4.0	—
Region 2 (%)	18.1	39.1	35.1	21.5	—
Region 3 (%)	8.5	19.8	35.9	30.4	—
Region 4 (%)	22.3	—	—	35.2	—
Region 5 (%)	21.0	—	—	—	—
Household composition					
Number of children	1.263	1.822	2.234	3.515	2.638
	(1.228)	(1.691)	(1.739)	(2.071)	(1.533)
Number of elderly	0.414	0.511	0.509	0.492	0.490
	(0.676)	(0.731)	(0.733)	(0.733)	(0.739)
Number of nonelderly	1.914	2.603	2.845	3.065	2.843
adults	(1.119)	(1.800)	(1.472)	(1.812)	(1.580)
Sample size (households)	1,890	1,926	2,618	1,983	541

Notes. Standard deviations of continuous variables are in parentheses. Expenditures are in national currency units. The regions are as follows: for Kazakhstan, 1 is central, 2 is south, 3 is west, 4 is north, 5 is east (excluding Almaty); for the Kyrgyz Republic, 1 is Chui, 2 is south, 3 is mountain; for Tajikistan 1 is Gorna Badakhshan, 2 is RRS, 3 is Leninabad, 4 is Khatlon.

education, and dependency. However, many of these characteristics are interrelated. Multivariate analysis of household poverty isolates the impact of the different household characteristics on poverty, holding other things constant, and probit models identify the overwhelming role of location in the capital city, the household head's education, and the number of dependents as key determinants of the probability of a household being above or below the poverty line.[5]

Poverty is one measure of the well-being of households. By focusing on poverty, however, much information about households is lost, because poverty analysis depends on arbitrary poverty lines to classify households as poor or nonpoor. It is also difficult to compare poverty across countries in which poverty lines may represent different consumption standards. A preferable approach to the analysis of material well-being is to examine the distribution of household income or expenditure.

Anderson and Pomfret (2002) estimate a human-capital model in which the per capita expenditure of households is affected by the level of human capital, the number of household members, the location of the household, and demographic characteristics of the household. The dependent variable is household expenditure per capita, based on a headcount of household members and the reported expenditures on goods (excluding vehicles), food, health, education, and other services, housing, utilities, communication, and transportation. Nonpurchased items, such as food grown on household plots, are valued and included in expenditure. Expenditure is preferred to income because the arrears problem in former Soviet republics during the 1990s meant that income often came in lumps so that many households reported zero income during the two-week survey period. Underreporting to avoid tax or other impositions is expected to be less prevalent for expenditure. The measure of household welfare assigns equal expenditure weight to all children and adults in the household.[6]

Household human capital is captured by measures of the education and health of the household head. The head's education level is assumed to be indicative of the household's human capital, and is proxied by dummy variables for college education, Tecnikum education, vocational or other technical training, and completed secondary education, with incomplete secondary schooling as the omitted education category. Health is measured by a dummy variable equal to one if the head reports

---

[5] See the probit analysis by Ackland and Falkingham (1997), by Pomfret and Anderson (1999), and by Falkingham (2000c), and additional references in Pomfret and Anderson (2001). In general, ethnicity proves to be a poor explanatory variable once education, location, and household size are considered, so that ethnic variables are not included here.

[6] In Anderson and Pomfret (2002) we test the sensitivity of our results to this assumption by estimating the model with an alternative dependent variable in which children, women, and the elderly are assigned lower expenditure weights than prime-working-age adult men. This affects the numerical results, but not the qualitative conclusions. The numerical results are also sensitive to the implicit assumption of no scale economies in the provision of household services; adjusting for economies of size with a scaling such as $E^* = E/n^\theta$, where E is household expenditure and n is family size, would soften the conclusion about the impact of family size on per capita consumption, but it is uncertain which equivalence scale would be appropriate. These size economies were small in the Soviet economy where housing costs were low, although they increased during the 1990s (Lanjouw et al. 1998). Lanjouw and Ravallion (1995) argue that household size matters for poverty studies because there are public goods in households and scale economies in housing, although studies of transition economies have found that the qualitative results are not sensitive to assumptions about size economies, e.g., Jovanovic (2001) reports that varying θ within a plausible range did not alter his results for Russia in any significant way.

good or very good health and equal to zero if health is reported to be average, poor, or very poor.

Household composition is measured by three variables describing the number of children under the age of 18, the number of elderly, and the number of nonelderly adults in the household. Other demographic characteristics include the age, gender, and marital status of the head of the household.

The location of the household is measured by a rural–urban dummy variable, and by region-specific variables. In the Kyrgyz Republic, households are classified into four geographical regions: resident of Bishkek; resident of Chui but not living in Bishkek; resident in the southern oblasts of Osh or Jalalabad; and resident in the mountain oblasts of Issyk-Kul, Narun, and Talas. Kazakhstan is divided into six regions: Almaty; southern oblasts other than Almaty; northern oblasts; central oblasts; western oblasts; and eastern oblasts. Tajikistan is divided into five regions: Dushanbe; Gorna-Badakhshan in the east; Regions of Republican Subordination (RRS) in the central western area; Leninabad (Sugd) in the northwest; and Khatlon in the southwest. In the regression equations for each of these three countries, the omitted category for regional location is the largest city: Bishkek, Almaty, and Dushanbe, respectively. For Uzbekistan, only the rural–urban variable is included, because a single oblast was sampled.

In addition to the national-level analysis, Anderson and Pomfret (2003) make two attempts to compare similar locations in different countries. They compare the Fergana oblast of Uzbekistan in 1999 to the parts of the Kyrgyz Republic in 1997 and Tajikistan in 1999 also located in the Ferghana Valley.[7] The Ferghana region of the Kyrgyz Republic is defined as the Osh and Jalalabad oblasts, while the Ferghana region of Tajikistan is the Leninabad (Sugd) oblast. They also compare the experience of households in the three capital cities: Almaty, Kazakhstan's capital in 1996; Bishkek, the Kyrgyz Republic in 1997; and Dushanbe, Tajikistan in 1999.

The results of the ordinary least-squares regressions are presented in Table 8.2 for Kazakhstan, Table 8.3 for the Kyrgyz Republic, and Table 8.4 for Tajikistan. The first and second columns in the tables for Kazakhstan and Tajikistan include the results from estimation of the model including regional variables and a rural–urban variable, while the third and fourth columns contain results from estimation of the model when the region variable is interacted with rural–urban residence. Table 8.3 contains results for the Kyrgyz Republic with a rural–urban variable and regional variables in 1993 and 1997 and using pooled data. The pooled model for the Kyrgyz Republic regresses the log of real per capita expenditure on the explanatory variables, with 1993 as the base year and a price index for 1997 equal to 369. Table 8.5 presents results from expenditure models for the Fergana oblast of Uzbekistan and for the

---

[7] The Ferghana Valley is the most fertile and most densely populated area of Central Asia. In the 1920s and 1930s, the Ferghana Valley was divided between the Kyrgyz, Tajik, and Uzbek Republics of the USSR with economically meaningless borders.

Table 8.2. Regression results: Kazakhstan 1996.

Variables	ln expenditure		ln expenditure	
	Coefficient	*t*-statistic	Coefficient	*t*-statistic
Intercept	8.542*	89.60	8.519*	89.31
Demographic traits				
Head is male	0.033	0.95	0.028	0.81
Age of head	−0.002	−1.12	−0.001	−0.92
Head is married	0.046	1.16	0.044	1.11
Education/health of head				
College graduate	0.272*	5.62	0.268*	5.55
Tecnikum	0.167*	3.63	0.165*	3.60
Vocational-technical training	0.114*	2.56	0.112*	2.54
Completed secondary	−0.001	−0.02	0.006	0.11
Head in good health	−0.032	−1.06	−0.029	−0.94
Location of household				
Rural community	0.117*	4.10	—	—
Central	−0.036	−0.70	—	—
Southern	−0.447*	−8.38	—	—
Western	0.089	1.43	—	—
Northern	0.295*	5.67	—	—
Other eastern (not Almaty)	0.038	0.74	—	—
Rural* central	—	—	0.095	1.56
Urban* central	—	—	−0.045	−0.81
Rural* south	—	—	−0.353*	−5.66
Urban* south	—	—	−0.432*	−7.32
Rural* west	—	—	0.029	0.36
Urban* west	—	—	0.218*	3.04
Rural* north	—	—	0.427*	7.47
Urban* north	—	—	0.284*	4.99
Rural* east	—	—	0.198*	3.43
Urban* east	—	—	−0.009	−0.16
Household composition				
Number of children	−0.174*	−14.04	−0.170*	−13.61
Number of elderly	−0.116*	−3.82	−0.108*	−3.56
Number of nonelderly adults	−0.058*	−4.18	−0.055*	−3.94
R-square	0.300	—	0.306	—
F-statistic	47.14*	—	39.12*	—
Sample size	1,890	—	1,890	—

Note: an asterisk indicates significant at the 5% level.

Ferghana Valley regions of the Kyrgyz Republic and Tajikistan. Table 8.6 presents the estimates for Almaty, Bishkek, and Dushanbe.

Three variables—location, children, and university education—are consistently significant across all four countries studied and play the largest role in determining

Table 8.3. Regression results: Kyrgyz Republic 1993 and 1997.

Variables	ln expenditure		ln expenditure 1993		ln expenditure 1997	
	Coeff.	*t*-statistic	Coeff.	*t*-statistic	Coeff.	*t*-statistic
Intercept	5.248*	58.26	4.887*	28.55	7.348*	89.94
Demographic traits						
Head is male	0.015	0.34	0.113	1.41	−0.089*	−2.09
Age of head	0.0005	0.45	−0.0005	−0.24	0.002*	1.99
Head is married	0.012	0.31	0.066	0.089	0.005	0.14
Education/health of head						
College graduate	0.285*	6.50	0.321*	4.04	0.215*	4.93
Tecnikum	0.144*	3.38	0.199*	2.60	0.074	1.74
Vocational-technical	0.081	1.90	0.120	1.69	−0.060	−1.26
Completed secondary	−0.056	−1.36	−0.105	−1.19	−0.063	−1.62
Head in good health	0.015	0.33	0.097	1.07	−0.011	−0.27
Household location						
Rural community	−0.264*	−8.63	−0.365*	−6.10	−0.177*	−6.42
Chui	−0.184*	−3.90	−0.083	−0.94	−0.256*	−5.74
South	−0.547*	−12.80	−0.373*	−4.51	−0.733*	−18.81
Mountain	−0.728*	−16.53	−0.459*	−5.08	−0.928*	−23.96
Household composition						
Number of children	−0.137*	−16.09	−0.118*	−6.78	−0.139*	−18.68
Number of elderly	−0.068*	−3.86	−0.077*	−2.16	−0.014	−0.84
Number of adults	−0.024*	−2.82	0.002	0.11	−0.073*	−8.37
Year						
1997	0.482*	17.90	—	—	—	—
R-square	0.309	—	0.151	—	0.553	—
F-statistic	125.95*	—	22.47*	—	214.50*	—
Sample size	4,531	—	1,913	—	2,618	—

Note: an asterisk indicates significant at the 5% level.

household expenditure. First, the failure to establish national labor markets even by the late 1990s in Central Asia highlights the lengthy process of institution building required for the effective functioning of a market economy. Second, the higher cost of children reflects the good record of the USSR in satisfying basic needs. (Unlike the elderly, whose living standards were by and large protected during the transition, children suffered from the decline in many social services, which pushed the costs of providing them onto their family.) Third, higher returns to education were expected in a market economy, but few observers distinguish between types of education. These findings support the view that, in a market economy, general-purpose education is most valuable, while vocational training is relatively less valuable than in centrally

Table 8.4.   Regression results: Tajikistan 1999.

Variables	ln expenditure		ln expenditure	
	Coefficient	t-statistic	Coefficient	t-statistic
Intercept	9.927*	114.43	9.920*	114.16
Demographic traits				
Head is male	0.020	0.35	0.021	0.36
Age of head	−0.001	−1.04	−0.001	−1.05
Head is married	0.070	1.51	0.072	1.55
Education/health of head				
College graduate	0.327*	6.97	0.329*	7.01
Tecnikum	0.260*	5.26	0.263*	5.31
Vocational-technical training	0.097*	2.25	0.097*	2.25
Completed secondary	0.023	0.57	0.026	0.64
Head in good health	−0.007	−0.26	−0.006	−0.23
Household location				
Rural community	0.027	0.79	—	—
Gorna-Badakhshan	−0.603*	−7.65	−0.583*	−7.82
RRS	−0.061	−1.06	—	—
Leninabad	−0.335*	−6.36	—	—
Khatlon	−0.344*	−6.38	—	—
Rural RRS	—	—	−0.052	−0.98
Urban RRS	—	—	0.059	0.66
Rural Leninabad	—	—	−0.309*	−6.11
Urban Leninabad	—	—	−0.337*	−5.74
Rural Khatlon	—	—	−0.312*	−6.29
Urban Khatlon	—	—	−0.377*	−5.83
Household composition				
Number of children	−0.088*	−12.80	−0.087*	−12.77
Number of elderly	−0.047*	−2.69	−0.047*	−2.68
Number of nonelderly	−0.006	−0.81	−0.005	−0.69
R-square	0.182	—	0.183	—
F-statistic	27.30*	—	24.43*	—
Sample size	1983	—	1983	—

Note: an asterisk indicates significant at the 5% level.

planned economies. The loss in value of vocational training was exacerbated by the
specificity of Soviet training.

8.2   Household Location

Location is an important factor in determining per capita household expenditure.
Urban–rural differences in per capita expenditure are significant in Kazakhstan, the
Kyrgyz Republic, and the Fergana oblast of Uzbekistan, although not in Tajikistan.

Table 8.5. Regression results: Ferghana region of Uzbekistan, Kyrgyz Republic, and Tajikistan (an asterisk indicates significant at the 5% level).

Variables	Uzbekistan		Kyrgyz Republic		Tajikistan	
	Coeff.	t-statistic	Coeff.	t-statistic	Coeff.	t-statistic
Intercept	8.183*	33.08	6.496*	50.12	9.744*	68.06
Demographic traits						
Head is male	−0.033	−0.18	0.082	1.15	−0.097	−0.89
Age of head	0.007	1.92	0.003	1.81	0.0009	0.45
Head is married	0.092	0.62	−0.142*	−2.41	−0.009	−0.10
Education of head						
College graduate	0.430*	3.09	0.273*	3.69	0.223*	2.50
Tecnikum	0.351*	2.50	0.106	1.48	0.261*	3.12
Vocational-technical	−0.050	−0.34	−0.114	−1.47	0.085	1.06
Completed secondary	0.115	0.93	−0.002	−0.03	0.018	0.25
Head in good health	−0.074	−1.06	0.064	1.28	—	—
Household location						
Rural community	−0.521*	−6.60	−0.229*	−6.10	0.063	1.19
Household composition						
No. of children	−0.123*	−4.99	−0.124*	−12.33	−0.105*	−7.22
No. of elderly	0.105*	2.23	0.033	1.22	−0.054	−1.77
No. of nonelderly adults	−0.021	−0.86	−0.059*	−4.64	−0.031*	−2.07
R-square	0.207	—	0.357	0.147	—	—
F-statistic	12.53*	—	41.66*	8.50*	—	—
Sample size	541	915	603	—	—	—

Note: an asterisk indicates significant at the 5% level.

Within each country for which we have a national survey, some regions are significantly wealthier than others and the estimated coefficients are large.[8]

In the Kyrgyz Republic, rural households' per capita expenditure is, other things being equal, on average 26% lower than that of urban households, although the gap did narrow between 1993 and 1997. Households in the northern oblast of Chui and the capital city of Bishkek are significantly wealthier than those in other regions of the country. The regional differences widen over the transition period. In 1997, a mountain-region household is estimated to have 93% lower per capita expenditure than an identical household in Bishkek. The gap is smaller for the other regions, but still 73% for the south and 26% for Chui, even though the latter is contiguous with Bishkek.

In Kazakhstan, living standards are highest in the north and lowest in the south and, within both the north and the south, rural households are better off than those in

---

[8] Spatial inequality is analyzed in greater depth in Anderson and Pomfret (2005).

Table 8.6.   Regression results: capital cities of
Kazakhstan, Kyrgyz Republic, and Tajikistan.

Variables	Almaty (Kaz.)		Bishkek (Kyrg.)		Dushanbe (Taj.)	
	Coeff.	*t*-statistic	Coeff.	*t*-statistic	Coeff.	*t*-statistic
Intercept	8.848*	33.90	7.584*	38.27	10.170*	41.77
Demographic traits						
Head is male	0.133	1.45	−0.200*	−2.23	−0.120	−0.64
Age of head	−0.003	−0.62	0.0003	0.11	−0.005	−1.23
Head is married	0.010	0.11	0.117	1.38	0.330*	2.05
Education of head						
College graduate	0.245*	2.05	0.073	0.67	0.243	1.67
Tecnikum	0.055	0.43	0.069	0.61	0.019	0.11
Vocational-technical	0.078	0.58	0.048	0.38	0.004	0.02
Completed secondary	0.005	0.03	0.126	1.08	−0.240	−1.59
Head in good health	0.037	0.40	0.163	1.78	0.138	1.39
Household composition						
Number of children	−0.214*	−4.44	−0.183*	−7.32	−0.145*	−4.87
Number of elderly	−0.294*	−3.23	−0.035	−0.77	−0.129	−1.59
No. of other adults	−0.136*	−3.37	−0.177*	−6.73	0.003	0.09
R-square	0.247	—	0.305	—	0.220	—
F-statistic	4.96*	—	15.39*	—	4.16*	—
Sample size	178	—	397	—	174	—

Note: an asterisk indicates significant at the 5% level.

the cities. Per capita expenditure is also relatively high in the rural eastern region and
the urban west. As in the Kyrgyz Republic, the estimated coefficients on location
variables are large. The size of the regional gaps is perhaps masked by the fact that
the omitted location (Almaty) was not an outlier in 1996. A household in the south
had 45% lower and a household in the north 30% higher per capita expenditure
than a similar household in Almaty, which means that per capita expenditure in a
household in the best location was more than 100% higher than that of an identical
household in the worst location. Preliminary results from applying a similar model
to the 2002 household survey suggest that the situation changed dramatically after
1996. In 2002 the same three sets of variables were significantly related to per capita
household expenditure but the location effect was stronger, and the other variables
weaker, than in 1996, and residence in Almaty had a far more positive impact than
residence in any other region (Pomfret 2005c).

In Tajikistan rural–urban differences were insignificant, but regional differences
were substantial in 1999. Households in Dushanbe and the surrounding RRS had
significantly higher expenditure levels than identical households in other areas of
the country. Per capita household expenditure in Gorna-Badakhshan was 60% lower

than in Dushanbe *ceteris paribus* and that in Leninabad and Khatlon was 34% lower than in Dushanbe.

In the Fergana oblast of Uzbekistan, per capita expenditure is 52% lower in rural areas than in urban locations, which is much larger than the effect of rural residence on expenditure in the Ferghana regions of Tajikistan and the Kyrgyz Republic. There is no difference in average expenditure in the urban and rural areas of Ferghana in Tajikistan, but rural expenditure is 23% lower than urban expenditure in the Ferghana area of the Kyrgyz Republic (Table 8.5). This may reflect national policies that have been especially harmful to cotton farmers in Uzbekistan. It could also reflect that the superior economic performance of Uzbekistan during the 1990s has resulted in relatively higher urban living standards. Anecdotal evidence from the southern Kyrgyz Republic indicates a return to the land by poor townsfolk due to depressed urban labor-market conditions, while Tajikistan experienced universally high poverty.

8.3 Household Composition

In all four countries, household composition is an important determinant of per capita household expenditure. The costs of large households are substantial. A recurring result is that additional children lower per capita household expenditure by a larger amount than additional elderly or nonelderly adults do. Unsurprisingly, the costs of additional children, in terms of the negative impact on per capita household expenditure, are larger in the cities.

In Kazakhstan, an additional child reduces per capita household expenditure by 17%, an elderly adult reduces per capita expenditure by 12%, and a nonelderly adult reduces per capita expenditure by 6%. In the Kyrgyz Republic, extra children reduce per capita household consumption by 12 and 14% in 1993 and 1997, respectively. An extra adult also reduces per capita household expenditure but, whereas elderly adults reduce it by 8% in 1993 and nonelderly adults have no significant impact, it is nonelderly adults who reduce per capita household expenditure in 1997, by 7%, while the elderly have no effect. In Tajikistan, each additional child reduces per capita household expenditure by 9%, and each additional elderly adult reduces it by 5%, but additional nonelderly adults do not affect per capita expenditure.

Comparing the Ferghana regions of Uzbekistan, Tajikistan, and the Kyrgyz Republic reveals similarities and differences. In all three countries, an additional child lowers per capita household expenditure by between 10.5 and 12%. The presence of a pensioner has no effect on per capita household expenditure in the Ferghana region of Tajikistan or the Kyrgyz Republic, but in the Fergana oblast of Uzbekistan the presence of a pensioner increases per capita household expenditure by 11%. This is consistent with the evidence, reported in Chapter 3, that Uzbekistan was relatively successful in maintaining its social policies during the transition from central planning. In contrast, nonelderly adults have no impact on per capita household expenditure in the Fergana oblast of Uzbekistan, but an additional nonelderly adult in the household lowers per capita expenditure by 3% in the Ferghana region of Tajikistan and by 6% in the Ferghana region of the Kyrgyz Republic. This suggests that, in the Ferghana Valley, the labor market provides enough income to cover the average expenditure of adults in Uzbekistan, but cannot cover expenditure needs of adults in the poorer countries of Tajikistan and the Kyrgyz Republic.

The effects of household composition on expenditure in the capital cities of Almaty, Bishkek, and Dushanbe are reported in Table 8.6. In all three cities, an additional child substantially lowers per capita household expenditure, *ceteris paribus*, by 21% in Almaty, by 18% in Bishkek, and by 15% in Dushanbe. The negative impact of children on material well-being is stronger in the cities than in the poorer and rural Ferghana Valley. Additional elderly adults have no effect on per capita household expenditure in Bishkek or Dushanbe, which is similar to the result for the Ferghana Valley, but the presence of a pensioner lowers per capita household expenditure significantly in Almaty. In Almaty, the effect of an additional elderly adult on expenditure is 29% and, uniquely, it is larger than the effect of an additional child. An additional working-age adult lowers per capita household expenditure in Bishkek by 18% and in Almaty by 14%, but has no effect in Dushanbe.

8.4   Education and Health

In all four countries, having a college-educated head positively affects household well-being. In Kazakhstan and in the Kyrgyz Republic, per capita expenditure is 27–29% higher in households with a college-educated head than in households whose heads failed to complete secondary school. In the Kyrgyz Republic, the effect of college education drops significantly during the transition period, from 32% in 1993 to 22% in 1997. The effect of a college-educated head is large in Tajikistan (33% higher per capita household expenditure than in households whose head failed to complete secondary education), and larger still in the Fergana oblast of Uzbekistan (43%). Overall, general high-skilled training has helped household heads to substantially improve their families' standard of living.

The effect of Tecnikum training is generally positive, but lower levels of vocational training have less impact on household expenditure and the impact is often not significantly different from zero. In Kazakhstan, having a head with Tecnikum training is associated with 17% higher expenditure than a household whose head failed to complete secondary school, while vocational training is associated with 11% higher expenditure. In the Kyrgyz Republic having a head with noncollege, post-secondary training had no effect on per capita household expenditure in 1997, although Tecnikum education yielded a 20% return in the early transition year of 1993. In Tajikistan having a head with Tecnikum training raises per capita household expenditure by 26%, while a head with vocational education raises expenditure by 10%.

In the Ferghana Valley, university education has large returns in all countries, and Tecnikum education has large returns in Uzbekistan and Tajikistan. There is no difference among the effects of other education categories. The largest returns are in Uzbekistan, at 43% for university education and 35% for Tecnikum education. In Tajikistan, returns to university and to Tecnikum education are similar, 22 and 26%. In the Kyrgyz Republic, the return to university education is 27%, but the return to Tecnikum education is not statistically significant and the point estimate is only 11%.

Completion of secondary education appears to have no benefits in terms of a head's ability to increase household expenditure relative to that of a household headed by somebody with only primary or incomplete secondary education. The second measure of human capital, self-reported health of the head, also has no impact on expenditure.

8.5 Demographic Traits and Year

The demographic traits of age, gender, and marital status of the household head are generally not significant determinants of household expenditure. The age coefficient is positive and significant for the Kyrgyz Republic in 1997, but elsewhere it does not differ significantly from zero. In the Kyrgyz Republic in 1997, expenditure is 9% lower if the head is male, and the negative effect is even more pronounced in Bishkek, but this variable is not statistically significant in the other countries or with the 1993 Kyrgyz data. Having a married head is positive and significant in Dushanbe and in the Ferghana region of the Kyrgyz Republic, but not in Almaty or Bishkek; nor is marital status significant in any of the national or other Ferghana Valley samples.

In the pooled expenditure regression results for the Kyrgyz Republic in 1993 and 1997 (Table 8.3) real per capita expenditure is 48% higher in 1997 than in 1993, holding other determinants of household expenditure constant. The fit of the human-capital model is substantially better in 1997 than in 1993; R^2 increases from 0.15 to 0.55. The interpretation by Anderson and Pomfret (2000) is that the Kyrgyz economy was becoming more similar to established market economies in which human-capital variables provide an accepted explanation of differences in living standards. Other R^2 values also track the degree of marketization. The R^2 for Kazakhstan (0.30) is higher than that for Tajikistan (0.18). In the Ferghana Valley, the R^2 for the Kyrgyz Republic (0.36) is higher than for Uzbekistan (0.21) or Tajikistan (0.15); the Kyrgyz Republic has had the most extensive transition from central planning, while in Tajikistan the ongoing political problems have impeded establishment of institutions needed for well-functioning markets.

8.6 Summary and Relations to Other Research

Analysis of the determinants of household living standards in the Central Asian transition economies during the second half of the 1990s indicates three strong relationships. First, location is very important; whether this reflects specific cultural factors of the region or the time needed to create national labor markets in these economically least-developed parts of the former USSR is uncertain. Second, the costs of large families and in particular the higher private cost of children in a market economy than in a planned economy that provided cradle to grave support are also significant. Third, education brings greater material reward in the market economy but, in the shift from central planning, people with high-level general education have been best able to take advantage of new opportunities. By contrast, narrower technical education has left many with obsolete skills yielding no returns in the market. These results are consistent with evidence from other formerly centrally planned economies, although they have not been emphasized in the transition literature. The first two relationships may be of special significance to Central Asia, with its relative economic backwardness and high birth rate, but the importance of high-level general-purpose education appears to be a general, but underappreciated, factor.

The literature on earnings in Eastern Europe has focused on labor-market institutions, and the relationship between the degree of labor-market regulation and the responsiveness of labor demand to changes in sales and of labor supply to changes in wages (Svejnar 1999). The strength of the regional variables in Central Asia suggests that national labor markets scarcely exist in these countries or that people respond poorly to financial incentives to relocate. In either case, the Central Asian countries are much further from having a well-functioning market economy than are Eastern European countries. This may reflect cultural factors such as the strength of the extended family (Buckley 1998). Jovanovic (2001), however, reports similar results for Russia, which suggests a common problem in the former Soviet Union due to economic obstacles such as poor infrastructure[9] or undeveloped housing markets, rather than features specific to Central Asian culture.

Analysis of changes over time in the Kyrgyz Republic suggests that, despite gradual improvement in the standard of living of households as the market economy developed, poverty reduction and improvement in household well-being may take many years. This could reflect the deep institutional obstacles to establishment of a market economy or the extremely poor physical infrastructure that sharply separates the regions of individual countries. Applying human-capital models over time indicates that market forces are taking firmer hold, but the fragmentation of national labor markets suggests that the process still has a long way to go in Central Asia.

The rural–urban division, while strongly related to poverty in simple cross-tabulations, is much subtler. In Kazakhstan, distinctions exist between the disadvantaged rural south and relatively affluent rural areas in other regions with differing

---

[9] In the product market context, Aghion and Schankerman (1999) emphasize the role of improved infrastructure in reducing transaction costs and hence increasing competition. Their argument is supported by the convergence of infrastructure in Poland, Hungary, and the Czech Republic towards Western European standards. In all three countries, the degree of competition appears to have been increasing. Similar causality works in labor markets; an oft-cited example is the impact of U.S. road building in eastern Thailand during the 1960s in creating a national labor market and contributing to the rapid economic growth in Thailand during the final quarter of the twentieth century.

agrarian bases, i.e., cereals and livestock rather than cotton. In the Kyrgyz Republic, the rural disadvantage applies to all regions, while in Tajikistan rural locations in the south and north do relatively better than those in the east or the center-west. The Ferghana Valley comparison highlights a possible explanation for these variations: in very poor areas experiencing severe economic decline, as in the south of the Kyrgyz Republic and much of Tajikistan, a retreat to the rural economy is a coping mechanism because self-sufficiency is preferable to destitution in economically decaying towns.

The increased cost of large households, and especially households with many children, is a recurring finding in the empirical literature on transition. In part, this is explained by cutbacks in the real value of social assistance. Pensioners, however, generally succeeded in maintaining their relative living standards, even when pension payments became large proportions of government budgets (Cangiano et al. 1998; Anderson and Becker 1999). The Soviet pension scheme related payments to the minimum wage and had generous coverage. During the early and mid-1990s, many transition economies actually eased eligibility before the normal age of 60 for males and 55 for females to cushion the effects of increased unemployment and other economic pressures, although the prevalence of payments arrears makes it difficult to assess the net impact.[10] One consequence was severe budget pressure as state pensions came to account for a large share of GDP, e.g., 15% in Poland from 1992 to 1994 (Cangiano et al. 1998, p. 14) and over 10% in Uzbekistan. Budgetary pressure contributed to the need for reform and major reforms were introduced, including in Kazakhstan in 1997, but these changes occurred only after the surveys on which our results are based.

The cost of children is more complex than the cost of pensioners, who are more or less nonworking adults receiving a state subsidy. The cost of children is more than simply their consumption minus child-support payments (Falkingham 2000b). In particular, parents faced a sharp reduction in kindergarten availability and increased private costs of schooling.[11] Cultural pressures not to send children to school in poor clothing or old shoes have added to these costs, as even poor parents are willing to incur high costs in order to send their children to school in decent dress (Howell 1996a). A reduction in freely available health services may also have impinged more on families with children.

The existing literature on education in transition deals mainly with estimating returns to years of education, without distinguishing between types of education. An exception is the comparative study by Newell and Reilly (1999), who use data

---

[10] In Kazakhstan in the mid-1990s, according to de Castello Branca (1998), half of those receiving pensions were below the normal retirement age.

[11] Kindergartens were often provided by enterprises and were one of the first noncore activities to be divested during transition (Klugman 1999). This is especially important in view of the relatively late age for starting formal schooling in the Soviet education system, normally seven. Many state schools introduced unofficial fees during the 1990s to help provide even basic education.

from nine transition economies to estimate rates of return to an extra year of post-secondary schooling. They distinguish between university and technical training, and the returns are generally higher to the former, but the evidence is spotty and the distinction between the two types of post-secondary education is not pursued. National studies have shown increases in the returns to education during transition to a market-oriented economy.[12] In Estonia, employment of university-educated workers rose absolutely, even as overall employment declined substantially, and the skill premium for university-educated workers relative to workers with only primary education increased from 11% in 1989 to 69% in 1995. Noorkiov et al. (1997) suggest that this change can be attributed to especially drastic labor-market liberalization in Estonia, but they do not focus on the specific qualities of university education. Rutkowski (2001) observes that, in Hungary, skilled manual workers were the hardest hit as their wages fell by 14% between 1992 and 1997, but he does not discuss the redundant nature of skills acquired in pre-transition vocational training. Jovanovic (2001) finds a larger and more consistently significant impact of university, as opposed to technical education, on household expenditure in Russia, but does not comment on it.

The clearest finding from Central Asian poverty studies and the cross-country household expenditure analysis concerns the importance of college education and the lack of evidence of positive returns to other forms of education. In a more detailed analysis of the Kyrgyz Republic, Anderson and Pomfret (2000) find that the return to university education increased while the returns to vocational training declined, and they interpret this result as support for the idea that general-purpose education becomes particularly valuable in disequilibrium situations (Schultz 1975). The benefits of a nonspecialized higher education would be especially apparent in dealing with the huge unanticipated shocks associated with the dissolution of the USSR. However, the benefits are also likely to be important in the uncertain world of a market economy, in contrast to Soviet planning in which rules of thumb were useful, initiative was not encouraged, and education was undervalued. In three of the Central Asian countries, prospects existed in the 1990s to benefit from the identification of profitable opportunities. The relatively unchanged, and desperately poor, economy of Tajikistan was the exception to this general finding. On the other hand, the fairly narrow vocational training offered in nonuniversity post-secondary institutions in the USSR had little economic value after the demise of central planning.

One corollary of these findings is that increased returns to education have benefited female at least as much as male workers so that the gender wage gap has generally narrowed since the end of central planning. Hunt (1998) has argued that, in East Germany where women's wages rose by ten percentage points relative to men's wages, four-fifths of the reduction in the gap was due to a selection process whereby

---

[12] In, for example, the Czech Republic (Vecernik 1995; Chase 1998), East Germany (Krueger and Pischke 1995), Hungary and Poland (Rutkowski 1996, 2001), Slovenia (Orazem and Vodopivec 1995), Russia (Newell and Reilly 1996; Brainerd 1998), and Estonia (Noorkiov et al. 1997).

poorly qualified women withdrew from the labor force. In other transition countries, however, little difference is found between the decline in male and female labor force participation rates.[13] Anderson and Pomfret (2001) find that better-educated female workers have been the biggest winners from transition in the Kyrgyz Republic, despite fears that the position of women would deteriorate in the Islamic countries of Central Asia.

8.7 Conclusions

The 1990s saw dramatic and traumatic economic and social change in Central Asia. The end of central planning, dissolution of the USSR and hyperinflation were accompanied by falling average living standards and rising inequality, as well as by large shifts in families' positions in the income distribution. Some people became very rich, and some had opportunities denied before 1991. Other people who might have expected a comfortable life under the old regime saw their living standards collapse, especially those with vocational training who were working their way up a state enterprise and had a family to support. Some who were at the bottom of the ladder in the Soviet era became more impoverished as they lost social benefits previously taken for granted.

The situation since the turn of the century has been less dramatic. Those who benefited from the privatization of state assets or from their political power base have little desire for further change, and may even be working towards reforms such as strengthening the protection of property rights. This is especially true of Kazakhstan, and less so for Uzbekistan, which fits better with Hellman's model of partial reform where vested interests resist further change because they have learned how to benefit from the distorted economy.

For those at the bottom of the economic and social pyramid, the nadir was generally in 1996 or 1997. Although conditions remain dire in the poorest areas of Tajikistan, and very bad in rural areas of the other southern Central Asian countries, the absolute poverty rate has probably been declining. This seems definitely to be the case in Kazakhstan and the Kyrgyz Republic. The evidence is least transparent in Turkmenistan.

Regional divisions remain important, as do environmental issues, with areas like Dashoguz in Turkmenistan or the Karakalpakstan autonomous republic in Uzbekistan or South Kazakhstan where widespread poverty is exacerbated by the negative effects of the desiccation of the Aral Sea. Within Central Asia, regional inequality could be critical for internal social and political stability in light of the ethnic distribution of the countries' populations. In the first post-Soviet decade, ethnic tensions were muted, but more recently there have been clashes in the Ferghana Valley and along the Turkmenistan–Uzbekistan border, which have often involved minorities

---

[13] Newell and Reilly (2001) report evidence from six Eastern European economies and five former Soviet republics. See also Ham et al. (1999) on the Czech and Slovak Republics.

living in economically disadvantaged regions, e.g., Uzbeks in the Dashoguz region of Turkmenistan or the Leninabad (Sugd) region of Tajikistan or in southern parts of the Kyrgyz Republic. In Kazakhstan the shift in relative advantage between the 1990s and early 2000s from the primarily Russian areas of northern and northeastern Kazakhstan to the financial and political capitals of Almaty and Astana may become a source of political tension.

What does the future hold for living standards across the region? With the establishment of market-based economies, wrenching economic changes like those of the 1990s are unlikely to be repeated. There will, of course, be variations in economic performance, but, short of political or social collapse or of war, the expectation is of less economic drama in the coming decades.

Part III

The International Context

9

The Role of Natural Resources

In the individual country chapters much of the explanation of national patterns of economic development was in terms of varying political responses to common initial conditions and challenges. Central Asia's post-independence economic history can also be explained in large degree by the region's resource endowments and by variations in the world price of the main primary-product exports. Uzbekistan's good economic performance during 1992–96 coincided with buoyant cotton prices, and after 1996 this economic boost was absent. Kazakhstan's fortunes revolved around world oil prices which were stagnant during the 1990s but soared after 1999. Turkmenistan's idiosyncratic path is fueled by natural-gas rents, while the Kyrgyz Republic and Tajikistan struggle because they have few readily exploitable and exportable natural resources.

This chapter analyzes the role of natural resources in Central Asia in greater depth. Outside the region, the focus has been on the Caspian Basin as a potentially large source of untapped oil reserves, but this mainly concerns Kazakhstan (and Azerbaijan). For Central Asia as a whole, cotton is of greater significance and it will be dealt with first.

9.1 Cotton

Cotton is by far the most important crop in Central Asia. Indeed the timing of the incorporation of the area south of the steppe into the Russian Empire in the 1860s partly reflected fears of a cotton famine due to the U.S. civil war. The cotton economy expanded during the Tsarist and Soviet eras, and especially rapidly in the period after the second world war. Major irrigation projects, of which the Karakum Canal in southern Turkmenistan was the largest and most environmentally disastrous, brought large new areas into cotton production at the cost of reducing the Aral Sea, the world's fourth-largest lake in 1960, to a couple of ponds by 2000. The mechanization of cotton harvesting was a propaganda coup in the 1960s aimed at showing the Third World how modernization was occurring in the poorest part of the USSR.

Much of the cotton output in the Soviet era went to cotton mills in the Russian republic. The cotton which was sold on world markets went through centralized

Table 9.1.   Cotton output, 2004–05 season (thousands of tonnes).

	Production	Exports
Kazakhstan	142	114
Kyrgyz Republic	48	44
Tajikistan	174	131
Turkmenistan	207	87
Uzbekistan	1,089	740
World total	25,412	7,247

Source: United States Department of Agriculture, Foreign Agricultural Service (www.fas.usda.gov/cotton/circular/2005/02/table05a.pdf).

foreign trade agencies, with little direct benefit to the growers.[1] After independence a major windfall to the southern republics was that they now controlled cotton sales. Cotton was readily sold through international brokers, such as Paul Reinhart in Winterthur, Switzerland, or Cargill in Liverpool, England, and its portability and high value–weight ratio meant that it could be transported by rail or air.

According to data from the International Cotton Advisory Committee, in 1990 Uzbekistan was the world's second-largest cotton exporter (397,000 tonnes) and Tajikistan the fourth largest (200,000 tonnes). Cotton was also a significant export for Turkmenistan and was regionally important for the southern part of the Kyrgyz republic and for South Kazakhstan. Acreage sown with cotton in Soviet Central Asia in 1988 was 3,133,000 hectares, of which 2,017,000 were in the Uzbek republic, 636,000 in the Turkmen republic, 320,000 in the Tajik republic, 128,000 in Kazakhstan, and 32,000 in the Kyrgyz republic (Lewis 1992, p. 144).

Since independence cotton exports are of great importance, accounting for 6.5% of GDP in Uzbekistan, 8.2% of GDP in Tajikistan, and 3.6% of GDP in Turkmenistan (Baffes 2004, p. 36). Uzbekistan increased its supplies to the world market, reaching a peak of 900,000 tonnes exported in 1998 and in 1999. Output, however, stagnated in Tajikistan and in Turkmenistan during the 1990s, because of poor maintenance of irrigation canals and also due to civil war in Tajikistan; both have had harvests of over a million tonnes in the past, but were producing only a fifth of that in the 2004–05 harvest (Table 9.1). In 2002 Uzbekistan was still the world's second-biggest cotton exporter (with 717,000 tonnes), but Tajikistan had slipped to ninth (147,000 tonnes). Poor management and diversion to domestic textile mills have dramatically reduced Turkmenistan's cotton exports to the point that they are now lower than Kazakhstan's (Table 9.1).

---

[1] The Uzbek republic, however, benefited by more than it was supposed to as the local leadership masterminded an overstatement of cotton output which directed billions of extra rubles into the republic. The Uzbek leadership was one of the first targets of Mikhail Gorbachev's anticorruption campaign, although long-term leader Sharif Rashidov avoided punishment by his timely death in 1986. After independence Rashidov was treated as a national hero in Uzbekistan and one of the main streets in Tashkent was named after him.

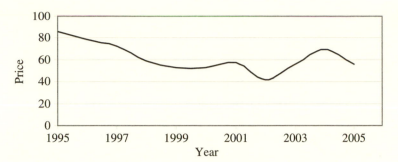

Figure 9.1. The world price of cotton, 1995–2005. Source: Cotlook 'A' (NE) index accessed on May 10, 2005, from www.cotlook.com/cdis/more_cotlook_indices.php.

One drawback of cotton dependence is the volatility of world prices (Figure 9.1). In January 1992 the price was $1.31 per kilogram. In May 1995 it peaked at $2.53. This is the context for Uzbekistan's success in limiting the negative impact of the transitional recession. It should, however, be pointed out that, although Uzbekistan was lucky in world price movements for its main export, it did succeed in realizing the earnings, while the other cotton regions of Central Asia were less successful in maintaining cotton output and in getting the crop to world markets. The world price dropped to $1.66 by October 1996 when Uzbekistan was starting to sell that year's harvest, and this provided the backdrop to the panic over the balance of payments that led to the hurried introduction of exchange controls. Worse was to follow as the world price of cotton bottomed at 82 cents in October 2001. Two years later it had doubled, but it then fell by about a quarter in the 2004–05 harvest season. In Uzbekistan and Turkmenistan the volatility mainly affects government revenues, because the state order systems insulate farmers from world price movements.

A second drawback of cotton dependence is the prospect that world prices may be in secular decline. The nominal price per kilogram was lower in January 2002 than in January 1952 ($0.96 versus $1.05). Given the price volatility, the nominal price comparison is of course sensitive to choice of dates, but it is indisputable that in real terms (e.g., relative to the price of manufactured goods) cotton prices have declined substantially over the last half century. Part of the decline is due to tastes and technology as artificial fibres have challenged cotton and as genetically modified cotton has raised the productivity of cotton producers in the United States, Australia, and China. Part, however, reflects policy decisions in high-income countries who provide huge subsidies to cotton producers. This has been especially true since 1985 in the United States, when the policy shifted from stockpiling to price supports, and since Greek and Spanish accession to the European Union in the 1980s.

The direct assistance to cotton production in the 2001–02 season amounted to $2.3 billion in the United States and $0.8 billion in the European Union. U.S. producer prices were 91% higher than world prices, and in Greece and Spain the producer prices were 144% and 184% above world prices. Other OECD producers

(Turkey and Mexico) provided smaller amounts of direct assistance to cotton producers.[2] Estimates of the effects of removing these production and export subsidies go as high as a 71% increase in cotton prices (using 2001–02 as the base year), and a 6% increase in the volume of Uzbekistan's cotton exports (Baffes 2004, pp. 18–19). If the assistance were to be removed overnight, the direct effects via the world price would raise GDP in both Uzbekistan and Tajikistan by around five percentage points, and this is not counting the indirect effects of greater price incentives (Pomfret 2005a). Unfortunately, the policies are unlikely to change so drastically: the 2002 U.S. farm bill is effective until 2007 and in the European Union the focus in agricultural policy reform is on items whose supply will be greatly increased by the 2004 cohort of new EU members, none of whom produces cotton in significant quantities.

Cotton prices have also been depressed by rich countries' polices towards imports of textiles and clothing. The Multifibre Arrangement (MFA) and its successor the Agreement on Textiles and Clothing, which took these products outside WTO rules and allowed substantial trade barriers to persist, not only reduced demand for textiles and clothing and hence demand for all fibres covered by the ATC, but also discriminated against cotton relative to other fibres.[3] These arrangements were phased out as part of the 1994 Uruguay Round Agreement, but the process was back-loaded and was only completed at the end of 2004. The demise of these restrictions was due to the more active participation of low-wage countries in multilateral trade negotiations. A lesson for cotton producers is that the WTO is likely to be the most effective forum for lobbying against the producer support programs that distort world cotton markets. Some West African cotton producers and Brazil have started to use this forum, and WTO accession by Uzbekistan and Tajikistan would add weight to these poor countries' case (see Section 10.2).

Domestic conditions within the cotton-producing countries of Central Asia have varied considerably since independence and are more difficult to document than world market conditions.

Turkmenistan and Uzbekistan have retained state procurement systems for cotton. In contrast, the neighboring Kyrgyz Republic eliminated state procurement in 1992 and Kazakhstan and Tajikistan did so in the mid-1990s. This is reflected in substantial differences in farmgate prices. Table 9.2 reports the local-currency price of cotton for the 1997 harvest season, and the U.S. dollar equivalent. The average border parity price was estimated by Goletti and Chabot (2000, p. 55) at $404 per tonne, which is not far from the prices received by farmers in the Kyrgyz Republic,

---

[2] The International Cotton Advisory Committee estimates that global support for cotton producers in 2001–02 was $5.8 billion, including an estimated (but doubtful) $1.3 billion in China. Australia (the third-largest cotton exporter after the United States and Uzbekistan) is recorded as having little or no government intervention, although underpricing of irrigation water subsidizes water-intensive crops like cotton.

[3] Will Martin estimated in 1996 that the MFA imposed an implicit tax of 20% on cotton relative to other fibres, and that ending the MFA would increase the world price of cotton by 4% (quoted in Baffes 2004, p. 18).

Table 9.2. Output price for cotton, 1997 harvest season.

	Kazakhstan	Kyrgyz Rep.	Tajikistan	Turkmenistan	Uzbekistan
Local-currency units	25,500 tenge	7,100 som	190,000 TR	1,000,000 manat	14,750 sum
USD at official exchange rate	349	394	388	240	242
USD at parallel exchange rate	—	—	—	188	105

Source: Goletti and Chabot (2000, p. 55).

Table 9.3. Cost per kilogram of nutrient (in U.S. dollars).

	Kazakhstan	Kyrgyz Rep.	Tajikistan	Turkmenistan	Uzbekistan
Nitrogen	0.50	0.50	0.50	0.12	0.25
Phosphorous	1.50	1.50	1.00	1.00	0.50
Potassium	0.16	0.16	0.15	0.04	0.07

Source: Goletti and Chabot (2000, p. 60), citing data from a European Union–Tacis 1995 report.

Tajikistan, and Kazakhstan, but substantially above the prices which farmers receive in Turkmenistan or Uzbekistan.

In their study of agricultural prices in eighteen developing countries, Krueger et al. (1988) found that overvalued exchange rates imposed a more serious burden on farmers than did trade barriers or other direct taxes. Uzbekistan introduced strict foreign-exchange controls in October 1996 and the black-market premium subsequently widened. Goletti and Chabot calculate that at the parallel exchange rate the local-currency price in Table 9.2 of 14,750 sum per tonne translates into $105 per tonne, or about a quarter of the border parity price. The burden of the overvalued exchange rate, represented by the gap between domestic and world prices, increased in the remainder of the 1990s. Turkmenistan's black-market premium only became substantial in 1998, so the effect of foreign-exchange controls is not very great in Table 9.2, but it has become a major source of price distortion since 1997.

In the more regulated systems of Turkmenistan and Uzbekistan, farmers receive subsidized inputs and appear to benefit from more reliable supply of seed and fertilizers and better-managed irrigation than farmers in the Kyrgyz Republic or Tajikistan. Goletti and Chabot provide data on differences in fertilizer prices (Table 9.3), and comment on the incentives to smuggle from Turkmenistan and Uzbekistan to neighboring countries. Smuggling may benefit the farmers involved, but provision of incentives to smuggle is socially inefficient. Farmers in Turkmenistan and Uzbekistan also benefit from advanced interest-free partial payments, although it is unclear how promptly these and the final payments are made available and the extent to which farmers are free to use monies credited to their bank accounts. Efficiency of water use does not appear to differ much among the Central Asian countries, apart from war-torn Tajikistan, and all five countries' cotton sectors appear to be wasteful of water relative to cotton growers elsewhere. In 1996–98, kilograms of seed cotton produced per thousand cubic meters of water used were 309 in Kazakhstan, 230 in the Kyrgyz Republic, 125 in Tajikistan, 256 in Turkmenistan, and 273 in Uzbekistan—all of these figures are much lower than in other cotton-producing countries, e.g., 462 in Syria, 487 in California, 610 in Australia, and 1,027 in Greece (Goletti and Chabot 2000, p. 62).

Uncertainty about the net benefits from liberalization of the cotton sector arise from coordination problems associated with supplying services with public-goods attributes,[4] such as research and extension services, quality control, and input credit (where there is potential for free-riding). In Africa, the francophone countries, which invest in public-sector agencies that deliver services to cotton producers, have performed better than the anglophone countries that liberalized their cotton markets in 1994–95, and among the latter those with more concentrated market systems (Zambia and Zimbabwe) fared better than those with more atomized market systems (Tanzania and Uganda). Poulton et al. (2004) ascribe this to a trade-off between the incentive benefits of competitive markets and the coordination benefits of more concentrated market systems. In Central Asia, the countries with state-controlled markets have also used the market system to transfer resources from the farm sector to the state budget.

Figure 9.2 presents a simple partial equilibrium model of the cotton market in Uzbekistan and Turkmenistan. Assuming a perfectly elastic demand for exports (D_w) at the world price (P_w) and given the domestic supply and demand curves (S_d and D_d), the free-market outcome would involve production of OQ_2, domestic sales of OQ_1, and exports of Q_1Q_2. With a two-tier pricing system of a controlled price (P_c) on a specified output (OQ_3) and a higher market-related price on additional output, then as long as farmers receive the world price for their extra output, the outcome will be the same level of output, domestic sales, and exports as in the free-market outcome. The only difference between these two outcomes is that the dual-pricing mechanism transfers $(P_w - P_c) \cdot OQ_3$ from farmers to the government; the tax rate is determined by the values of P_c and Q_3. If the demand and supply curves capture social as well as private benefits and costs, then both outcomes are efficient, and only differ in their distributional patterns.

The cotton sectors in Turkmenistan and in Uzbekistan diverge from the basic dual-pricing model combining allocative efficiency with state revenue raising due

---

[4] Pure public goods are nonrival and nonexclusive. Additional consumers do not add to the cost of providing a public good, whereas a "rival" good such as an apple cannot be consumed by everybody. Nonexclusive goods can be consumed without direct payment, e.g., individuals cannot be easily excluded from the benefits of national defense or of a pest-eradication campaign. The potential for free-riders to under-contribute to the cost of public goods while still enjoying the benefits means that they will be underprovided by the market mechanism.

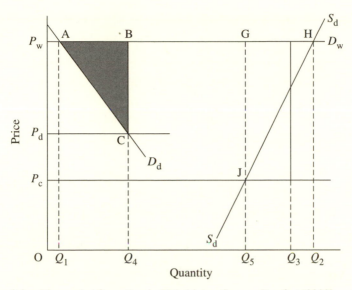

Figure 9.2. The market for cotton in Uzbekistan. Source: Pomfret (2000b, p. 274).

to three distortions. The following analysis (from Pomfret 2000b) is of Uzbekistan's cotton sector, but qualitatively the Turkmenistan system is the same.

Part of cotton output is reserved for domestic mills at a price (P_d in Figure 9.2) below the world price.[5] Subsidizing domestic mills through lower cotton prices stimulates domestic cotton sales, by $Q_1 Q_4$ relative to the free-market outcome, with an equal decline in cotton exports. Artificially low cotton prices for domestic mills reduce the government's revenue from the cotton tax by the area ($P_w BC P_d$), but the benefit to the mills ($P_w AC P_d$) is less than this amount and there is an uncompensated loss to the nation, measured by the shaded triangle ABC, from overexpansion of the textile industry. There is no direct impact on farmers; they receive price P_c on the $O Q_4$ units, whether the cotton ends up in domestic or foreign mills.

Secondly, practically all farmers' cotton output has been sold through state orders at the controlled price, with no sales at a price above P_c.[6] Thus, Q_3 is so far to the right as to be irrelevant and farmers' revenue is a rectangle with height $O P_c$, rather than a lazy-L with higher marginal revenue on units $Q_2 Q_3$. This is important not only because of the distributional outcome, but also because output decisions are made at the margin. If all output is sold at a price P_c, then farmers will cut

---

[5] In Uzbekistan P_d was less than half of P_w in 1992 (Connolly and Vatnick 1994, p. 209). In 1998 one-seventh of the cotton output went to domestic mills and the rest was exported.

[6] In Uzbekistan's state order system the percentage of the two main crops that must be sold to the state was gradually reduced during the late 1990s, but, if a farm produced less than its target output for cotton, then the entire crop had to be sold through the state order system. With the long-term decline in cotton productivity, this was a common outcome. Starting in 2002 procurement prices were liberalized in Uzbekistan, but the price officially received by farmers remained below the world price, and in practice it was hard for farmers to obtain money from the banking system (ICG 2005, p. 4).

Table 9.4.   Estimated transfers out of agriculture.

	Year	Coverage	Value	Reference
Turkmenistan				
Lerman and Brooks (L&B)	1998	Cotton and wheat	1,565 billion manat	11% of GDP
Pastor and van Rooden	1999	Cotton and wheat	2,880 billion manat	15% of GDP
L&B adjusted	1999	Cotton and wheat	7,330 billion manat	—
Uzbekistan				
Connolly and Vatnick	1992	Cotton	$367 million	—
Khan	1995	Agriculture	10% of GDP produced in agriculture	—
Herman	1996	Cotton and wheat	$1,533 million	8% of GDP

Sources and notes: see the appendix at the end of this chapter.

back supply (to OQ_5 in Figure 9.2), with a national welfare loss (GHJ) on foregone exports.

The third major distortion is the subsidization of inputs, which shifts the supply curve for cotton growers to the right. Whether the incentive to grow more cotton increases or decreases national welfare depends primarily on whether output is close to OQ_2 or to OQ_5. In the free market or the pure Chinese dual-pricing model, the optimum output (OQ_2) is achieved and input subsidies will induce undesirable over-expansion of cotton output. In Turkmenistan and Uzbekistan, where many marginal decisions are based on the controlled price of cotton and output may be suboptimal, input subsidies may be a correcting distortion in the cotton sector, although they may create undesirable distortions in the input markets.

Table 9.4 summarizes the publicly available estimates of transfers out of agriculture in Turkmenistan and Uzbekistan during the 1990s. The distortions and transfers are significantly higher in Turkmenistan, and the gap between the two countries is likely to have widened since 2000 as the exchange rate distortion in Turkmenistan has increased while that in Uzbekistan is being reduced.

How are the agricultural rents used? In Turkmenistan the difference between domestic cotton prices and world prices is divided between the cotton-marketing agency, the state budget, and the Agricultural Development Fund (ADF) "in proportions that are not transparently displayed" (Lerman and Brooks 2001, p. 8). The cotton marketing agency provides some services, e.g., extension advice and provision of some inputs not provided by state ginneries or other agencies, but its accounts have not been made public. The ADF was created in 1996 to manage centralized investments and to repay foreign debts associated with the agricultural sector, although it has also been involved in nonagricultural projects (e.g., construction of the Ak-Altyn Hotel in Ashgabat). The residual difference between revenue from cotton sales, payments to cotton farmers and to the cotton marketing agency, and transfers to the ADF should show up as state budget revenues. In the 1998 budget, cotton revenues are shown as $199 billion manat, which is much less than Lerman and Brooks's calculated residual (2,030 revenue minus 700 to farmers minus 355 to the ADF minus marketing agency costs).

The most likely explanation of the gap is that cotton, or revenue from cotton exports, was channeled through the myriad off-budget funds directly controlled by the president. Prestige construction projects in the mid-1990s, such as the national airport, the presidential palace, and the grandiose monuments in Ashgabat were paid for in cash or in cotton. Later, in the early 2000s, Turkmenistan appeared to be accumulating foreign debt at commercial rates, but in the 1990s the foreign contractors (e.g., Bouyges from France, Siemens from Germany, and Mitsui from Japan) were paid out of current income.

In both Turkmenistan and Uzbekistan cotton mills benefited from input prices below world cotton prices. In Turkmenistan the distortion became larger as funds were used in the late 1990s and early 2000s to build up a substantial cotton textile and apparel industry. By the end of 2000 this industry was absorbing a third of the cotton crop and probably had negative value-added at world prices; the value of the finished cotton products may even have been less than the value of the raw cotton used in their manufacture (Pomfret 2001). Uzbekistan's promotion of its textile industry was less extreme and the costs were being acknowledged by 2001 when the government indicated a shift to a less dirigiste industrial policy. Most of the agricultural transfers in Uzbekistan appear to go to general government revenue.

Agricultural rents are vulnerable to adverse supply responses. There is considerable evidence that the negative supply response to state marketing of crops like cotton or cocoa is small in the short term, when the rents are a ready source of government revenue, but becomes larger.

The most serious consequences of punitive taxation of an export crop are the long-run loss of sales and encouragement of illegal economic activities. In Figure 9.2 a uniform tax ($P_w - P_c$) on all output will reduce supply from the free market or dual-pricing level, OQ_2, to OQ_5; the value of output is cut by $(Q_2 Q_5) \cdot P_w$, government revenue is lower, farmers' income is lower, and there is a deadweight loss represented by the triangle GHJ. Just how big these costs could be in Uzbekistan or Turkmenistan is hard to estimate, because we do not know exactly where cotton output now is along the horizontal axis of Figure 9.2. If the supply elasticity of 1.5 used by Connolly and Vatnick for Uzbekistan is close to the true long-run value, then their 1992 data for P_w and P_c imply that the cotton output associated with a long-run price P_c would be zero! While implausible as the actual outcome, such a calculation is suggestive of how serious the supply response could be.

An indicator of the possible long-run consequences is Ghana's post-independence economic history.[7] In the late 1950s, when Ghana's per capita income was similar to

---

[7] The material on Ghana is drawn from Pomfret (1997b, pp. 190–91) and Bulir (1998); the quotation

that of South Korea, Ghana produced over 400,000 tonnes of cocoa a year, and cocoa accounted for over half of Ghana's exports and government revenue. By the early 1980s, when an impoverished Ghana finally introduced serious economic reforms, cocoa output had dropped to 200,000 tonnes:

> For Ghana, export taxes on cocoa proved a double-edged sword. They offered an administratively simple means of gathering significant, and sorely needed, revenue. But export taxes customarily do—and in Ghana certainly did—affect the marginal rate of return. Recent research indicates that one to two million rural workers migrated from Ghana in the 1970s; farmers made substantial shifts from cocoa to other food crops; and severe exchange rate distortions provided significant incentives for smuggling.

This summary already has a resonance with Uzbekistan's and Turkmenistan's situation, and could be an epitaph for their economic development in the next decade if cotton pricing policies do not change. Ghana has natural advantages for growing cocoa, but increasingly new plantings in the 1970s were adjacent to the long border with the Côte d'Ivoire and sales were in the Ivorian market where producer prices were some 50% higher than in Ghana, so that the decline in output and farmers' income may be overstated in official Ghanaian data, but government revenue from the cocoa tax was undoubtedly reduced by smuggling.

The negative-incentive effects will force the governments to choose between either current rent maximization and stagnating output or allowing farmers to retain a larger share of the export revenue. The policies of rent extraction provide incentives for smuggling cotton to neighboring states with freer markets. In the early 2000s there were frequent reports of cotton being smuggled over the porous border between Uzbekistan and Kazakhstan, where agricultural prices are less repressed.[8] Smuggling is widespread in the CIS, but providing strong incentives to smuggle through the cotton marketing system adds to the erosion of acceptance of the rule of law.

Full costing of the net benefits of cotton production is complicated by lack of information about harvesting techniques. In the Soviet era cotton mechanization was used as a propaganda tool to illustrate how the Communist system was modernizing agriculture in the Soviet Union's less developed regions. In practice, much of the picking was still done by hand, using students and other groups who were mobilized during the harvest season.

---

is from a summary of Bulir's work in IMF Survey, July 20, 1998, pp. 235–36. The five-volume World Bank study edited by Krueger et al. (1991–92) provides further case studies emphasizing the negative impact of similar agricultural taxation schemes on long-term growth.

[8] Early reports of smuggling between Uzbekistan and southern Kazakhstan are cited by Pomfret (2000b, p. 278), and extensive smuggling from Uzbekistan to the Kyrgyz Republic in 2003–04 is reported in ICG (2005, p. 5). Lerman and Brooks (2001) suggest that the subsidized price of inputs also stimulated smuggling of fertilizers from Turkmenistan to Kazakhstan.

Given the relative supply of capital and labor it seems unlikely that mechanization of cotton picking has ever been efficient in labor-abundant Central Asia (Pomfret 2002a). Since independence the share of the cotton harvest picked by machine has declined substantially as farms are unwilling to purchase new machines and even appear to let existing machines stay idle because the benefits do not even cover the running costs. One reason why people accept the backbreaking work of cotton picking in Uzbekistan is that they are paid in cash immediately, unlike payment for crops which can be delayed for months or be paid into restricted-access bank accounts. They are, however, paid more in southern Kazakhstan, where a skilled picker could earn 20,000 tenge ($135) a month in the 2002 harvest season by picking 100 kg a day (wages in Uzbekistan were as low as 25 soms per kilogram, or $2 per 100 kg, according to ICG (2003, p. 13)), and this led to substantial illegal temporary immigration from Uzbekistan.[9]

In Turkmenistan, Uzbekistan, and Tajikistan the Soviet-era practice of forced labor is maintained to varying degrees (ICG 2005, pp. 18–25). Despite official bans on child labor, children as young as nine are required to pick cotton. Apart from the negative impact on their education, they are exposed to various health risks from being required to spray pesticides or from only having access to insanitary water. University students complain that not only are they required to provide unpaid labor, but an unreasonable portion of their low student stipends is kept by the farm managers for food and accommodation costs. According to ICG (2005, p. 35) the use of forced labor does not reflect labor shortage, but rather the power of vested interests aiming to maximize net revenue from cotton sales and having the power to force children, students, and others to work for practically nothing. The extent of child labor is difficult to document in the face of official statements that forced labor is illegal but some children help their parents in the fields.

9.2 Oil and Natural Gas

During the Soviet era Central Asian oil resources were underdeveloped relative to the established oil-producing areas of Azerbaijan and the newer oil fields in Siberia. Technical difficulties of exploring and exploiting the offshore fields in the Caspian Basin may have convinced the Soviet authorities that it was not cost-effective, in contrast to the relatively low production costs in Siberia. Natural-gas production had a long history in Uzbekistan, but the old gas fields were becoming exhausted. In the final decade of the Soviet Union large investments were made in Turkmenistan's natural gas.[10]

After independence the approaches to the oil and gas sectors have differed substantially among the three countries with the largest potential reserves (Table 9.5).

---

[9] Rustam Temirov, "Uzbek illegal laborers exposed to abusive practices in neighboring Kazakhstan," *Eurasia Insight*, posted at www.eurasianet.org on May 11, 2003.

[10] Skagen (1997) analyzes the development of gas production in Central Asia up to the middle of the 1990s.

Table 9.5.   Energy resources.

	Natural gas (billions of m^3)	Oil (billions of tonnes)	Hydroelectricity (MW)
Kazakhstan	1,820	1.1	2,060
Kyrgyz Republic	—	—	2,950
Tajikistan	—	—	4,020
Turkmenistan	2,830	0.1	1
Uzbekistan	1,850	0.1	1,700

Source: EBRD Transition Report 2001, "Energy in transition."
Notes: proven reserves of oil and gas; current capacity for hydroelectricity.

Kazakhstan privatized the energy sector with a direct role for foreign firms, while Uzbekistan and Turkmenistan chose to maintain state ownership and minimize the role of foreign companies. Luong and Weinthal (2001) argue that this split reflects the fact that Uzbekistan and Turkmenistan had substantial alternative sources of export revenue from cotton and their leaders faced less contestation over rents than the leadership in Kazakhstan. While it is true that Karimov and Niyazov ruled over more ethnically homogeneous countries and could perhaps take a longer time horizon than Nazarbayev, who faced secessionist threats in the Russian-dominated areas of Kazakhstan, the physical nature of the resources also mattered.

As described in Chapter 3, exploitation of Kazakhstan's offshore oil fields was delayed for jurisdictional and technical reasons, but when the exploration became more serious in the late 1990s the discoveries were big.[11] In contrast, Turkmenistan's portion of the Caspian Sea has proven to be disappointing in terms of oil. Both the exploration and the subsequent exploitation of these offshore fields required the expertise of the largest international oil companies. Whether Kazakhstan could have negotiated better deals or retained more substantial ownership shares is a moot question, but there was no alternative to a direct role for foreign firms. Turkmenistan did in fact enlist oil majors in exploring its share of the Caspian Sea, but they withdrew, in part because of difficulties in dealing with the regime, but also, fundamentally, because they were not finding oil.[12]

Turkmenistan's retention of state control over natural-gas production reflected the fact that a passive position was all that was needed. The gas fields had been recently developed and the markets for the gas were dictated by the direction of pipelines.[13] In 1992–93, billions of dollars flowed into the government's coffers with minimum

---

[11] Although the existence of oil in the North Caspian Basin was known much earlier, the discovery of Kashagan East-1, announced in July 2000, was a major breakthrough (Belopolsky and Talwani 2001). Table 9.6 shows the increase in output between 1999 and 2003.

[12] ExxonMobil pulled out of Turkmenistan in 2002, citing disappointing drilling results as the reason, and Shell cut back its operations in 2003 due to poor prospects. However, Turkmenistan's oil output did increase from 0.5 million tonnes in 2002 to 2.6 million in 2003 (EBRD Transition Report 2003).

[13] Development of Turkmenistan's gas resources had encountered substantial technical problems, associated with high pressure and sulfur content. Lack of expertise in addressing these problems may have

Table 9.6. Global oil production in 1993, 1999, and 2003 (thousand barrels per day).

	1993	1999	2003
World	66,006	72,063	76,777
Saudi Arabia	8,962	8,694	9,817
Russia	7,173	6,178	8,543
United States	8,683	7,731	7,454
Iran	3,712	3,603	3,852
Mexico	3,132	3,343	3,789
China	2,888	3,213	3,396
Norway	2,377	3,130	3,260
Venezuela	2,692	3,248	2,987
Canada	2,184	2,604	2,986
UAE	2,443	2,302	2,520
United Kingdom	2,119	2,893	2,245
Kuwait	1,945	2,000	2,238
Nigeria	1,985	2,028	2,185
Algeria	1,329	1,515	1,857
Brazil	664	1,133	1,562
Libya	1,402	1,425	1,488
Iraq	455	2,541	1,344
Indonesia	1,586	1,408	1,179
Kazakhstan	490	631	1,106

Source: BP's "Statistical review of world energy."
Notes: countries ranked by 2003 production; Turkmenistan 210, Uzbekistan 166 in 2003.

effort. As described in Chapter 7, the ready cash came with the unstable situation of a bilateral monopoly: Turkmenistan's main customers in Ukraine and the Caucasus were heavily dependent on Turkmenistan's gas, but Turkmenistan was dependent on their paying their bills. This has imparted substantial volatility to the economy, notably during the 1997–99 episode when gas exports were essentially stopped. Finding new markets is contingent on new pipelines and there is little incentive to expand production beforehand. Unlike oil-pipeline construction, which typically depends upon oil producers guaranteeing to send specified amounts of oil through the pipeline, gas pipelines are built when the buyers at the destination guarantee to purchase sufficient quantities of gas to make the pipeline worthwhile. Faced with these problems, Turkmenistan has slipped from being the world's sixth-largest producer in 1993 to twelfth in 2003 (Table 9.7).

The expansion of oil and gas production in Uzbekistan has been less problematic than energy development in either Kazakhstan or Turkmenistan. Expertise has been sufficient to develop the oil and gas fields, and most production during the 1990s was for domestic consumption as Uzbekistan became energy self-sufficient. Exports

hindered further expansion after independence, but the demand side appears to have been the binding constraint on achieving higher revenues from gas sales.

Table 9.7.   Global gas production in 1993, 1999, and 2003 (billion cubic meters).

	1993	1999	2003
World	2,081	2,290	2,619
Russia	577	551	679
United States	520	542	550
Canada	139	177	181
United Kingdom	61	99	103
Algeria	56	96	83
Iran	27	56	79
Norway	25	49	73
Indonesia	56	71	73
Saudi Arabia	40	46	61
Netherlands	70	59	58
Turkmenistan	61	21	55
Uzbekistan	42	52	54

Source: BP's "Statistical review of world energy."
Notes: countries ranked by 2003 production; Kazakhstan 13 in 2003.

Figure 9.3.   The world oil price, 1990–2005.

started to grow after the turn of the century. Uzbekistan shipped 2.5 billion cubic meters of gas to Russia in 2002. A May 2004 agreement with Gazprom envisaged rapid expansion of sales to Russia, starting with 7.7 billion cubic meters in 2004.[14]

The fortunes of oil producers are hostage to volatile world prices (Figure 9.3).[15] In March 1998 when the world price hovered just above $10 per barrel, landlocked

---

[14] In June 2004 LUKoil signed a billion-dollar product-sharing agreement to develop Uzbekistan's southern gas fields of Kandym, Khauzak, and Shady, whose proven reserves are 280 billion cubic meters (see Sergei Blagov, "Investment strengthens Russian ties to Uzbekistan," posted at www.eurasianet.org on August 4, 2004.

[15] Natural gas is less sensitive to price changes because it is usually supplied under long-term contracts. The only spot markets for gas are in the United States. The strength of demand for natural gas is, however, influenced by the price of alternative energy such as oil. This was reflected in Turkmenistan's stronger bargaining position vis-à-vis Gazprom in 2005 (see Section 6.5).

Central Asia, with transport costs to deep-sea ports in excess of $10, did not look an attractive region for production.[16] Even after the CPC pipeline opened in 2001 and reduced the cost of transporting Kazakhstan's oil, it cost $6.5 per barrel to transport oil from Tengiz to Novorossiysk and another $2 to Rotterdam. Transport costs from the second-largest producing oil field, Kumkol, according to Raballand and Esen (N.D.), averaged around $12 per barrel. After the world oil price reached $30 in 2001 and edged up towards $50 in 2004, Central Asia became a much more attractive source of oil.

Much international interest in economic events in Central Asia has focused on the high politics of pipelines. Russia clearly wants to keep Central Asian energy producers dependent on Russian pipelines for as long as possible, while U.S. oil companies want to create new routes but their government rules out the geographically most sensible route through Iran. China's late entry further complicates the game between the great powers.

During the 1990s Russia was successful in maintaining its monopoly over oil and gas pipelines out of Central Asia, apart from the small gas pipeline from Turkmenistan to Iran. The driving force behind U.S. pipeline policy in the region was the desire to exclude routes via Iran, and other western companies would not proceed with the Iranian option in the absence of U.S. companies' participation,[17] but the U.S. government vacillated between supporting pipelines to Turkey or to Pakistan. Both of these routes are substantially longer and more expensive ways of getting oil to ports than going to Bandar Abbas in Iran, and the high cost deterred most private investors. The Turkish government strongly supported the Baku–Ceyhan route for which it has offered substantial investment guarantees and it has made U.S. support for Baku–Ceyhan one litmus test of U.S. commitment to its NATO ally in the Middle East. During the period 1995–97, however, the United States seemed more favorably inclined towards the trans-Afghanistan route to Pakistan, and this option was only abandoned in November 1998.[18]

---

[16] In 1999 major oil companies like Shell and BP Amoco were operating on the assumption that the world oil price for the next five years would average $10. The *Economist* ("Cheap oil," March 6, 1999) thought this was overoptimistic and that, due to new technologies and the availability of substitutes for oil, a more realistic projection was of prices between $5 and $10 per barrel.

[17] Companies from western countries other than the United States were also scared off by the reach of U.S. sanctions against companies doing business with Iran. The Australian resources company BHP completed a feasibility study for exporting Iranian gas to Pakistan and India, but backed away from any further involvement (Hunter 2000, p. 199).

[18] The years 1990–93 were a difficult period in United States–Pakistan relations, but starting in 1994 Pakistan abandoned attempts at friendly relations with Iran in favor of joining the United States in isolating the Iranian regime. An important weapon for Pakistan was support in Afghanistan of the Taliban movement, with its militant Sunni views (shared by Pakistan and Saudi Arabia) and hatred of Shias (the dominant group in western Afghanistan and in Iran). In 1995 Turkmenistan reneged on its agreement with the Argentinean company Bridas to build a pipeline to Pakistan, and the project was taken over by the U.S. company Unocal. In 1995–97 the U.S. government, while not overtly assisting the Taliban, looked favorably on their success in reuniting Afghanistan and restoring law and order (Hunter 2000). The situation changed in 1997–98 as the Taliban's type of law and order came under increasing criticism,

The decision to abandon the trans-Afghan route had the biggest impact on Turkmenistan, for whom South Asia offers tempting natural-gas markets. After the fall of the Taliban regime, the heads of state of Turkmenistan, Afghanistan, and Pakistan met in December 2002 in Ashgabat to try to reach a new agreement on the 1,500 km pipeline, but it is doubtful whether these countries alone could afford the construction costs of over $2 billion. The project would make more economic sense if the gas could also be supplied to India, but India has made it clear that it is unwilling to rely on a route through Pakistan for its energy sources.[19] Turkmenistan is thus left relying heavily on construction of a Baku–Erzurum gas pipeline running parallel to the first segments of the Baku–Ceyhan oil pipeline taking the gas to Turkish domestic markets, and on Azerbaijan allowing Turkmenistan access to the pipeline.[20] A proposed trans-Caspian pipeline to link Turkmenistan with the Baku–Erzurum pipeline is, however, on hold due to disputes over offshore fields being developed by Azerbaijan but claimed by Turkmenistan, and, as long as that conflict runs, there is no prospect of Turkmenistan's gas flowing through Azerbaijan. Other potential pipeline routes run through Russia and Iran, competing producer countries who have little interest in improving the access to, and hence making Turkmenistan's gas a competitor in, markets like Turkey or the European Union.

Oil-pipeline issues are more complex than those for gas pipelines because other transport modes, although inferior, are feasible. The geography of pipelines out of Central Asia is also influenced by Azerbaijan's position as a large producer. Azerbaijan's currently substantial output but lower proven reserves make its oil transport problems complementary to Kazakhstan's needs for some pipeline capacity now and even more in the future. The Turkish option of the Baku–Ceyhan pipeline is based on the calculation that combined oil flows from Azerbaijan and Kazakhstan will make it financially viable, despite a construction cost of $3.6 billion for the 1,760 km pipeline. Even so, and with Turkish offers of $2.7 billion in financial guarantees, the private companies and bankers, whose support is critical, were hesitant to sign on.[21] Only in November 2003 was agreement finally reached when the World Bank's International Finance Corporation affiliate committed $500 million and the

---

especially from women's groups, in the United States, and especially after the August 1998 bombings of U.S. embassies in East Africa by groups associated with Osama bin Laden, who operated out of Afghanistan with Taliban complicity. Unocal abandoned the pipeline project in November 1998.

[19] This may be changing as post-2003 détente between India and Pakistan included discussion of transport and pipeline links, but progress towards normal relations was slow in 2004.

[20] The oil and gas pipelines will be parallel, but they are separate projects with different consortia, although five transnational corporations are members of both consortia. Whether there are any synergies from the parallel routes is unclear, because it has not been done elsewhere. The viability of the $3.2 billion Baku–Erzurum pipeline was enhanced when the magnitude of Azerbaijan's huge offshore Shah Deniz gas field became apparent in July 1999.

[21] Unlike the CPC pipeline which is financed by shareholders (i.e., oil companies and governments), the BTC pipeline ended up being bank financed. Significant catalysts for change may have been the discovery of Kazakhstan's huge Kashagan oil field in the northern Caspian and the United States ending its adverse treatment of Azerbaijan in 2000.

EBRD committed $250 million in nonconcessional loans to a BP-led consortium. The Baku–Ceyhan pipeline was officially opened in May 2005.

Meanwhile, Kazakhstan had found alternatives to the Transneft Russian pipeline. During the late 1990s half of the output from Tengiz was transported by rail.[22] Some oil was shipped by barge across the Caspian to the Baku–Supsa pipeline to the Black Sea, which opened in spring 1999. After the CPC opened in November 2001, more substantial flows went to Novorossiysk on the Black Sea (see Section 3.4). Turkey opposed using Georgian and Russian Black Sea ports for Caspian oil, because the oil tankers taking the oil to the Mediterranean and beyond would have to pass through the Bosporus with potentially huge environmental costs from any accidents or spills.[23] Nevertheless, the CPC in particular showed that Transneft's monopoly was eroding and the future was likely to involve multiple outlets for Central Asian oil rather than a struggle to dominate the route with one single pipeline. Kazakhstan also sent some oil by railcar to northern Iran in a swap arrangement for oil in Iran's Gulf ports.[24]

At the end of the 1990s, Kazakhstan was also involved in negotiations over a pipeline to China, which would be even more expensive than Baku–Ceyhan but which China appears to be willing to pay highly for in the name of energy security. China ceased to be self-sufficient in oil in 1993 when oil production and consumption were 2.9 million barrels per day. By 2002 China's consumption had increased to 5.4 million barrels per day while production had only grown to 3.4.[25] Within China the debate was over whether to ensure energy security by buying equity shares in oil fields, as in Kazakhstan (see Chapter 3), or by building pipelines, or by accumulating a strategic oil reserve. In 1997, in the aftermath of the purchase of equity shares in Kazakh oil fields, China considered subsidizing the 3,000 km pipeline from Kazakhstan but the project was shelved in 1999. Some commentators saw this as part of a political deal with Kazakhstan including agreement over how to deal with Uighur separatists, while others saw it as being driven by the main Chinese oil companies (CNPC and Sinopec) whose position changed after reorganizations in 1998 made them more profit conscious. It may also be that as world oil prices hovered around $10 per barrel, investing $3.5 billion in a pipeline in the name of energy security was unjustifiable, but the project became worth resuscitating when

---

[22] In 1997, some 7,000 tonnes of crude oil were sent by rail from Tengiz to Urumqi in western China. TengizChevroil leased 5,000 railcars from various Russia and Kazakh companies in 1998, and 6,000 in 1999, to ship oil via the Russian rail network.

[23] Some oil going to Supsa avoided the Bosporus and bypassed Russia by using the rail ferry to the Ukraine port of Ilichovsk and thence by rail to Western Europe.

[24] Although the ten-year agreement signed in May 1996 specified quantities of 100,000 barrels per day, according to Raballand and Esen (N.D.) no more than 20,000 barrels per day were being sent to Iran in the early 2000s.

[25] Downs (2004) discusses the political debates within China about the appropriate reactions to energy security concerns. She emphasizes that western observers may be overstating the importance of the debate given that the major energy source in China is coal, of which China still has abundant supplies.

oil prices approached $50 in 2003 and 2004.[26] In September 2004 construction began on a pipeline from Atasu in central Kazakhstan to Alushankou on the Kazakhstan–China border, to be completed in 2006 and projected to carry 10 million tonnes by 2011.

9.3 Minerals

Before independence Kazakhstan's economy was centered on minerals rather than on hydrocarbons. The coal miners in Karaganda were the working-class elite and have in many ways suffered the biggest reversal of economic fortunes since 1991. Coal output declined from 130 million tonnes in 1991 to 58.5 million tonnes in 1999. Net exports of coal fell by two-thirds in the first half of the 1990s, and then plummeted further in 1998 as Russian demand collapsed.[27] Domestic coal consumption in Kazakhstan fell from 86 million tonnes to 36 million tonnes during the 1990s. By contrast, exports of nonferrous metals and of rolled steel were maintained reasonably well, although shipments were volatile during the 1990s, especially as sales to East Asia were affected by the Asian Crisis of 1997–98.[28]

One of the biggest mineral opportunities in Central Asia has been its gold resources. Gold production in Uzbekistan is around 80 tonnes a year and gold is the second-largest export after cotton. Although options on developing new gold mines have been granted to Lonrho of the United Kingdom and new joint ventures have been discussed with several Australian and Canadian mining companies, foreign participants have been deterred by the high start-up costs and failure to agree on benefit-sharing. In contrast, the Kyrgyz Republic moved quickly to bring in the technological expertise of Cameco of Canada in developing the Kumtor gold mine and output was over 17 tonnes in 1997, although the government has been accused of giving too-favorable terms to the foreign firm (see Chapter 5). Kazakhstan has also sought foreign partners to exploit its gold deposits, especially those at Vasilkovskoe and Bakyrichik, with a goal of producing over 40 tonnes a year by 2010, but the assignation of property rights has been complex (see Chapter 3) and progress slow. Tajikistan may have large gold deposits but exploration has been more limited than elsewhere and production was disrupted by civil unrest. Several Canadian companies are involved in mines whose combined production was over 2 tonnes in 1996, but the country's second-largest gold mine, the British–Tajik joint venture at Darvaz,

---

[26] At the same time, completion of a domestic pipeline network from west to south China in the early 2000s improved the economics of a pipeline from Kazakhstan's oil fields to the Chinese border. Russian energy policies under Putin (e.g., blocking the sale of Slavneft to Chinese buyers, dismembering Yukos which alone among large Russian oil companies was keen on selling oil to China, and focusing on a pipeline to the Pacific port of Nakhodka which would serve Japan better than China) also encouraged China to look to Kazakhstan.

[27] Exports to Russia were also discouraged by high rail tariffs on coal shipments.

[28] Kazakhstan was also hit by antidumping actions against its steel exports to a number of countries, including the United States and the European Union.

suffered 3 million dollars worth of damage during an attack in December 1996 and its output was cut in half.

Tajikistan's nonferrous metal sector is dominated by aluminum production, whose location reflects the abundant hydro power. The South Tajik complex was a model project combining economic development and regional policy in the Soviet south during the 1980s. The complex as a whole was far from completion when the USSR dissolved, but the modern aluminum smelter was the crown jewel of Tajikistan's economy.

9.4 Hydroelectricity

Tajikistan and the Kyrgyz Republic have substantial hydroelectricity capacity (Table 9.5) and even larger hydroelectric potential, but are not fully utilizing their current installed capacity (Kennedy et al. 2004, pp. 296–97). The huge dams on the two main Central Asian river systems, the Amudarya and Syrdarya, were constructed in the Soviet era primarily to regulate the flow of water to irrigate the downstream cotton fields during the summer growing season. Hydroelectricity generation was of secondary importance, and the two upstream countries were compensated by shipments of gas from Uzbekistan and coal from Kazakhstan to cover their winter heating needs.

The basic principles of the Soviet water arrangements have been maintained in annual agreements, but the upstream countries have been tempted to use the water to generate more power in winter, causing the downstream countries to complain about the inadequate flow of water when it is needed for irrigation. The disputes have become more bitter since the end of the 1990s. In the winter of 1999–2000 Uzbekistan cut off gas supplies to the Kyrgyz Republic, which retaliated by releasing more water for hydro generation and leaving less available for Uzbekistan to irrigate its cotton crop in the summer of 2001. Relations between Kazakhstan and the Kyrgyz Republic are less confrontational, and in March 2001 an agreement was reached under which Kazakhstan settled an outstanding $21.5 million debt and guaranteed supplies of fuel and coal in return for a guaranteed 750 million cubic meters of water for irrigation. The Kyrgyz Republic is seeking investment funds to increase its generating capacity, aiming at self-sufficiency in electricity in the near future, and also wants to introduce water charges, which are strongly opposed by downstream nations, especially Uzbekistan. Although Tajikistan would like to pursue similar plans, it is more constrained by both lack of domestic resources and attractiveness to foreign investors.

The Soviet Union did not have a single electricity grid. The northern Kazakhstan grid, based on coal, supplied electricity to Siberia as well as to the industrial towns of northern Kazakhstan. The United Power System (UPS) of Central Asia was developed in the 1960s to coordinate the seasonal hydroelectric resources of the Kyrgyz and Tajik Republics with the agricultural needs of southern Kazakhstan and the other four Central Asian republics. The installed generating capacity

Table 9.8.   Central Asian power trade, 1990 and 2000 (GW h).

	1990		2000	
	Exports	Imports	Exports	Imports
Kazakhstan	—	9,064	—	1,269
Kyrgyz Republic	3,978	—	2,376	319
Tajikistan	5,700	6,900	334	1,681
Turkmenistan	6,050	—	1,060	—
Uzbekistan	13,000	12,500	849	1,350

Source: Kennedy et al. (2004, p. 288).

Note: Biddison (2002, p. 7) reports that the annual value of the regional bulk power trade had declined from about $1 million in 1990 to approximately $100,000 by the early 2000s.

of the power stations in the UPS is about 25,000 MW, of which just over a third is hydropower and just under two-thirds thermal power stations, but according to Biddison (2002, p. 7) the actual working capacity of the UPS power stations is less than 19,000 MW.[29] It operated as an integrated power pool, whose main transmission lines cover southern Kazakhstan, the other four Central Asian countries, and part of Afghanistan.[30]

In the post-1991 environment all of the Central Asian countries have striven to increase their energy self-sufficiency (Table 9.8), and during the 1990s there was some attempt to create national grids. The national power systems are coordinated through the Unified Dispatch System in Tashkent, which is overseen by a Power Council consisting of ministers from the five countries, but is widely considered to be under Uzbekistan's influence. The national systems were inefficient and characterized by many power failures.

Since the turn of the century an important force in the development of the electricity sector has been the Russian joint-stock company Unified Energy System (UES). Throughout the CIS, UES has been increasing its influence, and a key component of its corporate strategy has been to complete a grid covering the entire former Soviet space, which it achieved in 2003 (Sabonis-Helf 2005). This has benefits to electricity users who gain in reliability and quality of supply, because shortfalls from one area can be met from areas which have surpluses which might otherwise be wasted, and it also has benefits on the supply side, because different types of power can be better balanced, seasonal surpluses managed, and peak loads better met. In Central

---

[29] Of the total UPS power, 51% is generated in Uzbekistan, 15% in Tajikistan, 14% in the Kyrgyz Republic, 11% in Turkmenistan, and 9% in southern Kazakhstan (Biddison 2002, p. 7). The largest hydropower stations are Nurek in Tajikistan (3,000 MW capacity) and Toktogul in the Kyrgyz Republic (1,200 MW capacity).

[30] Afghanistan's electricity supply is tiny, with installed generating capacity of less than 500 MW. Balkhenergo operates a transmission line from Uzbekistan to Mazar-i-Sharif and in the northeast a transmission line was opened in 1986 from Tajikistan to Kunduz, although this was disrupted during the 1990s. Other projects planned during the Soviet era, including a transmission line to Kabul, were never completed.

Table 9.9. Farmland resources, 1999 (thousands of hectares).

	Total cultivated cropland	Irrigated cropland	Pasture
Kazakhstan	30,135	2,313 (7)	18,233
Kyrgyz Republic	1,435	1,077 (75)	9,216
Tajikistan	860	719 (84)	3,600
Turkmenistan	1,744	1,744 (100)	3,070
Uzbekistan	4,850	4,309 (89)	2,280

Source: World Bank (2002, Volume 1, p. 4).
Notes: figures in parentheses are the percentage of the total cultivated cropland which is irrigated; in southern Kazakhstan 70% of the cropland is irrigated.

Asia this process began when Kazakhstan began joint operations with UES, but it gathered pace in 2004, when UES acquired assets through debt-for-equity swaps. In September 2004 UES acquired 50% of the Ekibastuz power plant in Kazakhstan. In 2004 UES also negotiated a shareholding in Tajikistan's Sangtuda hydroelectricity station. Perhaps more important for the Kyrgyz Republic and Tajikistan was that UES participation in hydroelectricity generation, plus the creation of a single grid, has helped to secure markets for their electricity in Russia.

The UPS and other hydroelectricity facilities were built with equipment from the USSR and Eastern Europe. They have been poorly maintained since 1991 and the increasing difficultly in obtaining parts, etc., poor design for metering usage, and generally antiquated control and monitoring systems mean that significant investment will be required in order to develop an efficient regional power market.

Two of the largest hydroelectricity projects begun during the Soviet era in the Tajik Republic stalled in the 1990s, and completion of the Sangtuda project, started in 1987 and destined to be the second-largest hydropower facility in Tajikistan, and of the Rugun hydro dam southeast of Dushanbe was not even discussed until after the turn of the century. Iran committed $200 million to the Sangtuda project, but in 2004 UES offered to invest $250 million in the project, apparently displacing Iranian involvement. Also, in 2004 RusAl announced plans to invest in the aluminum sector. These last two deals were part of the October 2004 agreement in which Russia offered substantial economic assistance to Tajikistan in return for bases and other military facilities in the country.

9.5 Other Natural Resources

Central Asia has a large and varied agricultural and pastoral sector (Table 9.9), but for the most part its output is either volatile or constrained by the region's aridity and scarcity of water. In the southern part of Central Asia the area watered by the two great rivers which flow into the Aral Sea has long contained highly fertile oases. Under Russian Tsarist and Soviet leadership the area was largely turned over to cotton fields, with harmful ecological consequences summed up in the disappearance of the Aral Sea, but earlier it produced a variety of crops and there is potential for finding niche markets for fruits and vegetables.

The ecology of the northern steppes and the mountain regions of the southeast is different, and the traditional pastoral nomadism has long been under pressure. The main innovation of the Soviet era was the Virgin Lands campaign begun in the late 1950s by Khrushchev which brought large areas of northern Kazakhstan under wheat. This remains a major crop, but harvests are volatile due to the marginal growing conditions. Both Turkmenistan and Uzbekistan have provided substantial incentives to their farmers to grow more wheat and hence reduce dependence on imports, but conditions there are even less clearly favorable to such cropping patterns.

Some of the obstacles to agrarian progress have been touched upon in the country chapters, but there are region-wide patterns. Land reform has been problematic, and actual developments are difficult to assess because of the gap between legislation and reality and because of the paucity of extensive fieldwork by researchers. The strongest legal commitment is in Turkmenistan, where the principle of private ownership is enshrined in Article 9 of the 1992 Constitution. In practice, however, land may not be transferred and Turkmenistan's government retains the right to reallocate land if it is not being used efficiently. In the most generous interpretation, "private land ownership" in Turkmenistan means inheritable use-right subject to the will of the government—an almost meaningless use of the term "private" (Lerman and Brooks 1998, p. 175). In practice, both Turkmenistan and Uzbekistan remain committed to tight state control over land and its use, while Kazakhstan and the Kyrgyz Republic are more open to substantive change in land tenure arrangements. Even in the latter two countries, however, land reform has stuttered along (see Chapters 3 and 5). Although the distinction between the attitudes of the two pairs of countries to land reform matches their general attitudes to reform, it may also reflect the far greater dependence of Uzbekistan and Turkmenistan on cotton (and reliance on rents from cotton for government revenue), which makes them more conservative with respect to land reform.

True land reform in all but the pastoral areas is also intimately linked to water. In much of Central Asia land is useless without access to water rights, and there is a general resistance to market-determined pricing of water. Without water pricing and with often unclear property rights, the profligate use of irrigation water inherited from the Soviet era has continued, and the maintenance of irrigation systems has deteriorated (World Bank 2002).[31] Institutional reforms, especially in the

---

[31] Even in the Soviet era maintenance was neglected. According to reports summarized in World Bank (2002, Volume I, p. 5n), about half of the irrigated area of Uzbekistan, Kazakhstan, and the Kyrgyz Republic was already in need of capital repairs in the early 1990s. Water use in Uzbekistan during the 1990s was about 14,000 cubic meters per hectare, compared with averages of 9–10,000 in countries such as India, Pakistan, and Egypt. Over-irrigation has contributed to widespread salinization, especially in Turkmenistan and to a lesser extent Uzbekistan, as well as environmental disasters such as the desiccation of the Aral Sea.

Kyrgyz Republic and Kazakhstan, have decentralized maintenance to farms who cannot afford it. Collapse of monitoring has led to piercing of irrigation channels to withdraw water illegally, especially in upstream areas. Downstream farmers are caught in a vicious circle, as diminished water flows increase the cost of maintaining irrigation facilities due to the greater accumulation of silt in irrigation channels.[32] Pumped systems are often out of commission due to unavailability of parts. Given the difficulty of farm-level response to degradation of the irrigation systems and increased salinization, the principal consequence has been substantial declines in agricultural yields and rural incomes.

Livestock production was especially important and especially hard hit by privatization in Kazakhstan. Suleimenov and Oram (2000) ascribe this to the more severe winters requiring heated barns and the disruption of power supplies during the transition from central planning. Privatization was less catastrophic in the Kyrgyz Republic where the farms were smaller and more flexible, and in Uzbekistan whose less dramatic change was associated with the best livestock sector performance of the three countries studied by Suleimenov and Oram.

9.6 Natural Resources and Economic Growth

A more rigorous debate on this old topic was ignited by Sachs and Warner (1995), who found a negative relationship between resource abundance and economic growth in cross-country regressions. Contributions since Sachs and Warner (1995) have refined the debate, establishing that the relationship is conditional (on variables proxying for institutions or on democracy) and that the negative relationship is stronger for oil and minerals than for agriculture.[33] The conditional nature of the resource curse is apparent from the success of some resource-abundant economies, such as Botswana or Australia or Malaysia. Even among oil producers, where there are many disappointing outcomes in the three decades since the oil-price increases of the 1970s, there are also cases of the oil revenues being used to create equitably distributed high incomes and future growth prospects (as in Norway or Alberta).

Identification of the transmission mechanisms from resource abundance to economic growth has focused on three links: through relative prices (Dutch disease

---

[32] Theesfeld (2004) argues that the political and economic changes associated with the collapse of communism undermined irrigation maintenance during the transition. The gap between formal and effective rules encouraged opportunistic behavior, and this was exacerbated by the shortening of people's time horizons and low levels of trust. Information asymmetries and corruption were symptoms of opportunism that made collective action difficult. Theesfeld provides detailed evidence from Bulgarian villages of such mechanisms constraining irrigation maintenance after decentralization of responsibility for irrigation.

[33] See, for example, the literature review and regression analysis in the first two sections of Sala-i-Martin and Subramanian (2003). Papyrakis and Gerlagh (2004) obtain a negative coefficient on their natural-resource variable (share of minerals in GDP) in a simple conditional convergence regression, but the coefficient becomes positive when measures of corruption, openness, and schooling are added to the right-hand side. Isham et al. (2003) distinguish between point-source resources (oil, natural fertilizers, and cotton) and coffee/cocoa, which have been associated with poor growth performance, and other natural resources, which have not.

effects), through volatility, and through rent seeking and distortion of institutions. To a large extent these can be seen as real productive-sector links, public-finance links, and political-economy links. The relevance to Kazakhstan with its dramatic post-1999 oil boom is clear: distorted institutions raise the prospect of resource abundance being a curse.

Dutch disease effects have long been part of the international trade theory literature. An increase in resource-intensive exports will be associated with a decline in output of other traded goods, primarily because exchange rate appreciation will make other traded goods less internationally competitive. If the latter have desirable externalities or there are costs to reversing their decline when the resource revenues dry up, then there is a negative effect on long-run growth. Although the Dutch disease literature has a lengthy theoretical pedigree, it appears to be the empirically least important mechanism.[34]

Resource exports typically have more volatile prices in world markets than other goods and services. This can negatively impact on growth if the earnings are invested in domestic projects whose marginal return is low, because the sudden increase in available funds is not matched by a comparable increase in good projects needing finance, or if the earnings are used for consumption that is costly to reverse.[35] If the bust following a boom requires cuts in domestic absorption that fall on those least capable of protecting themselves, then volatility can increase poverty directly as well as indirectly via slower growth.[36] Volatility can be addressed by investing some of the boom-period revenues in diversified assets, as for example Norway's oil fund or Alberta's Heritage Fund, which can be drawn upon as the resource runs out or when boom turns to bust.

The impact of resource abundance on rent seeking and on institutions depends upon the nature of the resource and also on preexisting institutions. Economic historians have traced the links between the nature of resource endowments and institutional development.[37] Agriculture that was technologically suited to production

---

[34] Sala-i-Martin and Subramanian (2003), for example, reject Dutch disease explanations of Nigeria's dismal growth record and emphasize the institutions link.

[35] The deleterious effects of volatility are emphasized in the case studies in Gelb et al. (1988), and are the focus of the analysis in Devlin and Lewin (2004).

[36] When the Indonesian government turned to the IMF for assistance after its 1997 crisis and reduction of the budget deficit was a key condition for such assistance, most of the immediate burden fell on cuts in cooking-oil subsidies, which fell disproportionately on the poor. The poverty-among-plenty aspect of Indonesia's experience is reflected in Transparency International's "Global corruption report 2004" (Transparency International, Berlin), ranking the leader of Indonesia at the time of the crisis as the most corrupt politician in the world, measured by the amount of public revenue diverted to his family.

[37] There are several strands to this intellectual history. An influential one in the twentieth century was the staple theory associated with Canadian economists, adopted by Douglass North to explain nineteenth-century U.S. history, and applied by Robert Baldwin to the twentieth-century Third World. Some resource rents are difficult to manage, and Atkinson and Hamilton (2003) find that countries suffer from a resource curse when their true savings, including the running down of natural capital, are negative. Dalmazzo and de Blasio (2003) argue that resource abundance may reduce the incentives to undertake difficult structural reforms. Auty (2001) makes a similar point in the context of high oil revenues.

on the family farm was associated with human-capital formation, democracy, and other institutional features amenable to economic development with relative economic equality, while resources such as minerals or plantation agriculture were associated with less democratic political systems and less favorable institutional development. The impact of a resource boom on inequality depends upon the nature of the resource; "point-based" resources such as oil have rents that may be relatively easily grabbed by a few.[38] However, institutions developed before the resource boom may be resilient; resource abundance has been a blessing for democratic oil-rich countries or provinces or states such as Norway, Alberta, and Alaska, which have judiciously managed their oil rents. The less happy outcomes are where resource abundance has led to despotic and corrupt political and institutional set-ups which inhibit development and impoverish the majority of people.[39]

9.7 Conclusions

Huge swings in world prices of cotton and oil have had asymmetric effects on the two largest Central Asian countries. Uzbekistan's relatively good performance in 1990–95 was helped by buoyant world cotton prices, but the country struggled in the face of the substantially lower prices in 1996–2000. Meanwhile, Kazakhstan struggled through the 1990s despite predictions of a windfall post-Soviet gain from improved terms of trade, but then rode an oil boom in the early 2000s. The country chapters in this book emphasize policy choices and their consequences, but short- and medium-term outcomes were strongly influenced by external forces as the countries entered world markets after the dissolution of the USSR.

The long-run relationship between resource abundance and economic performance is harder to assess. Resource booms create the potential for investment in physical and human capital to promote long-run economic growth, but global evidence indicates that resource abundance can be a curse. A more subtle interpretation relates the characteristics of the specific resource to institutional change, which is a fundamental determinant of long-run performance.

The Kyrgyz Republic and Tajikistan, by contrast, suffer from a paucity of readily exploitable natural resources and their isolated location.[40]

---

[38] Tornell and Lane (1999) analyze competition for, and dissipation of, rents as the source of the resource curse. Other authors have suggested other links, e.g., resource abundance reduces the incentive to invest in human capital (Gylfason 2001; Wen and King 2004), but these have not received much attention in the empirical literature.

[39] A problem with emphasizing the third mechanism is that details of the use or dissipation of rents have varied in economically significant ways. Indonesia, despite high-level corruption, used the 1970s oil boom to stabilize the economy and invest in universal primary education, which promoted long-term pro-poor growth, while in Nigeria and Venezuela the 1970s oil boom was followed by decades of economic decline and increasing poverty. Mexico squandered the initial windfall gains from the 1970s oil boom, but after the 1982 Debt Crisis use of oil rents was more socially beneficial. The variations may lie in details of national politics, but may also lie in the idiosyncrasies of the political leader, whose personality matters much more in dictatorships than in democracies.

[40] Raballand (2003a) analyses the costs to the Central Asian countries of being landlocked.

Appendix: Measuring the Transfers from the Cotton Sector

Using 1992 data, Connolly and Vatnick (1994, pp. 205–8) estimated that the gross transfer from Uzbekistan's cotton farmers was $1,034 million, but farmers received $667 million in input subsidies, so that the net tax on farmers from the state order system cum subsidies amounted to $367 million.[41] Of this transfer, $117 million went to domestic mills (area $P_w BCP_d$ in Figure 9.2), of which the deadweight loss (ABC) was $31 million.[42] These are large numbers for a country of 21 million people, in a period when senior government officials earned $25 a month. The 1993 World Bank report "Uzbekistan: an agenda for economic reform" estimated that in 1993 the cotton sector provided a sixth of government revenue. The transfer was even larger in 1994 and the first half of 1995 when world cotton prices increased faster than domestic prices in dollar terms, although the transfers declined when world prices fell sharply between July 1995 and July 1996.

The transfers from Uzbekistan's cotton farmers to the state increased sharply in the second half of 1996, reflecting their sensitivity to exchange rate changes. In August 1996 a producer price for raw cotton of 12,500 sum per tonne was announced, equivalent to about 39,000 sum per tonne of cotton fibre, which was 63% of the world market price of $1,600 per tonne.[43] By the end of 1996, depreciation of the sum had reduced the producer price to 44% of the world price[44] and the proportion would be even smaller if the unofficial exchange rate, whose premium had diverged further from the official rate during the period, were used (e.g., with the rate of about 100 sum to the dollar at the end of 1996 the farmers received $400 per tonne of fibre). The estimates for 1996 reported below are highly sensitive to the choice of exchange rate. With a continuing increase in the black-market premium on dollars in 1997 and 1998, the farmers' share of the world price continued to decline.

Subsequent estimates of the overall impact of transfers in and out of agriculture in Uzbekistan are fairly impressionistic. Khan (1996, p. 71) estimated, on the basis of information obtained during a 1995 ILO mission, that transfers out of agriculture amounted to a tenth of the GDP produced in agriculture. Herman (1999), using

---

[41] The model used by Connolly and Vatnick is more complex than Figure 9.2 because they assume a market-related price on above-quota sales, which is below the world price due to a (later-repealed) 5% export tax on cotton, but the consequences for their estimated effects are small.

[42] The deadweight loss component of the transfer to domestic mills is underestimated, perhaps severely, because Connolly and Vatnick use a low demand elasticity. The presumption that because Uzbekistan grows cotton it should do the processing is widely held, but there is no reason to expect Uzbekistan to have a comparative advantage in spinning and weaving.

[43] Note that in different sources cotton prices may be quoted for seed cotton or for fibre equivalent, which is approximately three times higher per tonne. Also it is not always clear how processing and transport margins, approximately $220 per tonne of fibre equivalent in the competitive U.S. market (Lerman and Brooks 2001, p. 9), are treated.

[44] See "Republic of Uzbekistan: recent economic developments," IMF Staff Country Report No. 97/98, October 1997, p. 13. This is in sharp contrast to China where farmers receive the full international price at the farmgate. Even though they then have to pay ginning fees of $220–300 per tonne and in Xinjiang an irrigation levy of about $100 per tonne, the net revenue to Chinese cotton growers is still 75–80% of the world price or at least double that received by Uzbekistan's cotton growers.

1996 data, calculated gross transfers from cotton farmers of $1,402 million and from grain farmers of $529 million, offset by $198 million in irrigation water subsidies and $200 million in other subsidies, to give a net transfer out of agriculture of $1,533 million, or 8% of GDP.[45] These seem more plausible than the "approximate accounting of transfers" by the IMF showing transfers out of agriculture in 1996 of 25.4–28.4 billion sum (about 15% of the total value of agricultural production) being more than offset by transfers into the agricultural sector of 29.5 billion sum, of which 23.0 billion is due to subsidized irrigation; the unexplained calculations appear to understate the costs to farmers from the state order system by using the official exchange rate to convert world prices into domestic prices.[46]

The most thorough publicly available accounting of the net resource transfers in Turkmenistan draws on an autumn 1998 farm survey supported by the World Bank for estimates of the direct input subsidies. The sampled farms reported spending 42,804 million manat on purchased inputs (fertilizers, chemicals, fuel, transport and machinery services, etc.), for which they receive a 50% subsidy. Given a total area sown by the sampled farms of 86,919 hectares, the subsidy was worth 246,250 manat per hectare. Extrapolating to the total area planted in cotton (548,000 hectares) and wheat (705,000 hectares) yields an estimated subsidy of about 300 billion manat. The 1998 output of cotton (700,000 tonnes) and wheat (1,200,000 tonnes) were respectively valued at 760 and 588 billion manat at procurement prices, and some 3,388 billion manat at international prices at the official exchange rate, implying an indirect tax of around 2,100 billion manat. Finally, farmers received an irrigation subsidy of 235 billion manat, according to the corresponding budget expenditure category. The net transfer out of agriculture amounted to 1,565 billion manat (i.e., $2,100 - 300 - 235$), or 11% of GDP (Lerman and Brooks 2001, pp. 10–11).

These estimates understate the tax on Turkmenistan's farmers because the calculations are at the official exchange rate. For cotton, the procurement price in 1998 remained at one million manat per tonne, even though the official exchange rate had been devalued from 4,165 to 5,200 manat per dollar and the tightening of foreign-exchange controls in late 1998 had led to a rapidly increasing black-market premium. By March 1999, when producers still depended on the 1998 procurement price, the unofficial exchange rate was 17,000 manat per dollar, at which the farmgate price of cotton was equal to less than $60 per tonne, when the world price was over $500 (Lerman and Brooks 2001, p. 7).

Adjusting Lerman and Brooks's net resource transfer estimates for the overvaluation of the official exchange rate is difficult, because the black-market premium

---

[45] All of these estimates are subject to data difficulties, but one key assumption is that payments are made promptly and are accessible. The common delays in payments to farmers, reported payments in kind (cottonseed oil and flour) in some districts, and most of all the use of limited-access bank accounts may be the most important source of bias, which means that the reported calculations will underestimate the tax on farmers.

[46] See "Republic of Uzbekistan: recent economic developments," IMF Staff Country Report No. 97/98, October 1997, p. 65.

was constantly changing. The general formula is $3,388x - 1,288 - 300 - 235$, where x is the ratio of the parallel to the official rate. This is highly sensitive to whether one uses the late-1998 parallel rate of around 8,000 or the March 1999 rate of 17,000; the former implies a net resource transfer of 3,389 billion manat, equal to almost a quarter of GDP, and the latter implies a net resource transfer of 7,330 billion manat, equal to over half of GDP.[47] The comparison with GDP is overstated because the export component of GDP is valued at the official exchange rate; for consistency, exports should be valued at opportunity cost prices, rather than administered prices. Nevertheless, the valuation at the official exchange rate, when there was a large black-market premium, ignores an added burden on farmers when imported consumption goods tend to have market-determined prices. It also represented an added gain to the government, as the domestic purchasing power of the dollars earned by exports increased while its obligations to the farmers, denominated in manat, remained unchanged. Perhaps the most that can be said is that the net resource transfers out of agriculture in the 1998 crop season were substantially greater than 1,565 billion manat and probably double that amount due to the foreign-exchange regime.

---

[47] However, it did not really matter to the farmer whether he was paid in December 1998 or March 1999 because he was unlikely to spend much of his revenue on imports. Pastor and van Rooden (2000, p. 12) estimate the transfers from wheat and cotton farmers in 1999 to have been 2,880 billion manat, or 15% of GDP, but they used an exchange rate of 9,000 (a proxy for what the equilibrium rate might have been if controls were removed).

10

International Economic Policies: Regionalism and Integration into the World Economy

The five Central Asian countries have all remained open economies with high trade/GDP ratios, despite adoption, especially in Turkmenistan and Uzbekistan, of import-substitution policies. Initially, their trade was heavily oriented towards CIS markets as a result of inherited links and infrastructure, but by 1996 over half of their foreign trade was outside the old Soviet area. The early expectation was of a struggle for influence among the region's neighbors and outside powers, reminiscent of the Great Game of the nineteenth century, but that expectation was only realized in the area of oil and gas pipelines (see Section 9.2). Otherwise trade has been on a multilateral basis with nonenergy exports being sold on world markets and imports being purchased from least-cost suppliers. In sum, all five countries are participants in the global economy and international economic polices are important.

This chapter analyzes the choices between regionalism and multilateralism, and the impact of WTO membership on the Central Asian countries. As background, the first section outlines the trade polices of the Central Asian countries since independence, and the second section describes the five countries' WTO status. The second section also considers what lessons can be drawn from the Kyrgyz Republic's experience as a WTO member since 1998. In the early years of the twenty-first century the Central Asian countries' relationships to the WTO became a more pressing issue. In December 2001 China's long-running WTO accession negotiations were successfully concluded. Russian negotiations are also moving forward and when they are concluded the Central Asian countries will be in a situation in which their two largest neighbors are WTO members. Section 10.2 includes analysis of the consequences for the Central Asian countries of Chinese and Russian WTO membership, and the consequences of the current Central Asian applicants' (Kazakhstan, Tajikistan, and Uzbekistan) own WTO accession.

Despite the actual multilateralism and the focus on WTO issues, there has been a huge number of regional agreements, both among the Central Asian countries and between Central Asian countries and their neighbors: Russia to the north, China to the east, and Iran and Turkey to the south. Section 10.3 reviews regional arrangements

Table 10.1. Share of exports (X) and imports (M) with the CIS, 1991–99 (percentages).

	1991		1992		1993		1994		1995	
	X	M	X	M	X	M	X	M	X	M
Kazakhstan	91	86	88	94	84	90	58	61	53	69
Kyrgyz Republic	97	80	94	96	88	91	66	66	66	68
Tajikistan	78	82	80	90	53	62	19	43	34	59
Turkmenistan	95	79	80	85	70	78	77	47	49	55
Uzbekistan	84	82	83	86	74	81	62	54	39	41

	1996		1997		1998		1999	
	X	M	X	M	X	M	X	M
Kazakhstan	56	70	46	54	40	47	26	43
Kyrgyz Republic	78	58	53	61	45	52	40	43
Tajikistan	43	57	36	64	34	63	46	78
Turkmenistan	68	30	60	55	26	47	N/A	N/A
Uzbekistan	21	32	33	27	25	28	30	26

Source: Islamov (2001, p. 173).

in which the Central Asian countries have been involved. Section 10.4 addresses other regional issues, focusing on water-resource management, security and border issues, and trade facilitation. The final section draws conclusions.

10.1   The Central Asian Countries' Trade Patterns and Policies

The five Central Asian countries' trade patterns changed substantially over the 1990s, although the timings and precise magnitudes of the changes are uncertain due to the variable quality of the trade data. The aggregate trade data have been discussed in Section 1.2. At the time of their independence, the Central Asian countries' trade was overwhelmingly oriented to former Soviet markets; Table 10.1 presents Islamov's reconstruction of trade shares by destination during the 1990s.[1] By 1996 over half of the Central Asian countries' international trade was with non-CIS countries (Kaser 1997, p. 179). The lead was taken by Uzbekistan, and reflects primarily the ability to sell cotton on world markets.[2] Kazakhstan was slower to diversify markets, unsurprisingly given its reliance on oil pipelines and mineral-processing links and its proximity to Russia, but the CIS share of Kazakhstan's trade had fallen to half in

---

[1] The IMF ("Common issues and interrepublic relations in the former USSR," IMF, Washington, DC, April 1992, p. 37) estimated similarly high ratios of 85–90% of the Central Asian republics' trade in 1988 being within the USSR.

[2] Breaking non-CIS trade down by country is not very interesting, because most exports went to cotton exchanges in the United Kingdom or Switzerland from whence the final destination was unknown (and was of little concern to Uzbekistan). Kazakhstan's oil also becomes anonymous once it leaves the country; in 2002, according to the IMF's "Direction of trade statistics," over a fifth of Kazakhstan's exports went to Bermuda.

Table 10.2. Central Asian trade matrix for 2003 (millions of U.S. dollars).

Exporter	Importer								
	Kazakhstan		Kyrgyz Rep.		Tajikistan		Turkmenistan		Uzbekistan
Kazakhstan	—	—	156	171	76	96	37	77	138	152
Kyrgyz Rep.	57	55	—	—	19	28	2	7	16	18
Tajikistan	5	7	4	3	—	—	2	4	67	74
Turkmenistan	3	49	1	0	26	32	—	—	11	12
Uzbekistan	82	90	36	39	121	133	42	46	—	—

Source: IMF "Direction of trade statistics," CD-ROM, December 2004.
Note: in each cell the first figure is exporting country data and the second figure is importing country data.

Table 10.3. Average import tariff, 2002 (percent).

Kazakhstan	7.8
Kyrgyz Republic	5.1
Tajikistan	8.0
Turkmenistan	N/A
Uzbekistan	15.3

Source: IMF data reported in Elborgh-Woytek (2003, p. 18).
Note: N/A denotes not available in the source.

1997 and dropped substantially further in 1999 during the export boom following devaluation of the currency. The pattern after 1999 is less clear in the four southern Central Asian countries, because the large devaluations in Russia and Kazakhstan increased the competitiveness of imports from these countries, and the share of CIS suppliers of imports increased by 2003 to 58% in the Kyrgyz Republic, 70% in Tajikistan, 49 % in Turkmenistan, and 40% in Uzbekistan.[3] In all five countries, however, the share of CIS markets in total exports continued to decline.

One symptom of the declining share of trade within the former Soviet Union is the very small intraregional trade flows (Table 10.2). To some extent this is a consequence of the lack of regional cooperation described in this chapter, although it also reflects the similarity of the five economies and greater opportunities for trade with complementary economies outside the region.

The Central Asian countries' tariff schedules have, in general, been fairly liberal (Table 10.3) and without great variance, although this has not been consistently true. The Kyrgyz Republic has bound most tariffs at 10% as part of commitments made during WTO accession negotiations, and actual tariffs average half of this level and applied tariffs are even lower because much intra-CIS trade is still duty-free. Kazakhstan has also had a liberal trade policy since mid-1996, when export duties were removed and the average tariff on imports fell to 12%; the average

---

[3] Data from IMF's "Direction of trade statistics," CD-ROM, December 2004.

tariff had fallen below 8% by 2002, but there are recurring complaints of ad hoc impositions which make trade policy less predictable. Uzbekistan's July 1995 tariff schedule had an average tariff of 18%, but included some high rates (such as 100% on automobiles). Both Turkmenistan and Tajikistan also levy protective tariffs as well as imposing a range of export restrictions (mainly in the form of surrender requirements on foreign exchange earnings). The last four countries also charge different rates for excise and other taxes on domestic and imported goods, which is in effect a tariff and would be illegal under WTO rules.

Episodes of illiberal policies have involved tariffs, nontariff barriers to trade, and restrictions on access to foreign exchange. Uzbekistan in 1996 and Turkmenistan in 1998 responded to balance-of-payments difficulties by reintroducing foreign exchange controls, which made other import restrictions largely irrelevant.[4] Uzbekistan has applied very high duties on automobiles to protect the UzDaewoo joint venture. Kazakhstan suddenly raised duties on intra-Central Asian trade in response to its 1998 crisis.[5] Border crossings have been temporarily closed, e.g., for several months in 1999 Uzbekistan unilaterally closed all but one of the posts along its border with Kazakhstan. Such actions are often unpredictable and may only be discovered upon arrival at the border.[6]

Customs officials operate with considerable discretionary power, and bureaucratic requirements impose substantial costs. Formal health, safety, and technical requirements can be onerous: for example, for goods entering into Tajikistan, sixteen different inspections are required, including quality control from which not even brand new Mercedes cars are exempt. There are, of course, good reasons for enforcing some of these standards, but their complexity is in many cases an excuse for customs officials to extract bribes in return for smoothing the process.

---

[4] The Kyrgyz Republic, in March 1995, and Kazakhstan, in July 1996, accepted Article VIII commitments to the IMF, guaranteeing full current-account convertibility and nondiscriminatory currency arrangements. Turkmenistan made circulation of foreign currencies illegal in December 1995, although the small private sector had reasonable access to foreign currency and the official and curb rates were close together until the second half of 1998, when tight exchange controls were introduced. In early 1996 Uzbekistan committed to formally adopting Article VIII, and its currency was de facto convertible, but the commitment was abandoned and controls were introduced in the second half of 1996. The introduction of currency convertibility was delayed until October 2003, and even then traders experienced difficulty in obtaining foreign currency.

[5] After the August 1998 Russian Crisis, which hit Kazakhstan hardest among the Central Asian countries, Kazakhstan introduced a 20% value-added tax on all personal imports from Russia, the Kyrgyz Republic, and Uzbekistan, and then in December 1998 enacted a law on "Measures to protect the domestic market from imported goods." Under this law, special tariffs as high as 200% were imposed on a number of goods imported from the Kyrgyz Republic and Uzbekistan in February 1999, when other restrictions such as import quotas on cement imports from the Kyrgyz Republic were also introduced. In April 1999 the 200% February tariffs were eliminated, but new licensing procedures, transit fees, and mandatory deposits on imports from the Kyrgyz Republic and Uzbekistan were introduced and the Kazakh tenge was floated, which led to an effective 50% devaluation.

[6] This can also affect domestic trade; for example, the main road between Uzbekistan's two largest cities, Tashkent and Samarkand, passes through a slice of Kazakhstan. Normally traffic flows freely but some days a long detour on side roads is necessary because the border is closed.

Table 10.4.   Status of WTO accession negotiations.

	Applied	Working Parties	Member
Kazakhstan	January 1996	7 meetings 1997–2004[a]	—
Kyrgyz Republic	1993	—	December 1998
Tajikistan	May 2001	1 meeting (March 2004)	—
Turkmenistan	Not applied	—	—
Uzbekistan	December 1994	2 meetings 2002–04[b]	—
China	1986	—	December 2001
Russian Federation	June 1993	25 meetings 1995–2004	—

Source: WTO website (www.wto.org), accessed January 31, 2005.

Notes: [a]Kazakhstan Working Parties met on March 19–20, 1997, October 9, 1997, October 9, 1998, July 13, 2001, July 15, 2003, March 4, 2004, and November 3, 2004; [b]Uzbekistan Working Parties met on July 17, 2002, and June 29, 2004.

10.2   The World Trade Organization

The first part of this section describes the current WTO status of the five Central Asian countries. The second part examines the experience of the only Central Asian country to have joined the WTO, the Kyrgyz Republic. The remaining parts analyze the consequences for the Central Asian countries of China's WTO accession in December 2001, Russia's expected WTO accession, and the accession of the Central Asian countries currently negotiating WTO membership.

10.2.1   WTO Status

With low average tariffs, the main obstacle to WTO membership has been Central Asian governments' unwillingness to formally abjure all of the nontariff barriers to trade described in the previous section. So far, only the Kyrgyz Republic among the Central Asian countries has joined the WTO, which it did in July 1998 (Table 10.4). Kazakhstan's application appears to be fairly far advanced.[7] Uzbekistan's accession process is at an earlier stage than Kazakhstan's. Tajikistan applied for WTO membership in May 2001. Turkmenistan has not yet made a formal application for WTO membership. The benefits of WTO membership should be accentuated by China's accession in 2001 and by Russia's impending accession. The remaining Central Asian countries' accession would then provide a common framework for formal trade policies and dispute resolution with respect to both intraregional trade and trade with all of the region's economically important neighbors.[8]

---

[7]The common belief is that, because of the Kazakhstan economy's close trade links with Russia, Kazakhstan's WTO accession will follow very soon after that of Russia.

[8]Pakistan and Turkey are WTO members, and Iran's accession is likely after a U.S. announcement in March 2005 that it would not oppose Iran's application. A major agenda item at the Eurasian Community's May 2002 Moscow summit was coordination of the WTO negotiations by Russia, Belarus, Kazakhstan, and Tajikistan. For more details on the Central Asian countries' WTO relations, see Pomfret (2003a, 2005b) and Michalopoulos (2003).

The Kyrgyz Republic was the first Central Asian country to apply for WTO membership. Given its liberal trade policies, including a low and even tariff structure and few nontariff barriers, negotiations went smoothly and the country became the first former Soviet republic to join the WTO. In the transition-country context, the Kyrgyz Republic was typical of a number of small countries with liberal policies whose accession negotiations were untroubling to existing members.[9]

Uzbekistan was the second Central Asian country to apply, and the Working Party on the accession of Uzbekistan to the WTO was established on December 21, 1994. This was during a period of substantial reform of Uzbekistan's economy, which had been initiated in January 1994 with a purposeful macroeconomic stabilization package. The reforms, however, began to lose momentum and were substantially undermined by the reintroduction of rigid exchange controls in October 1996. This reform slowdown and even reversal was reflected in snail's pace progress through the WTO accession process. Uzbekistan submitted its Memorandum on the Foreign Trade Regime in September 1998 and replies to questions were circulated in October 1999. The first meeting of the Working Party took place on July 17, 2002. The October 2003 reforms, which included establishment of currency convertibility, may signal a change of direction which could accelerate the accession process. The Working Party met for a second time in June 2004. Nevertheless, Uzbekistan has yet to begin bilateral negotiations with WTO members or to submit a formal offer.

Kazakhstan's Working Party was established on February 6, 1996. Bilateral market access negotiations in goods and services commenced in October 1997, and are continuing based on revised offers in goods and services. The process slowed down in 1998 following the Russian Crisis and its contagion effects on Kazakhstan, but has been revitalized since 2001. Kazakhstan has negotiated with the countries expressing interest in specific aspects of its application. Several rounds of formal offers have been made, of which the latest—in May and June 2004, for goods and for services, respectively—formed the basis for the Working Party's Factual Report in September 2004, potentially allowing the accession process to move into the final stages in 2005 and 2006.

In May 2001 Tajikistan lodged a formal request for accession, and a Working Party was established in July 2001. Tajikistan submitted a Memorandum on the Foreign Trade Regime, made an initial offer on goods and services in February 2004, and initiated bilateral negotiations. Thus, although the Working Party only met for the first time in March 2004, Tajikistan's negotiations are already further advanced than Uzbekistan's.

10.2.2   *The Experience of the Kyrgyz Republic*

The Kyrgyz Republic's WTO experience has become a disputed element in trade-policy debates elsewhere in Central Asia and in Azerbaijan. Opponents of WTO

---

[9] Slovenia joined the WTO in 1995, Bulgaria in 1996, Latvia and Estonia in 1999, Georgia, Albania, and Croatia in 2000, Lithuania and Moldova in 2001, Armenia in 2003, Cambodia in 2004.

membership cite the Kyrgyz Republic's poor economic performance since 1998 as evidence of a harmful effect of WTO membership. Such an interpretation is difficult to prove or disprove empirically given the many other candidates for explaining the country's disappointing economic performance in the final years of the century. The 1998 Russian Crisis, Kazakhstan's large currency devaluation, and the Kyrgyz Republic's massive banking crisis were major negative shocks to the Kyrgyz economy which coincided with WTO accession.[10] The weakened economy of the Kyrgyz Republic certainly failed to reap much in the way of immediate benefits from WTO membership, but it is hard to demonstrate that it suffered harm from accession.

A more robust criticism of the Kyrgyz Republic's accession experience is that the negotiators, whether due to inexperience or by intent, failed to make transitional arrangements or gain exemptions that would have protected Kyrgyz interests. Some learning process is reflected in Kazakhstan's lengthier and more detailed WTO negotiations and harder stance on some of the voluntary codes. The appropriate negotiating balance must reflect a country's preferences and compliance capabilities. It is generally unlikely that WTO provisions would harm a small open economy, although specific interest groups in the country may lose out, but immediate compliance may be problematic and a transition period desirable.

In this context it is worth emphasizing that the basic WTO principles, embodied in the General Agreement on Tariffs and Trade (GATT), are general in applicability. Every nation has its own specific features, but they do not imply that the WTO principles need to be modified. A red herring for many CIS countries (and China) in their WTO accession negotiations has been the pursuance of developing-country status in order to qualify for special and differential (S&D) treatment. All of the evidence suggests that S&D treatment has been of little value to its beneficiaries. Donor-determined schemes under the Generalized System of Preferences grant very limited preferential access to developing-country exports, and even this can be withdrawn at short notice if the developing country actually succeeds in increasing its exports substantially (Pomfret 1997a). On the other hand, the CIS countries have been slow to shed their "nonmarket" status, which allows the countries to be treated as nonmarket economies in antidumping determinations; this allows the importing country to disregard actual prices in the alleged dumping country when calculating dumping margins and instead to use constructed values, which are often biased in favor of the import-competing industry's claims. The situation may be changing as Russia gained acceptance of its market-economy status in 2002 during its

---

[10] Trend (2003, pp. 55–60) contrasts the 7–9% GDP growth of 1996 and 1997 with the 2–5% growth in the years 1998–2001. The Azerbaijani report mentions the other negative shocks, but focuses on WTO accession as the main cause of disappointing post-1998 growth, alleviated only by exports from the Kumtor gold mine whose growth was independent of WTO status. In a study of twenty-five transition economies during the period 1990–98, Campos (2004) found no robust relationship between WTO membership and the rate of economic growth, although he did find a positive effect of WTO membership on domestic reform (see also Bacchetta and Drabek 2002).

WTO negotiations. After several adverse antidumping determinations, Kazakhstan achieved recognition as a market economy from the United States in 2002. In sum, developing-country status may be difficult to negotiate and is scarcely worth the effort, while nonmarket status may be difficult to shed but in view of the salience of antidumping measures as protective instruments it is definitely worth the effort.

10.2.3   *Trade with China and the Impact of Chinese WTO Accession*

China joined the WTO in December 2001, over fifteen years after the application was lodged. The Chinese negotiations were affected by specific political factors, notably the lengthy delay following the June 1989 Tiananmen incident, which prevented conclusion of negotiations during the GATT era. The drawn-out negotiations meant that by the time they were concluded much of the necessary adjustment in China's external trade polices had already taken place before formal accession.[11]

In the literature on China's WTO accession there is little mention of the impact on the Central Asian countries. This is primarily because the Central Asian countries are minor trading partners or investment suppliers for China. Consideration of Central Asia arises largely in the context of energy supplies or security, neither of which has much to do with WTO status. Trade with Central Asia is much more significant for Xinjiang province, which borders three of the Central Asian countries, although physical barriers are substantial in the south. China is more important for the Central Asian countries' trade, although the numbers are still not large. To some extent this reflects official discouragement of further expansion of trade with China after an initial surge followed the Central Asian countries' independence, even though the surge was from a very low base. The evidence of the bazaars is that unofficial trade with China, in imported consumer goods, continues to flourish but is underrecorded. It would be even more substantial if transport connections were better.

In the thirty years preceding the dissolution of the Soviet Union, trade took place between Central Asia and China, but was quite restricted. Border crossings were closed in the early 1960s after the Sino-Soviet split, and only two—Horgos between Kazakhstan and China, and Torugart between the Kyrgyz Republic and China—reopened when relations improved in the early 1980s. The first railway between China and Central Asia opened in 1990, and since then has carried the vast majority of freight by volume (mainly minerals from Kazakhstan to China). Other border posts opened during the 1990s, but they could be closed unilaterally at short notice.[12]

---

[11] There is a huge literature on China and the WTO. Bhattasali et al. (2004) contains studies on the main aspects affecting the Chinese economy.

[12] The five ports of entry from Kazakhstan to Xinjiang Autonomous Region are Jimunai (reopened in 1991), Bakhty (reopened in 1990), Ala Pass (opened in 1990), Horgos (reopened in 1983), and Dulata (opened 1999), and from the Kyrgyz Republic Irkeshtam (reopened in 1998) and Torugart (reopened in 1983). Bakhty and Jimunai were the most active crossings in the first half of the twentieth century, but both were closed in 1962. The rail crossing at Ala Pass, the road crossings at Bakhty, Horgas, and Torugart, and Urumqi airport are open to third-country imports into Xinjiang. There are also informal border crossings with Kazakhstan at Mubeizite and Aheitubieke and with the Kyrgyz Republic at Biedieli which serve

Table 10.5. Trade between Central Asia and China (in millions of U.S. dollars): Chinese trade statistics.

	1997		1998		1999		2000		2001	
	M	X	M	X	M	X	M	X	M	X
Kazakhstan	95	433	205	431	494	644	599	958	328	961
Kyrgyz Rep.	71	36	172	26	103	32	110	67	77	42
Tajikistan	11	9	11	8	2	6	7	10	5	5
Turkmenistan	12	3	10	2	7	2	12	4	31	1
Uzbekistan	62	140	58	32	27	13	39	12	51	8

Source: "China's customs statistics," reported by Wu and Chen (2004, p. 1,066).
Note: "X" denotes Central Asian exports to China, "M" denotes Central Asian imports from China.

Cross-border trade between Central Asia and China grew rapidly in the early 1990s, although hard data are unavailable. The growth slowed in 1993–94 amid currency changes, and in the mid-1990s some Central Asian governments expressed concern about their markets being flooded by Chinese consumer goods, while Chinese traders and potential investors worried about the insecurity of property rights in Central Asia. Some commodity trade was dominated by bulk state purchases and could fluctuate from year to year, e.g., Uzbekistan's cotton sales to China fell from $133 million in 1997 to $29 million in 1998.

In 1998 Chinese customs statistics report formal exports to Central Asia of $456 million and imports of $499 million (Tables 10.5 and 10.6).[13] Wiemer (2000) reports estimates of shuttle exports at $300–600 million. Even with the highest estimates of shuttle trade, trade with Central Asia amounted to less than 1% of China's total trade. For Xinjiang Province, however, over half of international trade is with Central Asia, although Xinjiang has a below-average trade–GDP ratio for China. For Central Asia, trade with China is more significant, perhaps 5% of total international trade, but no more than that.

Trade was disrupted in 1999 following the Russian Crisis and related crises in Kazakhstan and the Kyrgyz Republic. Kazakhstan closed border posts and devalued its currency substantially, cutting demand for imported Chinese goods. This is likely to have had a negative impact on the shuttle trade. The official trade data, however, show continuous growth in Kazakhstan's exports to China, by far the largest single

---

local populations, and three river ports of entry from Kazakhstan which process small quantities. A port of entry from Tajikistan at Kalafen opened in 2000. Even when new roads are built, the physical barriers remain substantial; on a new road between China and Tajikistan opened in summer 2004 the first bus from Kashgar took twenty-four hours to reach Khorog and a further two days to reach Dushanbe—and in winter the road will be impassible.

[13] The main items were iron and steel ($202 million), copper ($87 million), aluminum ($5 million), and fuel ($40 million) imports from Kazakhstan and shoe exports ($80 million) to Kazakhstan and the Kyrgyz Republic.

Table 10.6.   Trade between Central Asia and China
(in millions of U.S. dollars): Central Asian trade statistics.

	1997		1998		1999		2000		2001	
	M	X	M	X	M	X	M	X	M	X
Kazakhstan	47	442	51	382	82	473	154	670	169	656
Kyrgyz Rep.	32	32	44	16	37	25	37	44	49	19
Tajikistan	2	13	1	5	3	3	12	3	0	0
Turkmenistan	7	2	6	6	14	5	16	8	35*	1*
Uzbekistan	68*	127*	64*	29*	30*	12*	43*	11*	56*	7*

Source: IMF "Direction of trade statistics."
Notes: "X" denotes Central Asian exports to China, "M" denotes Central Asian imports from China;
all data marked with an asterisk are constructed from partner country records.

element in Tables 10.5 and 10.6, over the period 1998–2000.[14] Trade between the Kyrgyz Republic and China stagnated after 1998 while the other three Central Asian countries' trade with China, especially their exports, remained tiny.

The potential for increased trade between Central Asia and China is substantial given their differing factor endowments and natural resources, but realizing the potential depends upon a favorable trade environment and improved physical infrastructure. China's WTO accession could, given these favorable conditions, kick-start trade with Central Asia. Pressure to improve entry into the financial sector and to the logistics sector as a result of China's WTO entry commitments should reduce trading costs within China, with particular benefit to China's inland provinces such as Xinjiang. Such improvements could also facilitate international trade, including trade with Central Asia, which is currently conducted to a large extent in cash and is hampered by prohibitive transport and other transactions costs. In 2003–04 there appears to have been a surge in Chinese exports to the Kyrgyz Republic, a significant part of which went to bazaars for on-sale to Uzbekistan whose own bazaars are restricted.

10.2.4   The Impact of Russian WTO Accession

Russia's WTO accession negotiations have progressed in fits and starts. Although the Working Party on the accession of the Russian Federation was established in June 1993, little progress was made until after 2001.[15] In spring 2002, as a positive step in reintegrating Russia into the global trading system, the European Union

---

[14] Even for this element, which is dominated by trade in minerals between official entities or large companies, there is a large discrepancy between the Chinese data and data collected by Kazakhstan. The substantially larger numbers reported by China most likely reflect the deficiencies of Kazakhstan's customs service, which is widely believed to be one of the most corrupt parts of the administration.

[15] In January 2001 Russia's tariff schedule was revised to reduce and unify tariffs, but exemptions and nontariff barriers remain on the books and, because of low administrative capacities and corruption, implementation is poor.

Table 10.7. Stock of DFI in 2003 (millions of U.S. dollars).

Kazakhstan	17,567
Kyrgyz Republic	501
Tajikistan	223
Turkmenistan	1,314
Uzbekistan	917

Source: UNCTAD "World investment report 2004," United Nations, New York and Geneva, 2004.

and the United States both granted Russia market-economy status, which reduces the scope for using constructed values in assessing antidumping duties. Concerns remain (especially in the European Union) over Russia's subsidized energy prices, and agriculture and services are other major sticking areas. Work commenced in 2004 on a draft report of the Working Party, suggesting that negotiations were reaching the endgame stage.

Existing empirical studies of the economic impact of Russian WTO membership tend to assume that it can be analyzed in a similar fashion to that of China. Thus, estimates of gains to Russia emphasize the benefits from increased investment and technology transfer (e.g., Jensen et al. 2002).[16] This suggests that the main impacts of Russian WTO accession on Central Asia are likely to be investment diversion and increasing import demand. The former is likely to be minor because the amount of DFI in Central Asia is small, apart from energy investments in Kazakhstan and to a much smaller extent Turkmenistan (Table 10.7). The potential of benefiting from a larger Russian market will be felt most by Kazakhstan as the Central Asian country most heavily involved in trade with Russia.

For the Central Asian countries trade relations with Russia are substantially more important than their trade relations with China (Table 10.8). For Kazakhstan, the most important Central Asian trading nation with both countries, exports to Russia have been at least double those to China and imports from Russia have been several times larger than those from China; this last point may be slightly offset by the shuttle trade, but no estimates of the unofficial cross-border trade with China bring imports close to the amount coming from Russia. The Kyrgyz Republic is the only one of the Central Asian countries for which the two large trading partners have been of roughly equal weight. For the other three countries, Russia is a significant trading partner in contrast to the small magnitudes of China trade.

10.2.5 Central Asian Countries' WTO Accession

If Russia's outstanding issues can be settled expeditiously, then Kazakhstan's WTO accession is expected to follow close behind that of Russia, due to the strong

---

[16] Jensen et al., employing a computable general equilibrium model of the Russian economy, estimate long-run gains from WTO accession equal to over 50% of current consumption, and these mainly capture increases in total factor productivity associated with liberalization of DFI. Placing more emphasis on trade flows, Lissovolik and Lissovolik (2004) and Babetskaia-Kukharchuk and Maurel (2004) use the gravity model to measure the impact of Russian WTO accession.

Table 10.8.   Trade between Central Asia and Russia (millions of U.S. dollars).

	1997		1998		1999		2000		2001	
	M	X	M	X	M	X	M	X	M	X
Russian Trade Statistics										
Kazakhstan	2,472	2,743	1,881	1,877	1,222	1,391	2,246	2,197	2,544	1,834
Kyrgyz Rep.	167	149	131	129	84	95	103	88	83	61
Tajikistan	90	97	77	59	66	111	56	237	69	129
Turkmenistan	265	156	94	43	60	77	130	473	139	39
Uzbekistan	875	1,016	485	521	240	466	274	662	364	580
Central Asian Trade Statistics										
Kazakhstan	1,969	2,288	1,712	1,611	1,351	1,139	2,460	1,784	2,891	1,748
Kyrgyz Rep.	191	99	204	84	109	71	133	65	85	65
Tajikistan	115	63	102	48	92	115	105	259	129	105
Turkmenistan	164	57	132	29	167	44	255	1,029	153*	35*
Uzbekistan	962*	923*	533*	474*	264*	423*	302*	602*	400*	527*

Source: IMF "Direction of trade statistics."

Notes: "X" denotes Central Asian exports to Russia and "M" denotes Central Asian imports from Russia; data marked with an asterisk are constructed from partner country records.

economic links between the two. The Kyrgyz Republic has been threatening to withhold consent for Kazakhstan's accession until unresolved transit issues are settled, but that is unlikely to be an insuperable obstacle.[17] Pressure would then be on Tajikistan and Uzbekistan to accelerate their accession negotiations.

The most important benefit of WTO membership would be to place all Central Asian trade on a common basis of international trade law, and potentially to separate trade from politics. The failure of the myriad preferential trading agreements described in the next section should have already clarified that they are not a practical route to realizing greater gains from trade. The main change in geographical trade patterns since 1991 has been the switch of trade towards more distant markets. Trade with Russia has atrophied from the enforced patterns of the Soviet Union, while trade with China has expanded far below potential, and trade among the Central Asian countries has generally stagnated since the completion of the first phase of transition in the mid-1990s.

The general pattern has been an increase in openness (i.e., trade/GDP) of the Central Asian countries, as elsewhere in the CIS, from 1992 to 1997 and then a decline

---

[17] The Kyrgyz position is reported in *Ukrayinska Pravda* September 2, 2003 (English version at www.pravda.com.ua/). WTO decision making requires consensus, but this principle is coming under increased scrutiny with the expansion of WTO membership and the potential for minor economic powers to derail complex global trade negotiations. A likely compromise in the Kyrgyz–Kazakh case is that the Kyrgyz Republic will be able to represent what other WTO members accept to be its legitimate concerns, but not to block Kazakh negotiations over grievances that are not central to WTO rights. Even that restricted power illustrates a benefit of joining the WTO sooner rather than later; once inside the organization, members can have a say on future developments.

in openness over the next half decade. Many of the proximate causes are country or region specific (Elborgh-Woytek 2003), but the lack of a stable institutional environment surely did not help. One indicator of the potential for international trade is the contrast between intra-Russian trade and international intra-CIS trade. Using a gravity model, Djankov and Freund (2002a,b) estimate that trade among Russian provinces is around 60% higher than trade between CIS countries, *ceteris paribus*, but the national-border effect is weaker for Kazakhstan than for the other Central Asian countries' trade with Russia. Clearly such estimates are no more than indicative in what remains a disequilibrium situation, but they suggest the large orders of magnitude by which the Central Asian countries' trade could increase.

WTO accession could bring further benefits by encouraging liberal policies and punishing backsliding on commitments. Such an environment would help to attract DFI, as well as making domestic investment more attractive. Without good policies and good governance, the impact of WTO membership will be largely nullified. With a positive domestic environment, WTO membership helps to ensure that a country can reap benefits from specialization and trade with diminished fear of protectionist responses in foreign markets. WTO membership would also grant some leverage to reduce existing illiberal polices, e.g., Uzbekistan and Tajikistan would want to join Brazil and West African countries lobbying for reduced subsidies to cotton producers in the United States and the European Union (Pomfret 2005a).

10.3 The Attraction of Regionalism

This section reviews regional organizations that involve one or more of the five Central Asian countries. The assessment of existing regional organizations focuses on arrangements within the former Soviet space, new organizations with an exclusively Central Asian membership, relations with southern neighbors in the Economic Cooperation Organization, and relations with Russia and China within the Shanghai Cooperation Organization (SCO). Other groupings involving Central Asian countries and their neighbors are based on cultural or geographical affinity (e.g., the Turkic Group, the Organization of the Islamic Conference, the Black Sea and Caspian Sea organizations) and contain no trade mandate.

10.3.1 *Arrangements within the Former Soviet Space*

The five Central Asian countries are all members of the Commonwealth of Independent States (CIS),[18] but that organization has had little impact on trade conditions. The CIS was initially conceived as a framework in which to maintain economic ties among the Soviet successor states. In both the political and the economic spheres,

---

[18] When the leaders of Russia, Belarus, and Ukraine met in early December 1991 to discuss the end of the Soviet Union, the Central Asian leaders reacted quickly to maintain some degree of continuity and this became embodied in the CIS, which replaced the Soviet Union on December 25. President Nazarbayev of Kazakhstan in particular was a key mover in ensuring that the successor to the Soviet Union would include all the non-Baltic republics rather than just the three Slavic republics.

however, the replacement of the Soviet Union by sovereign nations created conflicts that the CIS framework was unable to contain. Between 1992 and 1994, CIS politics were largely defined by regional conflicts in the Caucasus and in Tajikistan, in all of which (with the partial exception of Tajikistan) Russia opted for a unilateral solution. After 1994 Russia sought more multilateral approaches, but the decline in Russian power exposed by the Chechnya conflict and the freezing of the main intra-CIS conflicts encouraged the emergence of alternative political initiatives, such as the grouping of Georgia, Ukraine, Azerbaijan, and Moldova (GUAM).

In the early years of the CIS many agreements to form economic arrangements were signed, but these had zero practical impact. This was especially true in the final year of the ruble zone. Armenia, Azerbaijan, Belarus, Kazakhstan, the Kyrgyz Republic, Moldova, Russia, Tajikistan, and Uzbekistan reached an agreement in May 1993 to set up an economic union, and they signed a formal treaty to that effect in September 1993. Georgia signed some of the provisions, and Ukraine became an associate member, so that the union included all the former Soviet republics except for the Baltic countries and Turkmenistan. The economic union treaty was supported by a host of other formal agreements on trade, payments, customs procedures and classifications, legal harmonization, and so forth, but neither the economic union nor subsequent proposals involving the CIS as a group made any practical progress (Sakwa and Webber 1999, pp. 386–90).

The reality of intra-CIS economic relations is more complex. During the early 1990s, national borders were poorly monitored, and goods and people continued to pass fairly unimpeded.[19] The situation gradually changed, especially over the second half of the 1990s, with the erection of formal customs posts at crossing points of what had been interrepublic borders. Actual monitoring continued to be erratic and the distinction between legal and private levies by customs officials was not always transparent. By the early 2000s, several CIS member states had introduced visa requirements for citizens of other CIS countries.[20] Within the CIS, and especially among members of the Eurasian Community, goods and people still cross some borders unimpeded, but the pattern is towards more and more onerous barriers.

Much of the maneuvering within the CIS has reflected strategic or political decisions, without economic content. Russia appears to view the organization as a vehicle

---

[19] In the confused situation following Russia's January 1992 price reform, the newly independent Central Asian countries imposed export taxes and bans to restrict the outflow of goods. The export barriers were generally removed by the mid-1990s, although Uzbekistan, Turkmenistan, and Tajikistan continued to tax farmers through a state order system for cotton, which was effectively an export tax, but with little impact on intraregional trade (apart from the incentive to smuggle) because cotton is exported to markets beyond Central Asia.

[20] The most important is Russia, which generally tolerated freedom of movement prior to the outbreak of the second Chechen war in 1999, but has since viewed illegal immigrants as a security risk. Russian officials estimate that perhaps four million illegal immigrants were working in Russia in 2002 (compared with 300,000 guest workers with proper documentation). Legislation, which took effect on November 1, 2002, expanded law enforcement officers' powers to deal with illegal immigrant labor. The summary deportations include an instance when 120 Tajiks were flown to Dushanbe in November 2002, and a similar incident a few days later involving 80 Tajiks.

for exerting political leadership in the former USSR, and sees the Collective Security Treaty (CST) as the main instrument.[21] During the mid-1990s Russia attempted to reestablish its influence over Central Asia. Faced with a delicate ethnic balance between Kazakhs and Russians, President Nazarbayev of Kazakhstan tried to deflect the impending Russian dominance into a more cooperative structure by promoting a customs union. Uzbekistan and Turkmenistan were more overtly resistant to Russian regional designs, and to falling too much under the influence of any multilateral organization. Uzbekistan's withdrawal from the CST and Turkmenistan's neutrality reflected suspicion of Russian motives and a desire to distance themselves from Russian influence.[22] Turkmenistan, with substantial (but declining) export earnings from natural gas and cotton, adopted an autarchic political position, seeking UN guarantees of its neutrality. Uzbekistan, after adopting a macroeconomic stabilization program in January 1994, by contrast became more prominent on the international stage as President Karimov sought to portray himself as the region's leader.[23] Concerns about potential Uzbek hegemony tended to push Kazakhstan and the Kyrgyz Republic, which also fears Uzbek irredentist claims to its territory, closer to Russia.[24]

One of the leaders in trying to retain the CIS as a formal regional trading arrangement since the collapse of the ruble zone has been Kazakhstan's president, Nursultan Nazarbayev, who in 1994–95 advocated a Eurasian Union (Kalyuzhnova 1998, pp. 49–50). In a 1994 comment, President Nazarbayev, frustrated by lack of implementation of the many agreements signed by CIS members, observed:

> Since the time of the establishment of the Commonwealth of Independent States, roughly 400 agreements have been adopted. However, as yet there have been no substantive results because individual national governments continue to reject certain provisions and interpret the meaning of the agreements in their own interest.
>
> Nazarbayev (1996, p. 234)

---

[21] In contrast, Russia showed little interest during the 1990s in pursuing closer economic ties, even with Belarus, which sought economic union, and still less with the Central Asian countries.

[22] Uzbekistan withdrew from the CIS Collective Security Treaty in 1998, and aligned itself with the GUAM grouping. Turkmenistan's president skipped CIS summits in Yalta in August 2000 and Sochi in August 2001, although he did attend the February 2002 informal summit at Chimbulak in Kazakhstan. Turkmenistan's relations with Russia were revived by Russian assistance in bringing Boris Shikhmuradov, a leading dissident who had been in exile in Moscow, to trial in Ashgabat in connection with the November 2001 assassination attempt on Turkmenistan's president.

[23] In 1995–96 Uzbekistan became the most prominent regional ally of the United States. On occasion only Israel and Uzbekistan voted with the United States at the United Nations, and at the May 1996 ECO summit Uzbekistan's denunciation of Iran was so vitriolic that the summit ended a day earlier than planned. In July 1996 President Karimov was warmly received by President Clinton in Washington, DC. For more details of Uzbekistan's evolving foreign economic policies, see Bohr (1998), Pomfret (2000b), and Spechler (1999).

[24] There was also an older political split insofar as Yeltsin, Akayev, and (eventually) Nazarbayev opposed the August 1991 coup, while Karimov and Niyazov initially supported it.

In December 1994, Kazakhstan announced the formation of a customs union treaty with Russia and Belarus, which came into effect on July 15, 1995. The Kyrgyz Republic acceded in 1996 and Tajikistan in 1999, making it a Union of Five.

Despite the formal agreements between 1994 and 2000, there was little evidence of implementation by the Central Asian countries. Echoing Nazarbayev's earlier reservations about the CIS, the Kyrgyz Republic's President Akaev was quoted in 1999 as saying that the customs union agreements existed "on paper only" (Zhalim-betova and Gleason 2001, p. 4). Indeed, members were operating in contradictory directions in terms of their actual policies. For example, it seemed likely that, as part of the custom union's common external trade policy, the tariff bindings which the Kyrgyz Republic agreed to in its 1998 WTO accession negotiations would be unacceptably low for Russia or Belarus, and a similar issue would arise if Kazakhstan were to join the WTO.[25]

A formal agreement on the common external tariff (CET) for the customs union, signed in February 2000, envisaged a CET consisting of tariff lines that were common to Belarus, Kazakhstan, and Russia with the remaining tariff lines to be set at a subsequent stage. The implementation period was five years, but by 2005 the CET covered only 6,156 of the 11,086 tariff lines identified in the Union's classification system.[26] The remaining tariffs are set independently by each member of the Union's successor organization.

In October 2000 the Union of Five was renamed the Eurasian Economic Community and a new treaty was signed in Astana, which came into effect in May 2001. The institutional framework has been strengthened in a bid to ensure better implementation. The organization is managed by an Interstate Council (chaired by President Nazarbayev), an Integration Committee, an Inter-Parliament Assembly (in Saint Petersburg), and by a Eurasian Community Court. The voting and financing formula gives Russia 40%, Belarus and Kazakhstan 20% each, and the Kyrgyz Republic and Tajikistan 10% each, with a two-thirds majority being required on "major policy issues." Thus, Russia has veto power, but to implement new measures Russia will generally need the support of at least one other member, and at least two others on major policy issues. Within the new framework any member failing to abide by Community rules can be expelled.

The functional areas of the new Community differ little from those agreed within the earlier frameworks. The emphasis is on free intra-Community trade with a common external tariff, as well as a common market for labor and capital, common policies towards migration, and more general policy harmonization. A specific intention

---

[25] In the mid-1990s Kazakhstan's WTO accession seemed more imminent than proved the case. According to Webber (1997, p. 56), President Nazarbayev indicated in September 1996 that Kazakhstan would leave the customs union when it acceded to the WTO. Apart from any treaty obligations, both Kazakhstan and the Kyrgyz Republic seem well aware that protecting their markets for the benefit of Russian producers is not in their national interest.

[26] See Patrizia Tumbarello, "Regional integration and WTO accession: which is the right sequencing? An application to the CIS." IMF Working Paper, February 2005, p. 9.

is to coordinate WTO accession negotiations, but even this attempt at a common external trade policy is dubious given that the Kyrgyz Republic is already a WTO member and that Belarus appears to have differing WTO goals than Russia. At the May 2002 summit in Moscow, Moldova and Ukraine were granted observer status, although President Nazarbayev as Chair emphasized that they would need to bring their legislation in line with that of the Eurasian Community's existing members before closer integration could be discussed.[27]

In contrast to its predecessor organizations, the Eurasian Community is intended to operate as a regional international organization rather than as an interstate agreement. At the political level it has very strong support from Kazakhstan, but the attitude of the other signatories is more lukewarm, and at the May 2002 summit Belarus President Alyaksandr Lukashenka openly criticized the implementation record of other members. Kazakhstan's ambitious aspirations were reflected in statements by the governor of the National Bank of Kazakhstan, Grigori Marchenko, that the Community should aim to have a single currency and that "preliminary procedures for the introduction of a single currency might take only five to seven years."[28] Later in 2002 Russian Prime Minister Kasyanov expressed hope that the Eurasian Community would adopt the Russian ruble as a common currency. In practice, however, Eurasian Community integration plans stalled in 2003.[29]

An alternative grouping among CIS countries emerged in February 2003 when the leaders of Russia, Belarus, Ukraine, and Kazakhstan reached a tentative agreement to create a Single Economic Space (SES). Russia promoted the SES concept, but the other three countries bridled at suggestions of establishing supranational institutions or of adopting the Russian ruble as a common currency.[30] The defeat of the Russian-supported candidate in Ukraine's December 2004 presidential election led to cooling of relations between Russia and Ukraine, which effectively mothballed the SES. After May 2005, Uzbekistan distanced itself from the United States and rebuilt bridges with Russia, culminating in Uzbekistan's accession to the Eurasian Community at the October 2005 Saint Petersburg summit. The broadening of the Eurasian Community is, however, unlikely to be accompanied by deeper economic integration. Both Kazakhstan, with its increased integration into global oil markets

---

[27] The presumed eagerness of other states to join the Community was not shared, e.g., President Kuchma was quick to deny any such desire by Ukraine.

[28] Quoted in the *International Herald Tribune*, sponsored section, April 24, 2002.

[29] For an optimistic analysis of the Community's prospects, see Zhalimbetova and Gleason (2001). In June 2004, however, Belarus President Lukashenka told the Community's General Secretary that "member states have got practically nothing from the Eurasian Community."

[30] Even as Russia was promoting the SES concept at a political level, in 2002–03 Russia was raising tariffs and nontariff barriers on specific imports from CIS countries, such as steel from Ukraine (Yudaeva 2003). By the end of 2003 the SES appeared to have joined the list of defunct schemes, and the concluding communiqué of the January 2004 Astana summit between Presidents Putin and Nazarbayev made no mention of the SES. At a May 2004 SES summit in the Crimea, however, Nazarbayev called for SES members to form a customs union, but Ukraine was not interested. During 2004 senior Russian officials also called for closer integration, using the ruble as a common settlement currency in the SES, although other countries were unresponsive.

and lessened dependence on Russian pipelines, and the Kyrgyz Republic, which pointedly ignored demands to follow Uzbekistan's lead and close the U.S. base on its territory, began to show unease with Russia's authoritarianism in 2005, and looked for countervailing links outside the region. Both the Eurasian Community and the SES reflect a more assertive Russian stance in leading regionalism in the former Soviet space, but so far none of the intra-CIS arrangements has had any impact on trade relations.

10.3.2   *Organizations with an Exclusively Central Asian Membership*

During the second half of 1993 the presidents of Kazakhstan and Uzbekistan made several statements on the need to maintain a common economic space in Central Asia amid the discord of the CIS and imminent breakdown of the common currency area.[31] After the collapse of the ruble zone in November 1993, the presidents of Kazakhstan, the Kyrgyz Republic, and Uzbekistan agreed to create an integrated economic space, announced in the Tashkent Declaration of January 1994 and formalized in the Cholpon–Ata Treaty signed by the heads of state on April 30, 1994. Initially called the Central Asian Economic Union, and intended to be modeled on the European Union, this organization evolved into the Central Asian Economic Community (CAEC) when Tajikistan joined in 1998.

The CAEC was viewed as a forum for resolving disputes within Central Asia, and also as a vehicle for promoting collaborative projects. The promotion of collaborative projects would require investment, and thus one of the main positive initiatives of the CAEC was the creation of an Interstate Central Asian Bank of Cooperation and Development, which was founded in June 1994 with head office in Almaty and branches in Bishkek and Tashkent. In the mid-1990s the Bank granted several small credits, such as $300,000 to an Almaty firm producing electric meters, $300,000 to an Uzbek firm producing blood products, and $300,000 to a Kyrgyz firm manufacturing electric motors. The modest scale of these credits illustrates that the Bank was playing a primarily symbolic role. By January 1997, the participating countries had given the Bank only some two-thirds of its charter capital, and it was clearly incapable of drawing substantial external funds into Central Asia for investment in collaborative projects. In April 1997 Uzbekistan openly expressed its disillusionment with the Bank's work.[32] The CAEC member countries insisted

---

[31] The original commitment to an integrated economic space was made at a time when many intra-Central Asian trade arrangements were based on barter. Kazakhstan banned barter transactions in 1994. Uzbekistan and the Kyrgyz Republic traded Uzbek natural gas for Kyrgyz hydroelectricity and other goods "to be named," but when Uzbekistan's need for the electricity declined in 1998 the agreement collapsed and Uzbekistan demanded hard-currency payment for its gas (because none of the three Kyrgyz customers could pay, Uzbekistan's gas exports to the Kyrgyz Republic fell to a fraction of their 1997 level). Annual water–energy agreements continue to provide a framework for Kazakh–Kyrgyz relations in these areas, but are subject to frequent disputes.

[32] Uzbekistan's disillusionment was partly driven by the introduction in the previous autumn of strict exchange controls, which made it practically impossible for borrowers in Uzbekistan to access funds from the Bank, which made hard-currency loans and required repayment in hard currency. In the view of

that the Interstate Central Asian Bank of Cooperation and Development allocate resources proportionately to each country's contribution, so that little attention was paid to profitability or to externalities in the form of enhanced regional integration. Apart from the activity of the Interstate Central Asian Bank of Cooperation and Development, the CAEC had little in the way of practical achievements. Officials claimed to have made some contributions in tax harmonization and elimination of double taxation, but these are difficult to document, and the CAEC had little impact on intraregional trade.[33]

On February 28, 2002, the four leaders proclaimed the Central Asian Cooperation Organization (CACO) as the successor to the CAEC. The Central Asian leaders attempted to distinguish the CACO from its predecessor by emphasizing improved effectiveness. By some counts, at the CAEC meetings the Central Asian leaders passed over 250 resolutions, but the implementation record fell far behind the statements of intentions. The founding agreement of the CACO, however, continued to voice lofty aspirations while paying little attention to institutionalizing implementation, and despite a flurry of activity in 2002 under CACO auspices[34] there seemed little change from its predecessor. In May 2004 Russia became a CACO member, and this signalled the end of the organization as one with exclusively Central Asian membership.[35] With Uzbekistan's accession to the Eurasian Community in October 2005, the CACO was formally absorbed into the almost identical organization (Belarus was the only country not in CACO).

As an alternative forum for regional cooperation, the Special Programme for the Economies of Central Asia (SPECA) was launched in 1998 with the support of the two United Nations regional organizations: the Economic and Social Commission for Asia and the Pacific (ESCAP) and the Economic Commission for Europe (ECE). The presidents of Kazakhstan, the Kyrgyz Republic, Tajikistan, and Uzbekistan signed the Tashkent Declaration on March 26, 1998, creating SPECA, and in September 1998 Turkmenistan officially indicated its intention to sign the Declaration and to participate in SPECA projects.

The main purpose of SPECA is to support the Central Asian countries in strengthening their cooperation in order to both stimulate their economic development and facilitate their integration with the economies of Asia and Europe. Through consultation with the participating countries, five priority areas were identified and working groups set up as instruments to develop and implement the program in each priority

---

Gleason (2001, p. 1,087), "The key obstacle to greater sub-regional economic cooperation at the end of the century was Uzbekistan" because of its inconvertible currency and protectionist trade policies. There is some truth to this, but the reasons for the lack of cooperation were deeper and more widespread.

[33] For more details on the CAEC see Rumer and Zhukov (1998, pp. 118–19), Dieter (1996), and Raballand (2003b).

[34] The October 2002 CACO summit in Dushanbe was combined with the meeting of the four heads of state of the International Fund to Save the Aral Sea. A regional business forum held its first session in November 2002 in Tashkent.

[35] Afghanistan also obtained official observer status in the CACO in 2004.

area. SPECA's achievements have been limited. In part, this is because it has no self-funding mechanism. Two of the working groups have been single-project dominated, with their activities determined by available funding, while the other three working groups have little concrete to show (two have not even been set up, and the third's achievements are limited to bilateral issues between two countries).[36] The lack of achievement also reflects incomplete participation—Uzbekistan and Turkmenistan have not attended the meetings of the Regional Advisory Committee, the governing body of SPECA which is responsible for strategic decisions. The SPECA concept was formally adopted in April 2000 at the Eurasian Economic Summit in Almaty, a forum in which Kazakhstan, the Kyrgyz Republic, and Tajikistan were participants and the other two countries were not.

The existence of SPECA is symptomatic of the proliferation of institutions for regional cooperation in Central Asia. If the CAEC/CACO had been an effective regional organization, there would have been little need for SPECA. Precisely because of the political obstacles to the smooth running of CACO, however, SPECA could have a positive role to play if it were to be accepted as a forum for technical cooperation, rather than having the political connotations of a European-Union-style organization that the CACO and Eurasian Community embody. In practice, however, SPECA fell victim to the political split in Central Asia, becoming identified with the Eurasian Community's Central Asian members and spurned by the other two Central Asian countries.

In 2005 political events prompted a realignment of regional affiliations. The March 2005 overthrow of President Akayev, following the color revolutions in Georgia and Ukraine, prompted a more active Russian role in Central Asia. This shift was abetted by the May 2005 Andijan massacre, whose condemnation by the European Union and the United States encouraged President Karimov to close the U.S. base in Uzbekistan and foster closer ties with Russia. One consequence of Uzbekistan's pro-Russian tilt was that at the October 2005 CACO summit in Saint Petersburg CACO was folded into the Eurasian Economic Community. The shift to a Russo-centered organization was, however, tempered by the Kyrgyz Republic agreeing to the continued use of the U.S. base on its territory, despite Russian pressure to follow Uzbekistan's example in ordering the Americans out. Kazakhstan also sought to distance itself from the autocratic regimes of Russia and Uzbekistan, especially as the opening of new pipelines was diminishing its economic dependence on Russia. Although the realignment in 2005 was politically driven, it mirrors an economic division between the more liberal trade regimes of the Kyrgyz Republic and Kazakhstan and the less liberal orientation of Russia, Belarus, and Uzbekistan.[37]

---

[36] The energy and water group has been supported by a UN-funded project on efficient water use, the foreign investment promotion group has organized a conference in Dushanbe, the transport and border crossing group has served as a forum for discussion of transit issues between Kazakhstan and the Kyrgyz Republic, and the industrial restructuring and technical assistance with pipelines groups have not met.

[37] Kazakhstan and the Kyrgyz Republic have powerful economic motives for not forming a customs

Although the formal agreements have had little impact, the need for regional cooperation in Central Asia is self-evident. Action on the Aral Sea and other water-management issues has to involve all five Central Asian countries to be effective (see Section 10.4.1 below). Transport and transit matters also require some degree of regional cooperation, although the individual countries' needs vary and neighboring countries should also be involved. The Central Asian regional organizations have, however, made no attempt to coordinate trade policy on a preferential basis, and by 2004 there was no effective regional organization composed solely of the five Central Asian countries.

10.3.3 *Relations with Southern Neighbors*

The Economic Cooperation Organization (ECO) offered to the newly independent countries a regional trading arrangement that could promote a southward reorientation of their trade from the patterns imposed within the Soviet economy. ECO's founding document is the 1977 Treaty of Izmir, signed by Iran, Pakistan, and Turkey, although the organization was dormant between the 1979 Iranian revolution and 1985.[38] The three founding members then attempted to revive the organization by offering preferential tariff treatment to one another, but the list of eligible products was extremely restricted. At the eighth ECO summit in Dushanbe in September 2004, Iran proposed committing to an ECO free-trade zone by 2015, but no practical steps were taken.

In 1992 the five Central Asian countries, together with Afghanistan and Azerbaijan, became members of the ECO. The members of the expanded organization contained over 300 million people, and included all non-Arab Islamic countries west of India.[39] In 1993 the ECO gained observer status at the United Nations General Assembly, and it was later accorded observer status at the WTO. In 1996 the Council of Ministers approved a restructuring, which included the establishment of a permanent ECO Secretariat in Tehran.

The ECO members have established eight regional institutions: a trade and development bank, an insurance institute, a shipping company, an airline, a reinsurance company, a chamber of commerce, a science foundation, and a cultural/educational institute. In 1995 it was agreed that the bank would be in Istanbul, and subsequently ECO issued a statement of intent that the reinsurance company would be located in Pakistan. Amidst bickering over location and funding, implementation has

---

union in which the external tariff would largely be determined by Russia. They would suffer both trade destruction, as the higher tariffs reduced aggregate imports, and trade diversion, as imports were sourced preferentially from Russia or Belarus instead of from the global least-cost supplier. Tumbarello (2005, Table 4) estimates that implementing the customs union would have negative net welfare effects of $31.8 million for Kazakhstan and $3.5 million for the Kyrgyz Republic, and, although her numerical estimates are model specific, they clearly capture the sign of the welfare effects.

[38] The Treaty was modified at a 1990 meeting in Islamabad and subsequently adopted as the Basic Charter of ECO. For a more detailed account of ECO's history, see Pomfret (1999b, 2000a).

[39] The Turkish Muslim Community of Cyprus is not a member of ECO, but its representatives have observer status.

proceeded slowly. The shipping company operated two leased multipurpose cargo vessels in the Persian Gulf and some ships plying the Caspian Sea, but despite being the sole profitable ECO project the shipping line ran into financial difficulties due to the failure of some ECO members to make their contributions to the capitalization fund (Afrasiabi 2000, Part II).

The ECO heads of state have met frequently since 1992, and the summits have typically included grand declarations. The implementation record is, however, poor.[40] This is highlighted by the history of the ECO transit agreements. Only eight countries signed the 1995 transit trade agreement, and the two nonsignatories, Afghanistan and Uzbekistan, straddle some of the most important routes in the region. The agreement officially entered into force in December 1997, but by early 1999 only five national governments had ratified the agreement. The modified, and much watered down, 1998 transit agreement had, as of mid-2000, only been approved by Azerbaijan and Tajikistan, whose geographical position makes them marginal countries to an ECO-wide transit arrangement. The unwillingness of key member countries to accept the principle of unhindered passage of goods in transit is a major obstacle to any concrete achievement by ECO.

As with the CAEC/CACO, the practical impact of ECO has been limited. In both organizations a fundamental obstacle to regional integration is the similarity of the member countries' economies, which all tend to be specialized on a small group of primary products (oil, gas, minerals, and cotton). Trade between the five Central Asian countries and their southern neighbors has expanded since 1992, but from a low base and more slowly than many observers expected. Moreover, it has done so on a nondiscriminatory MFN basis rather than within a regional trading arrangement such as the ECO founding members appear to have envisaged in the early 1990s.

10.3.4   *Relations with Russia and China*

Another overlapping configuration, dubbed the Shanghai Five, emerged from a meeting in 1996 of China, Russia, Kazakhstan, the Kyrgyz Republic, and Tajikistan, its intention being to demilitarize borders. At a summit in Dushanbe in July 2000, China, Kazakhstan, the Kyrgyz Republic, Russia, and Tajikistan, with Uzbekistan as an observer, took up a number of themes related to trade facilitation as well as discussing issues such as countering Islamic terrorist groups. Although the countries had met since 1996 to discuss security issues, the extension into economic areas was a fresh departure in 2000, and the group changed their name to the Shanghai Forum and invited other countries to join them. Despite the intention to cover matters such as trade facilitation, the subsequent history of the organization has centered on political rather than economic matters. At the June 2001 summit Uzbekistan became the

---

[40] In recent years, the attendance record at summits has also been poor. The 2004 ECO summit in Dushanbe was attended by the presidents of Iran, the Kyrgyz Republic, and Tajikistan and by Hamid Karzai, Afghanistan's president-in-waiting, by the prime ministers of Azerbaijan, Pakistan, and Turkey, and Turkmenistan was represented by the deputy speaker of the country's toothless parliament.

sixth member and the group was renamed the Shanghai Cooperation Organization (SCO). At the 2004 SCO summit Mongolia was admitted as an observer.

The years 1998–99 saw the division of Central Asia into two opposing camps as Uzbekistan aligned with GUAM and Kazakhstan, the Kyrgyz Republic, and Tajikistan joined Russia in the Union of Five and its successors. This division eased in 2000 and 2001, in part due to the incursion of Islamic fighters into the Ferghana Valley, presenting a common problem to the three countries whose territory was involved. China played a catalytic role in bringing the Central Asian countries together. In 1997–98 China had been an economic anchor in East Asia and had sought closer relations with the United States, but it gradually came to resent a perceived asymmetry in this rapprochement, which brought little gain to China. After the U.S. bombing of the Chinese embassy in Belgrade in spring 1999, China pursued a more anti-U.S. course, embracing Japanese proposals for Asian monetary cooperation (which were opposed by the United States) and promoting the SCO as a more formal successor to the Shanghai Forum (Pomfret 2005d). Although Russia saw the SCO as a vehicle for its leadership in Central Asia, for the Central Asian leaders, especially Uzbekistan, the SCO was palatable because of China's counterweight.

The SCO is the only international group formed by China, and it receives extensive press coverage in China. Russia was also enthusiastic in the early years of the Shanghai Five, hoping the grouping would help Russia to retain leverage over Central Asia, but Kazakhstan, the Kyrgyz Republic, and Tajikistan all reached border delimitation agreements with China in the late 1990s without consulting Russia. From 1998 to 2001 the organization evolved into a Sino-Russian vehicle for opposing U.S. hegemony and for mutual tolerance of anti-separatist measures in Chechnya and Xinjiang. The military side remains important and joint operations planning in 2001 represented the first cooperation between the Russian and Chinese military since the early 1960s. Russia and China are united in their support for the 1972 Anti-Ballistic Missile (ABM) Treaty and opposed to U.S. plans to revise it. The final statement at the 2001 SCO summit called the ABM Treaty "a cornerstone of stability, peace and nuclear deterrence," and cooperation against terrorism was a major theme.[41] The SCO, however, failed to respond to the September 9 assassination of Ahmad Shah Massoud or the September 11 terrorist acts in the United States. Chiefs of national border guard services met in Almaty on April 24, 2002, to coordinate responses to terrorism, the drug trade, and illegal migration, but there are doubts about the sincerity of such meetings when the Russian military and influential

---

[41] It was decided to establish an antiterrorist center in Bishkek. In May 2001 the CIS Collective Security Treaty (CST) signatories had already created a rapid-reaction force with some 2,000 soldiers from Russia, Kazakhstan, the Kyrgyz Republic, and Tajikistan committed to fighting potential insurgencies in Central Asia, and the CST would appear to be aimed at preempting Chinese (or Uzbek?) participation in joint antiterrorist action in the region. It took until December 2002 for SCO experts to meet in Bishkek to discuss the rules and activities, funding and staffing of the antiterrorist center, and then in September 2003 it was announced that the Bishkek center had been canceled and an antiterrorist center would be opened in Tashkent in 2004.

Central Asians are believed to be participating in the drug trade. Earlier in the year Chinese Foreign Ministry official Zhou Li called for a coordinated response against "the three forces" (i.e., radical Chechen, Uighur, and Uzbek organizations),[42] but it seems unlikely that China would welcome foreign troops in Xinjiang.

After the June 2004 SCO summit, Uzbekistan and Russia signed a strategic partnership agreement that could be a harbinger of greater coordination among SCO members. China announced plans to extend $500 million in loans and credits to Central Asian countries. However, this seems to be running on two tracks: at the security level, Uzbekistan was reacting to reduction of U.S. assistance due to its human-rights record—a consideration given less weight by Russia and China; and on the economic level, the Central Asian countries welcome infrastructure and other investment from both Russia and China, but Russia does not want to see China gaining economic influence in Central Asia.

More fundamentally the Central Asian governments do not share the Sino-Russian agenda of opposing U.S. hegemony. Since September 2001 the Central Asian governments have generally been willing to cooperate with the United States, providing bases and so forth, rather than coordinating antiterrorist action under the aegis of the SCO. After the 2001 summit at which Uzbekistan became a member, President Karimov in a speech on Uzbekistan TV stated that "This organization must never turn into a military political bloc. .... It should not be against any country." Splits among the Central Asian leaders are also evident. A Tajik official was reported in Russia as saying that "None of us is apt to welcome the Uzbek imperialists."[43] Although relations with China are cordial, potential conflicts could surface if China proceeds with plans to divert water from rivers originating in Xinjiang and flowing into Russia and Kazakhstan.[44] Opinions on the future prospects of the SCO, or whether it has a future, are split.

A looser organization is the Central Asia Regional Economic Cooperation (CAREC) program. CAREC is an ADB-supported initiative to encourage economic cooperation in transport, energy, trade policy, and trade facilitation. Despite slow progress since its launch in 1997, CAREC in 2004 established a Trade Policy Coordinating Committee which had its first meeting in September 2004. This may signal a willingness to take definite steps on trade facilitation among the CAREC members,

---

[42] Reported in the *Far Eastern Economic Review*, January 17, 2002.

[43] The statements by President Karimov and by the Tajik official were both reported in "Russia has misgivings about Shanghai Cooperation Organization," *Eurasia Insight*, posted at www.eurasianet.org on June 20, 2001. Uzbekistan's cooperation with the United States cooled in 2005 as the United States criticized handling of the demonstrations in Andijan, and President Karimov sought support from Russia and China.

[44] Horsman (2001, pp. 79–81) discusses China's position concluding that "China is unwilling to engage in meaningful cooperation or compromise in the pursuit of its water demands" (see also Section 10.4 below). If Kazakhstan were sufficiently aggravated, it might reinstate its agitation over Chinese nuclear testing at Lop Nor and treatment of Uighurs, two issues over which Kazakhstan (and the Kyrgyz Republic) has since the mid-1990s agreed to exercise restraint.

Table 10.9. Membership of regional agreements involving Central Asian countries mid-2005 (see text for details).

	CIS	Eurasian Community	SES	CACO	SPECA	ECO	SCO	CAREC
Kazakhstan	×	×	×	×	×	×	×	×
Kyrgyz Rep.	×	×	—	×	×	×	×	×
Tajikistan	×	×	—	×	×	×	×	×
Turkmenistan	×	—	—	—	×	×	—	—
Uzbekistan	×	—	—	×	×	×	×	×
Russia	×	×	×	×	—	—	×	—
China	—	—	—	—	—	—	×	×
Iran	—	—	—	—	—	×	—	—
Pakistan	—	—	—	—	—	×	—	—
Turkey	—	—	—	—	—	×	—	—
Afghanistan	—	—	—	—	—	×	—	—
Azerbaijan	×	—	—	—	—	×	—	×
Armenia	×	—	—	—	—	—	—	—
Belarus	×	×	×	—	—	—	—	—
Georgia	×	—	—	—	—	—	—	—
Moldova	×	—	—	—	—	—	—	—
Ukraine	×	—	×	—	—	—	—	—
Mongolia	—	—	—	—	—	—	—	×

which do not include Turkmenistan, but do include Azerbaijan, Mongolia, and Xinjiang Autonomous Region of China.

10.3.5 Prospects for Regionalism

Table 10.9 summarizes the membership of the regional arrangements described in this section. These arrangements have often been in implicit competition, reflecting differing and mutually exclusive political pacts. The evolving patterns have incorporated concerns for closer or more arms-length relations with Russia and, to a lesser extent, China, and internal competition for and suspicion of hegemonic leadership within Central Asia. Such ebbing and flowing of interest in alternative regional permutations has inhibited the institutional development of any regional organization involving the Central Asian countries. Although most have an economic content, at least in their stated goals, their economic impact has been minimal. None has reached a stage of seriously discussing preferential trade policies, and none has posed a threat to multilateralism in the Central Asian countries' trade policies.

10.4 Other Regional Issues

There are other reasons for regional cooperation besides trade policies, and three of these are of particular significance for Central Asia: water-resource management (including the desiccation of the Aral Sea and related energy supply issues), security,

and trade facilitation. The failure to take any common action on the desiccation of the Aral Sea is symptomatic of the inability of Central Asia's leaders to cooperate on a pressing regional issue. Security matters have been dominant since 1999, and have entered the international spotlight since September 2001. Trade facilitation, while more mundane, is an area in which stepwise progress could be made to reduce foregone opportunities for mutually beneficial trade, due to impediments such as unnecessary delays or bureaucracy at border crossings or in transit, and official or unofficial taxes on traders.

10.4.1 *Water Issues*

The dissolution of the USSR threw into question the 1921 and 1940 agreements between Persia and the Soviet Union that defined the legal status of the Caspian Sea. After 1991 each of the five littoral states set out to claim a stake in the hydrocarbon and marine resources of the sea. When talks among the five nations did eventually begin in 1996, they broke down among disputes over principles and over shares. The two countries with the potentially least valuable segments of the Caspian Sea, Turkmenistan and Iran, sought to maximize the extent to which the sea would be treated as a common property resource, while Russia, Azerbaijan, and Kazakhstan wanted national zones. The latter three countries worked out bilateral arrangements for the sea's territorial division, based roughly on the length of national coastlines, which gave Kazakhstan 27%, Russia 19%, and Azerbaijan 18%. Iran argued that if there were to be a territorial division, each country should receive 20% of the sea, whereas Iran was only allocated 13% under the Russian-backed arrangements. During the 1990s Azerbaijan was energetic in selling exploration rights to its claimed offshore zone, which led to disputes with both Turkmenistan and Iran. The most dramatic confrontation came in July 2001 when the Iranian navy, supported by fighter jets, forced away at gunpoint a vessel chartered by BP to explore an offshore area claimed by Azerbaijan.

The impasse in delimiting the Caspian has delayed exploitation of its hydrocarbon resources, affected pipeline plans, and prevented sensible management of the sturgeon stocks from which Caspian caviar comes. In April 2002 the five presidents met for the first time, in a conference convened by President Niyazov in Ashgabat, but the two-day meeting ended without any joint resolutions. Despite the acrimony, a November 2003 meeting involving the five states together with two UN agencies (the United Nations Environment Programme, UNEP, and the United Nations Development Programme, UNDP) reached the first substantive all-party agreement on Caspian issues when they agreed on a set of environmental measures.[45] This

---

[45] The states pledged to tackle such issues as industrial pollution, oil refinery and tanker leaks, and the energy industry's potential environmental impact on marine life, including the endangered sturgeon. Of course, implementation may be another matter, but the presence of the UNEP and the UNDP as coordinating agencies and the release of a joint communiqué noting that "the meeting passed in an atmosphere of friendship and mutual understanding" were interpreted on all sides as indications that the Caspian countries were finally taking cooperation seriously.

could foreshadow a series of issue-based agreements where alliances may shift. Iran and Turkmenistan may make common cause on delimitation, while Iran teams up with Russia on military technology rules and with Kazakhstan on transportation matters. That would make agreement, with cross-issue trade-offs, more likely than in the past negotiations on a single resource-sharing decision, which have become deadlocked. More materially, discovery of the huge Shah Deniz gas field and Kashagan oil field may be persuading the littoral states that there are enough resources under the sea for everybody to benefit as long as a peaceful resolution is found.

The Aral Sea poses a more environmentally serious but also more intractable problem because the states involved can only see short-term economic costs from addressing the environmental disaster. The problem is straightforward. Ever-increasing demands on the water of the two river systems feeding the Aral Sea, the Amudarya and Syrdarya rivers, have so far reduced the amount of water reaching the Aral Sea, the world's fourth-largest lake (after the Caspian, Lake Superior, and Lake Victoria) as recently as 1960, that between 1960 and 2000 the Aral Sea's area fell by half, its volume by 80% and the shoreline receded by 60–80 km as it subdivided into two small lakes.[46] The fisheries and other sea-based activities were destroyed by the end of the 1980s. The shrinking of the Aral Sea has changed climate patterns, increasing extremes of heat and cold, shrinking growing seasons, and reducing crop yields. Exposure of the sea bed has been accompanied by dust storms carrying toxic chemicals (a legacy of the fertilizer-intensive nature of Soviet cotton farming) for thousands of kilometers. One almost sci-fi concern is that the major biological warfare testing station of the Soviet Union was on Vozrozhdeniye Island in the Aral Sea, which is no longer an island, and that deadly biological agents, including the word's largest accumulation of anthrax spores, may spread.[47]

The most directly affected regions—the autonomous republic of Karakalpakstan and Khorezm in northwest Uzbekistan, South Kazakhstan and Kyzylorda in southern Kazakhstan, and Dashkoguz in northern Turkmenistan—are among the poorest areas of the respective countries. Morbidity rates have risen in the affected areas, especially in Karakalpakstan and Dashkoguz, where high levels of anemia contribute to underweight babies and high infant mortality rates. Respiratory diseases, dysentery, hepatitis, typhoid, and tuberculosis, associated with poor water supply and sanitation, are also prevalent. The full extent of the health problem is difficult to assess because few outsiders travel to Karakalpakstan and Dashkoguz, and the authorities conceal much of what happens there. In Kazakhstan, where the authorities are more open, mutations are reported.

The solution is straightforward in principle: reduce the quantity of water being taken out of the river systems. A major component should be to increase the efficiency with which water is used in Central Asia, where profligate practices were encouraged

---

[46] Weinthal (2002, Chapter 4) points to the cotton monocultures of Uzbekistan and Turkmenistan imposed by the USSR as the principal culprit (see also Pomfret 1995, pp. 28–30).

[47] See "Poisoned island," *The Economist*, July 10, 1999.

in the Soviet era. In the absence of improved water-use efficiency, however, reduction in the amount of water available for irrigation will make any agriculture denied water infeasible in the arid conditions of Central Asia. This would be especially disastrous for Turkmenistan, most of whose agriculture draws on water carried by the Karakum Canal, a 1,300 km open channel westwards from the Amudarya River, which has been the single main contributor to the shrinking of the Aral Sea.[48] President Niyazov seems, if anything, intent on enhancing the irrigated agricultural area in Turkmenistan, and some observers have speculated that if Turkmenistan proceeds with plans to build a huge artificial lake in the country's desert that could trigger war with Uzbekistan.[49] In international negotiations on how to deal with the Aral Sea crisis, agricultural change has been kept off the agenda.

In 1993 the five Central Asian countries established the Interstate Fund for Saving the Aral Sea (IFAS), and under the IFAS the Interstate Commission for Water Coordination (ICWC), with a secretariat in Khujand, Tajikistan, is the implementing body responsible for managing the seasonal allocation of water. The rotating chairmanship of the IFAS and lack of funds from the national governments have limited the effectiveness of these bodies. The technical management institutions for the two river systems are both headquartered in Uzbekistan and mainly staffed by Uzbek nationals, which inhibits other countries' confidence in their activities even though they report to the ICWC, so that their actual control over water flows is dependent on the agreement of national entities such as power companies. Between 1994 and 1997 the IFAS and external donors came together in the Aral Sea Basin Program, administered through a special office of the World Bank with $60 million funding, but in 1997 the World Bank closed the office due to lack of effective progress in coordinating actions with respect to the Aral Sea.

The World Bank, which played the lead role in negotiations in the mid-1990s, tried to streamline the institutional arrangements and to focus narrowly on water. This failed because, for example, the headgates of the Toktogul Reservoir were under the control of the Kyrgyz Ministry of Energy over whom the ICWC had no authority (Weinthal 2002, p. 1,845).[50] For international organizations and foreign economists the least confrontational solution would be to use the price mechanism to allocate a

---

[48] There would also be intracountry conflicts of interest. Much of the irrigated area of Tajikistan is marginal agricultural land with poor farmers who would be hard hit by reduced availability of water, while in Uzbekistan the areas where irrigated agriculture should be discontinued rather than reformed are concentrated in Kashkadarya province (World Bank 2002, Volume I, p. vii).

[49] Expression of such views at an April 2003 Moscow conference on water in the CIS is reported in "Clashing approaches becloud Central Asia's water future" posted at www.eurasianet.org on May 28, 2003. Water conflicts between Turkmenistan and Uzbekistan already existed as a result of Turkmenistan's construction of a canal to (inefficiently) bypass Uzbekistan and secure its own water, and accusations by Uzbekistan that Turkmenistan has been failing to maintain pumping stations at Karshi and Amu-Bukhara that serve Uzbekistan or clean drains through which water passes from Turkmenistan to Uzbekistan. More generally, however, the downstream nations, Turkmenistan and Uzbekistan, share a suspicion of any change to the status quo.

[50] On the other hand, the attempts by USAid to create new structures linking water and energy issues were naive considering the entrenched power of the existing bureaucracies.

reduced amount of water to competing demands. Apart from the Kyrgyz Republic, which adopted legislation in July 2001 making water a tradable commodity, and some quarters in Kazakhstan, however, most Central Asian policymaking elites have a deep antipathy to the concept for cultural reasons associated with the role of water in this arid region, and also because of concerns about fairness and opportunities for corruption, technical monitoring problems, and the inability of the poorest farmers to afford any but negligibly low prices for irrigation water.[51]

At least initially, the Central Asian leadership looked for technical fixes. Weinthal (2002, p. 195) argues that it was the (mistaken) prospect of funding for such schemes that led them to welcome international financial institutions' involvement in the Aral Sea after the dissolution of the Soviet Union. A Soviet-era scheme to divert waters from the River Ob in Siberia to Central Asia is sometimes revived, usually by Russian politicians considering the geopolitical benefits of increasing Central Asian dependence on Russia. In an April 2003 conference in Moscow, for example, Yuri Luzhkov, mayor of Moscow and an influential Russian politician, who has campaigned for the Ob-diversion project, declared that "This idea will be realized."[52]

A more likely outcome is continuation of negotiated water–energy swaps. Existing intrastate agreements, administered by the ICWC, have essentially maintained the pre-1992 status quo under which Kazakhstan, Turkmenistan, and Uzbekistan are allocated over 70% of the water in the Amudarya and Syrdarya river systems, while the upstream countries the Kyrgyz Republic (source of 25% of the water) and Tajikistan (source of 55%) are allocated 0.4% and 11%, respectively; 16% is allocated to the Aral Sea and a small proportion to northern Afghanistan. The upstream countries agree to release water for the irrigation needs of the downstream countries in return for guaranteed deliveries of other energy sources in winter, although these agreements are regularly breached and the specific terms, which are largely barter arrangements, have been frequently revised. The Kyrgyz–Kazakh agreements have been reasonably stable, with Kazakhstan supplying coal and oil, but agreements with Uzbekistan have been more volatile, leading the Kyrgyz and Tajik governments to threaten to (or actually) produce more hydropower in winter and hence have less water available for release during the cotton-growing season.[53] The conflicts are

---

[51] Water is implicitly priced in the energy-for-water barter agreements because there is no exogenously determined price for the energy component of the swaps. Despite the downstream countries' reservations about using prices in international trade in water, where they are importers and hence satisfied with a zero price, water pricing is likely to come eventually to the downstream countries because it is the most efficient way to allocate water domestically.

[52] Luzhkov argued that Russia had plenty of water to sell and the $34 billion project was necessary to forestall a huge wave of Central Asian immigrants pushed into Russia by water-related economic failure in Central Asia. These views expressed at an April 2003 Moscow conference on water in the CIS are reported in "Clashing approaches becloud Central Asia's water future," posted at www.eurasianet.org on May 28, 2003.

[53] Weinthal (2002) argues that despite their flaws these agreements have been critical in preventing interstate armed conflict over water resources. She sees international actors such as nongovernmental organizations, the World Bank, and other agencies as crucial facilitators of agreement, often providing or

becoming more severe over time, because the annual releases from the reservoirs exceed the average inflow, a situation which was exacerbated by the dry conditions in 2000 and 2001.[54]

Kazakhstan has a water conflict with China over the Ili and Irtysh rivers similar to the upstream–downstream conflict in the Syrdarya and Amudarya rivers. China plans to extract water from both rivers in order to stimulate the economy of Xinjiang province. Horsman (2001, pp. 79–81) argues that Kazakhstan, as the downstream nation, is impotent to influence China's actions, while China does not accept the principles of international riverine law or even the explicit constraints of conventions or agreements which it has signed, such as the requirement to consult downstream countries when making environmental impact assessments. The Ili feeds Lake Balkhash, which is in danger of shrinking like the Aral Sea, while the Irtysh provides water for large industrial towns in northeastern Kazakhstan, Oskemen, Semey (formerly Semipalatinsk), and Pavlodar as well as the national capital of Astana, before entering Russia and eventually joining the Ob River.

10.4.2 *Security Issues and Border Controls*

The establishment of new border posts was a consequence of the creation of the new independent states in 1991 and border tensions were inherent in the imprecise delimitation of republican borders within the Soviet Union, but the role of borders as a major source of tension was exacerbated by the 1999 explosions in Tashkent and the increased activity of the Islamic Movement of Uzbekistan (IMU). The introduction of visas has added to border tensions, but the strictness of visa enforcement appears to be related to security concerns.[55] Especially in the southern part of Central Asia, a vicious circle of heightened security concerns, more onerous visa restrictions and border-crossing procedures, and violent clashes has emerged. Policy statements

---

identifying side-payments which lubricate a deal. Horsman (2001), however, argues that all parties, but especially Uzbekistan and Turkmenistan, are so defensive about their perceived national interests and suspicion of any change in the current arrangements, that all attempts at multilateral solutions have been doomed.

[54] Prior to 1991 annual releases from the Toktogul reservoir averaged 2.7 km^3 in winter and 8.0 km^3 in summer, which was below the long-term average inflow of 12.3 km^3, but between 1995 and 2000 the annual release was 13.5 km^3 (Biddison 2002, p. 4). So far there have been fewer disputes over Amudarya water, because the sole major upstream power station on the Nurek reservoir in Tajikistan has operated below capacity and also because Afghanistan has not fully used its water entitlement. In the future, economic stability and growth in Afghanistan could lead in short order to increased use for irrigation because the right bank of the Amudarya is suited to gravity irrigation without the need for investment in pumping facilities.

[55] Although changing residence was restricted in the USSR, there were no restrictions on crossing republic borders. In the 1992 Bishkek Accord, CIS members committed to visa-free movement within the CIS. In 1998 some Central Asian countries (e.g., Turkmenistan and Uzbekistan) introduced visa requirements for CIS citizens, but enforcement was fairly lax, especially for people living close to a border. The de facto visa situation since 1998 is difficult to monitor, but in 1999 visa enforcement by Uzbekistan became stricter, and exemptions for residents close to the border were terminated. This was followed by retaliatory visa measures by Uzbekistan's neighbors. The general visa environment was also influenced by Russia's announcement in August 2000 that it was terminating its compliance with the Bishkek Accord.

emphasize coordinated action against terrorism, but since 1999 border closures and international incidents have become more frequent.

Precise delimitation of the sometimes vague Soviet borders has proceeded at varying speeds and degrees of smoothness (ICG 2002). Kazakhstan and the Kyrgyz Republic had more or less resolved their border by 1996 and a final agreement was signed in 2001. Kazakhstan and Uzbekistan reached agreement on 96% of their border in November 2001. Negotiations over disputed sections of the borders with China took time, often due to the inhospitable and mountainous terrain, but proceeded reasonably smoothly, apart from domestic opposition within the Kyrgyz Republic in 2001 to a secret treaty under which land was transferred to China. Borders within the densely populated Ferghana Valley and between Uzbekistan and Turkmenistan have been more contentious.[56] Nevertheless, in Central Asia, unlike in most other parts of the CIS, there have been no official claims of other countries' recognized territory nor serious secession movements.

In the Ferghana Valley the situation is complicated by the arbitrariness of borders, which were meaningless until 1991 but are now national boundaries, and by the presence of enclaves. The Ferghana Valley also contains the most fervently Islamic segments of the population, and was the channel through which IMU fighters entered Uzbekistan in 1999 and 2000. Uzbekistan subsequently tightened visa requirements, and took steps such as laying mines to deter IMU fighters from entering Uzbekistan through Tajikistan and the Kyrgyz Republic. By mid-2004 some sixty-eight Tajik civilians and thirty Kyrgyz civilians had been killed by the land mines.[57] Laying mines along the border involved decisions about where the border actually lay, and this opened up disputes with Tajikistan and the Kyrgyz Republic, whose governments were already alarmed by Uzbekistan fighter planes' incursions into their airspace without prior permission as they sought to bomb IMU targets.

The events of September 2001 and the overthrow of the Taliban government in Afghanistan provide a major milestone. All of the Central Asian leaders, along with those of Russia and China, gave verbal support to the U.S.-led war on terrorism. Uzbekistan and the Kyrgyz Republic went further by providing material assistance such as making air bases available to the U.S. military, and Tajikistan allowed overflight by U.S. military aircraft. These developments upped the international

---

[56] Relations between Uzbekistan and Turkmenistan have been hampered by mutual antipathy between the two presidents, who did not meet between September 2000 and November 2004. At the November 2004 reconciliation summit some border issues were addressed, but the minorities issue was not. The minorities issue concerns the different policies whereby Uzbekistan provides education and other services in Turkmen for Turkmen speakers within Uzbekistan, whereas Turkmenistan assimilates its large Uzbek minority.

[57] The mining was strongly resented by the Tajikistan government, and was a major source of tension along Tajikistan's northern border where twenty-two Uzbek paratroopers were detained in March 2004. In June 2004 Uzbekistan announced a change in policy, pledging to begin demining its borders. See Kambiz Arman "Border issues ruffle relations among Central Asian states," posted at www.eurasianet.org on February 25, 2004, and Erica Marat and Said Dilovarov, "Uzbek de-mining pledge strives to mollify neighbors," posted at www.eurasianet.org on July 15, 2004.

perceptions of Central Asia's strategic significance. Russia, although officially supporting the United States, attempted to reassert its own influence, and especially
after the expansion of NATO in Eastern Europe at the November 2002 Prague summit, President Putin tried to obtain recognition of Russian hegemony over Central
Asia and the Caucasus as a quid pro quo for his acquiescence in the NATO enlargement. President Karimov of Uzbekistan, however, had a fairly high profile at Prague,
meeting President Jacques Chirac and Secretary of State Colin Powell, who praised
"the practical actions of Uzbekistan in the international fight against terrorism."[58]

Although the general perception in 2002 was of a widening of the fissure between
those Central Asian countries more and less amenable to Russian influence in the
region, after the U.S.-led invasion of Iraq in March 2003 there was a general shift
towards closer relations with Russia and, to a lesser extent, China. This was especially clear in the case of the most authoritarian countries, Turkmenistan and Uzbekistan, which began to have concerns over whether the United States might one day
use their own human-rights abuses as an excuse for military action. Russia and China
were less concerned about human-rights issues, and opposed foreign intervention
in what they considered domestic matters.

A further twist to the border issue arose after Uzbekistan introduced high taxes
on private imports in July 2002 in a poorly articulated attempt to reduce the black-
market premium on the currency and to regulate the informal trading sector. One
consequence was a large increase in the number of Uzbeks shopping in nearby towns
in Kazakhstan or the Kyrgyz Republic.[59] The Uzbekistan government responded by
tightening border controls in order to regulate the inflow of "substandard consumption goods" and to enforce tax collection. In late December, Uzbekistan began to
close border crossings, even going so far as blowing up a bridge into the Kyrgyz
Republic near the Kyrgyz town of Kara Su in mid-January 2003.[60]

The presence of enclaves is a particularly tough problem to resolve in the Ferghana Valley. The largest enclave, Sokh (population 50,000), a piece of Uzbekistan's

---

[58] Quoted at www.press-service.uz/eng/vizits_eng/ve21112002.htm by the press service of the president
of Uzbekistan. President Rahmonov of Tajikistan also publicized improved ties with France and the United
States, making visits to the two countries in December 2002 as a signal of displeasure with Russia's
deportation of Tajik guest workers. By contrast, on February 18–19, 2003, President Nazarbayev of
Kazakhstan, facing U.S. and EU criticisms of his regime's corruption and human-rights record, made an
official visit to Russia, where he is not criticized for such things.

[59] In the less regulated Kyrgyz and Kazakhstan economies, prices of consumer goods were often a third
of those in Uzbekistan and, although the Uzbek authorities claimed this was due to the shoddy nature of
the goods available in those countries' markets, the number of Uzbek cross-border shoppers grew. By late
2002, guards at the Chirchik border crossing into Kazakhstan reported a daily flow of 3,000 Uzbeks on
weekdays and 6,000 at the weekend, with each person carrying $100 of their own cash and $200–300 for
friends. In Chimkent, traders reportedly praise President Karimov for making them rich, and in January
2003 media reports in Kazakhstan referred to 50,000 Uzbeks visiting Chimkent every day and spending
around $4 million.

[60] The bridge was quickly replaced by a makeshift bridge that the Uzbek customs officials guarded at
a charge of 100 sum per user. During this period the markets at Kara Su near Osh and Dordoi in Bishkek
became the largest in Central Asia, mainly due to demand by shoppers from Uzbekistan.

territory surrounded by the Kyrgyz Republic's Batken province, has been viewed by Tashkent as a potential base for IMU militants, and even as a potentially seceding Islamic republic. To counter the perceived threat Uzbekistan has sought a corridor along the Sokh river which would link the enclave to the rest of Uzbekistan, but an agreement in 2001 with the Kyrgyz government in Bishkek to provide such a corridor in return for a similar corridor to a smaller Kyrgyz enclave surrounded by Uzbekistan was denounced by Batken provincial officials and residents because of the impact on water rights and the splitting of the province. The standoff illustrates the complexity of border issues in the Ferghana Valley once Pandora's box is opened. Meanwhile, tighter border controls inhibit local movements in a region where such restrictions are historically unknown.

There have also been conflicts between Tajikistan and the Kyrgyz Republic over access to enclaves. Residents of the two Tajikistan enclaves, Vorukh and Western Kalacha, which are both surrounded by Batken province of the Kyrgyz Republic, have long complained about their isolation from the rest of Tajikistan, but the increasing inconvenience of border checkpoints has exacerbated their dissatisfaction. Tajikistan has informally sought land corridors, but the Kyrgyz Republic opposes such proposals as interfering with the movement of Kyrgyz citizens. In October 2002 Tajikistan established two new border posts in the Isfara region, which according to the Kyrgyz authorities violated an agreement prohibiting establishment of new checkpoints on disputed territories. The Kyrgyz Republic retaliated by establishing a border post at Kok-Terek. In December 2002 an intergovernmental commission on border issues met in Bishkek and identified about seventy-one land plots, totaling about 21 km^2, that are claimed by both the Kyrgyz Republic and Tajikistan. On January 4, 2003, residents of Tajikistan's Vorukh enclave (population 30,000) destroyed a Kyrgyz border post and residents of the surrounding Batken province of the Kyrgyz Republic responded by destroying a Tajik border post. The economic base to these actions is that the new border posts, staffed by ill-trained and corrupt customs officials, disrupt local trade networks that have existed in the valley for centuries.[61] The added economic hardship in an already poverty-stricken area provides a fertile ground for populist agitators to channel anger into ethnic hatred.

Border relations between Uzbekistan and Turkmenistan have also had tense episodes. Parts of both the Khorezm province of Uzbekistan and the Dashgauz province of Turkmenistan, in which a substantial Uzbek minority lives, lie in the historically integrated Khorezm oasis. The introduction of border posts and of visa restrictions and charges fueled local protests in the early 2000s.[62] At the national level, the long-strained relations between the two countries' presidents were exacerbated by accusations that Uzbekistan facilitated the entry of Boris Shikhmuradov

---

[61] They also add to the cost of long-distance trade by increasing the number of delays and tolls.

[62] In June 2001 four people died in a clash between Uzbekistan citizens and Turkmenistan border guards. In January 2002 Uzbekistan introduced a $6 visa charge on any Turkmenistan resident crossing the border, and Turkmenistan retaliated in January 2003 with a similar charge, to be paid in U.S. currency. These costs are substantial for people in what are relatively poor areas of both countries.

into Turkmenistan before the November 25 assassination attempt on Turkmenistan's president. Uzbekistan denies the accusation, but tensions between the two countries remain high as Turkmenistan's president continues to blame Uzbekistan for aiding those plotting to kill him. A summit between the two presidents in late 2004 signalled some improvement, or at least a joint recognition that relations should not be allowed to deteriorate further.

10.4.3   Trade Facilitation

Trade facilitation and soft infrastructure are impediments to trade not included under trade policy as discussed above or the hard infrastructure of trade (roads, bridges, ports, etc.). The border restrictions described in the previous subsection represent major obstacles to trade facilitation. Among other examples of poor soft infrastructure to be analyzed in this subsection are internal breakdowns of law and order which undermine the security of traders, arbitrary levies on traders, changes in trade or trade-related regulations, taxation systems which discriminate against traders by being imposed on traded goods both as exports and as imports, rudimentary communications networks which make it difficult to obtain information about current conditions in the foreign market and en route, and poorly developed banking and insurance services which are exacerbated in some countries by poor payment mechanisms due to inconvertibility or lack of confidence in national currencies. Predictability in areas such as customs duties, fees, and so forth is itself a positive factor in facilitating trade, but a feature of Central Asia's post-independence economic history has been volatility.[63] More generally, regional peace is a prerequisite for flourishing trade, and trade is undermined by regional competition for influence and by interstate conflicts.

The hard infrastructure of the transport and communications systems has been an impediment to developing trade within the region and exports to nontraditional destinations. The inherited networks of the former Soviet republics emphasized links to Russia at the expense of links to the east or south. Since independence, national infrastructure spending has often focused on improving internal communications within each new state, rather than strengthening the regional network. This has been clearest in Turkmenistan where the national highway system has been upgraded and a new south–north road is being constructed across the desert from Ashgabat to Dashoguz, and the railway system is also being "nationalized" by linking Kerkishi

---

[63] Examples of such volatility were given in the country chapters, but some were especially drastic. In October 1996 Uzbekistan suddenly reintroduced tight foreign exchange controls in response to a balance-of-payments problem triggered by falling cotton prices. Similarly draconian controls were imposed by Turkmenistan in December 1998. After the August 1998 Russian Crisis, which hit Kazakhstan hardest among the Central Asian countries, Kazakhstan imposed special tariffs as high as 200% on a number of goods imported from the Kyrgyz Republic and Uzbekistan and in April 1999 the Kazakh tenge was floated, which led to an effective 50% devaluation.

directly to the rest of Turkmenistan.[64] In 2004 Uzbekistan completed a 341 km rail link between Khorezm and Karakalpakstan to replace the existing railway which passes through Turkmenistan. Elsewhere, such nation-building transport projects have been less pronounced (e.g., in the Kyrgyz Republic a domestic Bishkek–Osh rail link is a low priority, although the Bishkek–Osh highway has been a high, and expensive, priority and a road is being built between Osh and Jalalabad to avoid the existing road's transit of Uzbekistan). Duplication of routes has also occurred as governments have tried to increase their options: Uzbekistan, for example, has constructed a rail link to Kazakhstan's Caspian port of Aktau in order to provide an alternative to the old trans-Caspian mainline to the port of Turkmenbashi. While some diversification of routes may be beneficial and avoiding border crossings reduces costs in the current environment, much of this expenditure would be unnecessary in a regionally integrated Central Asia.

Border enforcement has at times been lax and at other times rigorous, with occasional total closure. In the early 1990s several border crossings with China were opened which had been closed since the Sino-Soviet split of the early 1960s (see Section 10.2.3 above), but during the 1990s they were subject to unpredictable closure; for example, the Kazakhstan–China border crossing at Bakhty was unilaterally closed by Kazakhstan in October 1998 and then reopened in December 1999. Several other border crossings have been temporarily closed, e.g., for several months in 1999 Uzbekistan unilaterally closed all but one of the posts along its border with Kazakhstan. Such actions are often unpredictable and may only be discovered upon arrival at the border. In July 2000 Kazakhstan increased the bond required from customs agents from \$5,000 to \$20,000. This was expected to reduce the number of customs agents from seventy-five to fifteen, and was justified by government officials in terms of concerns about the financial stability of smaller brokerage firms, but exporters to Kazakhstan were concerned about the anticompetitive impact of the reduced number of agents.

Customs policies and practices remain a major problem in the region. Apart from uncoordinated opening times and other physical problems, the customs services still have a philosophy of control rather than facilitation. All countries in the region undertake inspection of all vehicles, increasing border dwell times. The trader or trader's representative must be physically present, and the lack of post-verification systems means that decisions cannot be checked later, which is open to abuse as officials on the spot enjoy discretion in interpreting complicated rules and schedules. In some cases this seems to be the point of complex regulations, and allocation of remunerative jobs in the customs service is a way for politicians to keep their clients happy.

---

[64] Kerkishi, on the east bank of the Amudarya River, has a rail link to Bukhara in Uzbekistan on the Central Asian main line. Dashoguz, which has historically been linked to the Khiva oasis, is also served by rail and road via Uzbekistan. Both of the recent projects have little economic justification, but contribute to nation building by physically linking the most isolated parts of Turkmenistan to the capital.

Transit rights have varied, and it is difficult to even establish transit rates, which are often levied irregularly by local police. An often-cited figure from the late 1990s is of lorries traveling through Kazakhstan from other Central Asian countries to Russia paying on average ten such levies, amounting to an average of $1,700. One response has been to travel in convoy, with greater safety in numbers but also greater bargaining strength. Another response has been to use agents who will clear the way; for $5,000, it is claimed, drug shippers can make all records disappear with respect to a truck crossing Kazakhstan and going to Russia with a cargo of narcotics.[65]

Concerns about transit charges in Kazakhstan have been voiced by Uzbekistan, complaining that the charges are in contravention of agreements reached within the CAEC/CACO on transport facilitation. These complaints include unofficial and local levies, as well as national measures (such as Cabinet of Ministers resolution #1397 "About transportation fees for crossing Kazakhstan," passed on May 5, 1999, which imposed additional charges of $300 per shipment). Kazakhstan's regulations also impose additional fees if the truck's weight or size exceeds certain limits and if the truck deviates from its previously specified route.[66] Agreements on the use of refrigerated rail cars also broke down and were not renewed in 1999, leading Uzbekistan to find alternative routes for shipping perishable goods. Any railcars passing through Kazakhstan are subject to a $14 per railcar fee, which Uzbekistan claims is contrary to agreements. When tensions between the two countries have risen, the Kazakh authorities have closed part of the Tashkent–Samarkand main road which passes through Kazakhstan territory, imposing a long detour along minor roads for travellers between the two largest cities of Uzbekistan. Using these practices as justification, Uzbekistan has introduced its own restrictive measures. State Customs Committee resolution #200, dated May 14, 1999, imposed a fee of $300 on trucks transiting across Uzbekistan.

Bilateral relations between Kazakhstan and the Kyrgyz Republic appear to be smoother. With the help of the ADB, the two countries signed a Cross-Border Agreement on November 15, 1999, to ease the movement of people, goods, and vehicles across the common border. To try to ensure that this does not become just another paper agreement, implementation has been given a contractual basis by writing it into the conditions of the ADB loans and technical assistance grants to the two countries for the Almaty–Bishkek regional road rehabilitation project. Among its terms, the Cross-Border Agreement provides exemption from export and import duties on transit trade, attempts to standardize customs documentation and procedures, and

---

[65] The cases in this paragraph are reported in "Expanding regional trade cooperation: the case of Kazakhstan, Uzbekistan and the Kyrgyz Republic," Draft Final Report prepared by Development Alternatives Inc. for the Asian Development Bank under TA No. 58181-REG, Regional Economic Cooperation in Central Asia (Phase II), October 23, 2000, pp. II, 22–24.

[66] The maximum weight of trucks allowed to enter Kazakhstan is 36 tonnes, which is less than international standards (normally between 38 and 54 tonnes) and Uzbekistan's 40 tonne limit. Lack of agreement on the limit makes it likely that an Uzbek truck entering Kazakhstan will have to pay $100–150 for exceeding the Kazakhstani limit.

brings truck weights and dimensions, as well as vehicle inspection and clearance procedures, on to a common basis.

Turkmenistan, which has the only railway south from Central Asia and the main port on the east coast of the Caspian Sea, could be a significant route for other Central Asian countries' international trade, but is reported to levy high transit fees. This hard line, although shortsighted, is not surprising given the extent to which Turkmenistan has suffered from transit fees charged by Russia on gas exports to Ukraine and the Caucasus. Nevertheless, it is a stark example of the tragedy of the anti-commons by which the imposition of a series of high transit charges along roads crossing several countries chokes off the trade so that nobody benefits.

High freight rates, and delays, on the international rail route between Xinjiang and Kazakhstan play a similar role in discouraging trade. The high costs of rail transport seem particularly associated with the border crossing. Exporters in Xinjiang appear to be willing to accept the cost of shipping containers from Urumqi by rail to the Pacific and then by sea to Western Europe, rather than facing the uncertainties of the much shorter transit through Kazakhstan and Russia, and European exporters to Xinjiang are also reported to favor the longer route.[67] The rail crossing through the Ala Pass is primarily carrying iron and steel from Kazakhstan to China; out of the 3 million tonnes of recorded overland trade between the Central Asian countries and China, over 2.1 million pass by rail to China. The huge imbalance by weight implies much unused capacity on trains in the reverse direction, but little or no attempt is made to attract custom by offering low freight rates. By contrast, truck traffic carries far more freight from China to Kazakhstan than vice versa, implying another unused-capacity scenario. These back-hauling inefficiencies are exacerbated by petty restrictions on the rights of trucks crossing the international border.

Following the nationalization of Soviet assets, each successor state took possession of locomotives on its territory, and since 1992 the general practice has been to change locomotives and crew at each national border, with added delays. Improving service on domestic routes has generally taken precedence over what became international routes after 1991.[68] The disintegration of the old market area has been exacerbated by the large migrations of the early 1990s, which left the Central Asian countries more homogeneous as a result of emigration of people who felt strangers in their new country and had a national homeland to go to. Over a fifth of the ethnic Russians in Uzbekistan and the Kyrgyz Republic and almost half of the Russians

---

[67] In 2000 Kazakhstan proposed the establishment of a secretariat in Astana to formulate better logistics and to implement tracking and other procedures to make the trans-Kazakhstan route more attractive. On this and other Central Asian routes little freight is containerized, and the substantial investment needed to cater to containerization might be justified by the boost it would give to international trade as well as intermodal domestic trade.

[68] Data on train times indicate that travel times fell and service improved between Russian cities at the same time as the time taken to travel between Russian cities and the new national capitals of Central Asia increased. From Tashkent, the transport hub of Soviet Central Asia, it took on average 11% longer to travel to nine Russian cities in 1996 than it had in 1989 (Djankov and Freund 2000, p. 28).

living in Tajikistan in 1989 had emigrated by 1996. Part of the economic loss from these human outflows arises from the absence of a diaspora with trade-facilitating networks, which could have substituted for the poor enforceability of contracts.

The frequent people movements that are a component of a flourishing trade environment are also discouraged by high visa costs and bureaucratic procedures for non-CIS citizens trying to enter the Central Asian countries. Between China and Kazakhstan visa charges are, by agreement, identical, ranging from $70 for single entry up to $400 for an expedited multiple entry visa, and the bureaucratic procedures include requiring a formal letter of invitation from Foreign Affairs offices. In 2000 both Kazakhstan and Uzbekistan introduced visa requirements for CIS citizens entering their countries. The trend in the region is towards greater restrictions on people movements.

Payment mechanisms are poor and financial services limited. The small-scale shuttle trade is overwhelmingly cash based. The limited convertibility of the Uzbek sum, and Turkmen manat, and limited international acceptability of the convertible Kyrgyz som and Kazakh tenge encourage reliance on vehicle currencies, especially the U.S. dollar. Currency scarcity and lack of financial services discourage trading operations that run up a large deficit or surplus.

After independence most CIS member countries introduced a value-added tax (VAT) as their main form of indirect tax. The VAT has many advantages, but in Central Asia the original VAT systems discouraged trade because most CIS countries administered the tax on the origin principle: all goods produced within the country were taxed whether they were for the domestic market or for export. The origin principle simplifies collection procedures, but discriminates against exports because sales to a country levying taxes on the destination principle will lead to double taxation. Some countries, e.g., the Kyrgyz Republic, have tried to avoid the double-taxation outcome by exempting exports to non-CIS markets from VAT, but that is a partial solution with the negative consequence of discouraging intra-CIS trade in a discriminatory manner. Kazakhstan changed to a destination-based VAT in January 1997, which should have favored exporters, but the outcome is complicated by the currency crises of 1998. Goods imported into countries on the origin principle from Kazakhstan or from countries outside the CIS may avoid tax altogether. Variations in application of VAT and in VAT rates on specific items have created incentives for smuggling, which increases international trade but not necessarily in a desirable fashion.

The poor coverage and quality of trade information cause several difficulties. Large recorded bilateral trade balances are a source of distrust, even though the imbalances may not be real. The Central Asian countries' exports to China, for example, tend to be primary products whose movements are well documented, but in return the Central Asian countries import consumer goods carried by thousands of shuttle traders. The large negative trade balance between the Kyrgyz Republic and Tajikistan reflects, to some unknown but probably large extent, unrecorded exports of narcotics coming from Afghanistan. More important for actual trade is the poor flow of information on tariffs, fees, opening hours of customs posts, and so forth. This is reinforced by lack of commitment to predictability and minimization of sudden unannounced changes. Dissemination of information about potential trading partners through trade fairs has been a common feature of provincial trade promotion in China, but such fairs do not have a tradition within Central Asia. Other information modes, such as the internet, could become important in the future, but still have limited use in Central Asia.

The impediments to trade described in this section tend to be very specific and often individually minor, but it is important to see the big picture of their overall effect. Specialization and trade is the source of prosperity for individuals and countries alike. The increased output and choice offer prospects of mutually beneficial win–win situations. If impediments to trade are sufficiently large, however, trade will be choked off and there is no prospect of realizing the potential gains. Without trade it is not always clear how much has been lost—because the alternative with-trade situation is not observed—but global development experience over the last half century clearly shows that all of the top-performing economies have been open to trade and autarchic economies such as Myanmar or North Korea have been among the poorest performers. Participation in international trade does not guarantee economic success, but nonparticipation guarantees failure in the long term.

The trade situation in Central Asia in the 1990s represented a tragedy of the anti-commons,[69] where excessive ability of official and unofficial regulators to tap the gains from trade forestalled potential win–win situations. A practical example (and just one of thousands) occurred in 1999 when the high shipment costs across Kazakhstan made Kyrgyz vegetable exports to Russia unprofitable. When Kyrgyz onions were not exported, Russian consumers missed their onions, Kyrgyz producers swamped the domestic market driving down prices, and Kazakhstan received no transit charges. Thus both Kazakhstan and Russia were absolute losers. The only winners were Kyrgyz consumers, but even for the Kyrgyz Republic the net loss was undoubtedly substantial, because the Kyrgyz–Russian onion trade was so clearly a case of efficient specialization and the onions could be more valuable earning foreign currency to pay for imports than adding to the amount of domestically consumed onions. Because the numerous individual fee leviers across Kazakhstan each tried to maximize their own "tax" on the transit trade, the trade was choked off, to almost everybody's disadvantage. Moreover, if the trade is cut off for some time, it will not

---

[69] The tragedy of the commons arises from too many people having access to a common resource, such as fisheries: each fisher has an incentive to catch as much as possible because any individual conservation strategy will be ineffective as fish left in the water will be caught by other fishers. The tragedy of the anti-commons arises when too many people have the potential to hold up an activity by levying taxes or imposing other costs. As in the tragedy of the commons, each holdup agent will ignore potential externalities of their actions and try to maximize current benefits, in this case leading to too little rather than too much of the activity actually taking place (Buchanan and Yoon 2000).

be a simple matter to restart it, because connections will have been lost and new channels to Russian wholesalers will have to be established.

Why do these lose–lose situations arise? Each individual with the power to levy a fee along the road from the farm in the Kyrgyz Republic to the onion market in Russia thinks only of maximizing their own returns. Given that the trader has started out on the enterprise, he or she will be willing to pay the extra cost as long as the shipment retains value, but at some stage the trader will look at the total costs and decide it is not worth trying to make a new shipment. There is a coordination problem, because each levier of fees will not consider this possible effect of their combined actions. The solution in more established areas of flourishing intraregional trade is for the government to exert its influence to prevent a tragedy of the anti-commons.

To some extent the internal levies described as occurring especially in Kazakhstan, but also in other countries, are an example of the cost to traders arising from the failure to establish the authority of the central government or even a breakdown of law and order. Enforceability of contracts is critical to the smooth operation of a market economy, and so is protection from arbitrary intrusion into property rights. These are inadequately addressed by the national governments, although with the ongoing process of nation building this may be happening. In Central Asia since the early 1990s, contracts have been especially difficult to enforce when the dispute is between people in different jurisdictions, and an obstacle to international cooperation to promote the enforceability of contracts is the mutual mistrust between the political entities.

A related problem arises when fees are levied or regulations imposed in differing countries. This is most obviously apparent for Uzbekistan, which is double land-locked and hence any exports must cross at least two other countries in order to reach an ocean port, but in practice it also applies to much of the trade of the other Central Asian countries due to the nature of the inherited transport system. The problem is complicated because there are genuine reasons to charge fees for road and rail use and to regulate on axle size of lorries and so forth, but, if the sum of the fees or the heterogeneity of the rules chokes off trade, then nobody benefits.

How large are the social costs of impediments to trade within the region? Measurement of something that does not happen is always difficult, and even rough estimates are hard to make when we have little idea of potential areas of comparative advantage or of the relevant demand and supply curves. The burdens of trade impediments are likely to be heaviest in markets where supply is elastic. If demand is also elastic, then relatively small impediments will cut trade volumes far below potential. This is likely to best describe household or labor-intensive activities, like those of the Kyrgyz onion farmers, underlining the regressive impact of trade impediments that are likely to hit the poor hardest. Beyond basic necessities, the demand for nonluxury consumption goods is likely to be more price elastic, so that the nonrich members of the community will be hit as consumers.

10.5 Conclusions

All five of the Central Asian countries that became independent in late 1991 are export-oriented economies, and thus trade relations have been an important policy element. Although all declared their intention to participate in the global trading system, they have, to varying degrees, pursued trade policies incompatible with WTO rules and have, with the exception of the Kyrgyz Republic, been cautious about accepting the obligations imposed by WTO membership. At the same time they have all signed on to myriad regional agreements which might threaten adherence to the most-favored nation principle at the heart of the WTO-based system.

The striking feature of the regional arrangements described in Section 10.3, however, is the general lack of progress in establishing or implementing preferential trade policies. Despite many proposals for regional trading arrangements, in practice the Central Asian countries have in their trade policies clearly chosen the path of policy autonomy combined with nondiscriminatory multilateralism. Buying imports from the global least-cost supplier and selling exports in the best market makes considerable economic sense, and is supported by the failure of the many discriminatory trading arrangements in Latin America and Africa during the second half of the twentieth century (this experience is documented in Pomfret (1997a)). This is significant for WTO negotiations because, as already mentioned, proposals to turn, say, the Eurasian Community into a customs union or free-trade area would require WTO approval insofar as it includes WTO members.

The positive feature of this de facto multilateralism is that the region remains well-placed to take advantage of opportunities offered by China's recent WTO accession and Russia's imminent accession. Central Asian countries which are or become WTO members will benefit from a rule-based environment in their trade with all neighboring economies except Afghanistan, and rules which are generally the most desirable for small open economies. The costs in terms of restrictions on import-substitution strategies and other antiliberal trade policies and in terms of reduced potential for political grandstanding via economic proposals in regional fora are minor—and indeed the tying of governments' hands in such activities should benefit the countries' citizens.

What are the prospects for improved international relations in Central Asia during the first decade of the twenty-first century? At the institutional level, existing regional organizations have been strengthened, at least on paper, as the Union of Five became the Eurasian Community, the Shanghai Forum became the Shanghai Cooperation Organization, and the Central Asian Economic Community was succeeded by the Central Asian Cooperation Organization, which was absorbed into the Eurasian Community in 2005. Whether the implementation ability of the new organizations will exceed that of their predecessors is still uncertain. The events of September 2001 stimulated declarations of concerted action against terrorism, but the immediate consequence was to widen the fissure between the Eurasian Community members and the countries which were more skeptical about Russia's role in the region. Moreover, recent developments within the region, especially increased territorial disputes, are creating a climate which is inimical to cooperation. Whether justified on security grounds or not, new border-control measures are unpopular among the local populations who have no history of such restrictions, and as assertions of the new states' territorial rights they augur poorly for interstate cooperation.

Yet, there are benefits from regional cooperation, and if these could be realized it would help to defuse political tensions. The costs to Central Asia of forgoing benefits from international specialization and trade arise from the tragedy of the anti-commons, where people promoting self-interested goals are choking off trade that would be mutually beneficial. This tragedy can be mitigated by government actions to discourage or regulate antisocial behavior by local authorities, customs officials, and others under their jurisdiction. The national governments can also benefit by implementing policies to reduce other impediments to trade such as cumbersome visa regulations, poorly developed financial systems, and capricious changes in border crossings, but that requires an appreciation that many of the forgone trade opportunities represent win–win situations.

In the early twenty-first century this situation is fluid. There is some fatigue with regional arrangements that have had little effect, but the need for regional cooperation on water and security is widely recognized. If the Central Asian governments feel that they have completed the nation-building task that was their top priority after 1991, then perhaps they can now move on to discuss regional cooperation with less fear of their sovereignty being undermined.

Part IV

Prospects

11

Shared Problems and National Economic Differentiation

When the five Central Asian countries became unexpectedly independent during the second half of 1991, they faced three huge negative economic shocks: the end of central planning, the dissolution of the Soviet Union, and hyperinflation. All experienced a transitional recession; output fell, inequality widened, and poverty increased. Their national experiences, however, diverged during the first decade after independence, both with respect to economic performance and with respect to the type of economic system created.

Individual economies were hampered by the inherited infrastructure, which prevented especially Kazakhstan and Turkmenistan from realizing potential energy exports in the 1990s, and also by poor economic policies. The Kyrgyz Republic and Tajikistan had the least favorable initial conditions and have remained economically disadvantaged, especially Tajikistan which had the added burden of a long civil war. Uzbekistan was the most successful in terms of economic performance during the 1990s, but major policy errors limited both its international economic influence and future prospects. Since 2000 economic performance has diverged sharply as Kazakhstan's boom contrasted with positive but slower growth in the other economies.

By the turn of the century, the national economies, with the possible exception of Turkmenistan's, had changed substantially from the centrally planned economy of the Soviet era and all were in one form or another market-based economies. Although the transition from central planning in Central Asia has created less-well-functioning economies than in Eastern Europe, the initial conditions were far more adverse, including the absence of anything comparable to the incentive of potential EU membership. The outcome after a dozen years could have been better, but to dismiss the countries as having unreformed economies, or more colorfully as "that depressing collection of Soviet-era relics,"[1] ignores the substantial changes that have occurred.

Kazakhstan, despite false steps in the 1990s, remains the most likely to succeed. The country's higher income levels, more abundant human capital, and natural

---

[1] "One down, four to go: revolution reaches the steppe," *The Economist*, April 2, 2005.

resources are enduring advantages, even if the potential benefits were frittered away during the 1990s. With new oil fields being developed and with new pipelines providing alternative outlets for Kazakhstan's oil, the prospects for substantial oil revenues in the medium term are rosy. The elite, although it derived its wealth and power from an unfair and distorted privatization process, is now keen to establish a rule of law in order to protect its economic gains, and favorable institutional developments are possible but by no means certain. As elsewhere, much rests on the nature of the political transition from the incumbent presidency.

At the other extreme, Turkmenistan, despite its natural-resource wealth, faces the grimmest immediate prospects with a regime that pursues poor economic policies and is resistant to change. On the basis of its small population and abundant natural gas, the country after independence laid claim to being the "Kuwait of Central Asia." The reality has been a highly personalized regime living off the resource rents, with nothing like the level of competent economic management of Kuwait. If the president continues to use the rents to ruthlessly suppress any potential rivals, the regime could be stable for as long as the president's health holds out. However, the poor state of the president's health and the absence of obvious successors raises the specter of rapid and unpredictable change at some point. From the perspective of the economy, almost any change would have to be better than Turkmenbashi's policies.

The Kyrgyz Republic introduced the best policies, but experienced disappointing outcomes. The problems arose from failure to establish the institutions necessary for a well-functioning market economy. Corruption was rampant and, even if President Akayev was the least repressive of the Central Asian leaders, his family and friends used their monopoly over the levers of power to enrich themselves. More generally, the Kyrgyz experience illustrates the huge obstacles to establishing in short order all the institutions necessary to support a well-functioning economy. In 1991 the scale and time-span of the transition from central planning to a market economy for the less-developed former Soviet republics, even if they adopted good policies, was underestimated by everybody.

Political factors are also critical in Tajikistan, where establishment of effective public administration and rule of law are necessary preconditions for progress. Even with those condition met, the economic prospects are not good for Tajikistan or for the Kyrgyz Republic, both poor landlocked countries whose economic potential depends upon good regional relations to export, for example, hydroelectric power.

Uzbekistan in the 1990s was economically the most successful of all Soviet successor states and in day-to-day matters the economy remains well-managed, but bedeviled by poor economic policies in key areas. If the interrelated issues of currency convertibility, farmgate prices, and government revenues can be addressed, the economic prospects should be reasonably good, but if they are not addressed Uzbekistan's economy could easily slip into the stagnation familiar from many import-substituting countries of the 1950s and 1960s. As elsewhere in the region, loosening of state control over the economy may be inseparable from political reform, allowing more freedom and pluralism.

On the international stage, the countries remained fairly insignificant despite their combined population of over fifty million and their resource abundance. They continue to be export oriented but have been slow to participate in the global economy in any role other than as primary-product exporters. As the national economies were established, they diversified their international economic relations away from the previous almost total intra-USSR orientation. This multilateralism of trade and other relations was desirable, but has had as an undesirable side effect the disintegration of Central Asia as an economic region. Despite the dozens of regional summits and innumerable paper agreements for free-trade areas or common economic space, the reality has been of increasing barriers to economic interchange within the region. Any scenarios of the Central Asian countries' acting as a group have foundered on intraregional rivalries. Apart from the continual struggle for regional hegemony between Uzbekistan and Kazakhstan and antipathy between the presidents of Uzbekistan and Turkmenistan, the tensions have been particularly taut in the Ferghana Valley, at times on the verge of armed conflict. The lack of regional cooperation is both economically costly and also dangerous, in terms both of the threat of war and of the inability to address major environmental problems such as the desiccation of the Aral Sea.

Political change in Central Asia has lagged far behind that of Eastern Europe or Baltic transition economies, and a civil society has been slow to emerge. During the 1990s political success in Central Asia was measured by survival of the new states and avoidance of interstate wars. National survival, however, became readily identified with the incumbent leaders' survival. No election in post-Soviet Central Asia has met international standards of fairness. The presidents have suppressed opposition, with varying degrees of brutality, and all are suspicious of pluralism. They often cite the Chinese model, but they have created personal super-presidential systems rather than mimicking the more collective leadership of post-Mao China.

The main conclusion of this book is that, despite much shared background and common initial conditions, the five countries, and especially the two larger economies, Kazakhstan and Uzbekistan, have been moving along differing trajectories and that is likely to continue. While the three smaller countries will remain minor players in the global economy, both of the larger countries could become significant middle-sized economies, but in their own right rather than as part of Central Asia. For each country, however, the heavy hand of the state deters the emergence of dynamic market economies in Central Asia. The critical question in the early twenty-first century is how the political and economic environment will evolve, and whether it will create a better or worse environment for economic development.

The events of September 2001 and the overthrow of the Taliban government in Afghanistan led to a new importance for the region in terms of U.S. influence and Russian and Chinese reactions. Within Central Asia, however, the most striking developments since 2001 have been in domestic rather than in international politics. Apart from in Tajikistan, the presidents were all men who were appointed as first secretary of their Soviet republic by Mikhail Gorbachev. Although the regimes are repressive, signs of opposition to the incumbent presidents have been multiplying, either in the political arena in the more open societies of the Kyrgyz Republic and Kazakhstan or in demonstrations and violent acts in Uzbekistan and Tajikistan. In Turkmenistan all domestic opposition has been muzzled, but an opposition in exile has emerged.

In March 2005, the first major political change in Central Asia occurred in the Kyrgyz Republic. The ingredients of the revolution were typical: after a fixed election demonstrations began in the economically disadvantaged south of the country, and then spread to the north where enough people were dissatisfied with the corruption and favoritism of the regime. The Kyrgyz Republic was, however, different from the rest of Central Asia in its degree of openness. Although some prominent opposition leaders were jailed on trumped-up charges, political discussion was open and a number of political heavyweights with governmental experience from the less dictatorial periods of the 1990s were available as credible leaders of a new government. Moreover, despite his tendencies towards authoritarianism, President Akayev at the end refused to use force against the demonstrators, ensuring a peaceful initial transfer of power, whatever the future might hold for his country.

Later developments in 2005 showed little clear pattern. Although the post-Akayev election in the Kyrgyz Republic was probably the fairest yet seen in Central Asia, the new government was slow to establish a coherent strategy and a succession of high-profile assassinations suggested that democratic institutions were far from secure. In Uzbekistan there was little pretence of pluralism as the government used its power to violently suppress demonstrations in Andijan in May and then sentenced dozens to prison in a series of show trials. In Kazakhstan the political situation is peaceful as the population benefits from the oil boom and is dismayed by the violence in the country's southern neighbors; according to not fully reliable opinion polls, President Nazarbayev would have won a fair election in December 2005, but old habits die hard and widespread abuses ensured a massive victory for the president. For the moment Tajikistan and Turkmenistan are out of the headlines, but the former remains unstable and the latter's future depends on Turkmenbashi's precarious health. The overwhelming issue in all of the countries for the second decade since independence is how the succession from the presidents of the 1990s will be handled. The economic issue concerns the environment that the next generation of leaders or new regimes will provide for economic activity. If the succession is to a regime that continues to self-enrich a few people from the natural-resource rents of the region, then the country's prospects will be dim, but Kazakhstan, the Kyrgyz Republic, Uzbekistan, and Tajikistan have taken initial steps towards economic development in a market setting which could be built upon in an appropriate institutional setting.

References

Ackland, R., and J. Falkingham. 1997. A profile of poverty in Kyrgyzstan. In *Household Welfare in Central Asia* (ed. J. Falkingham, J. Klugman, S. Marnie, and J. Micklewright), pp. 81–99. Basingstoke: Macmillan.

Afrasiabi, K. 2000. Three-part series on ECO. (1) The economic cooperation organization aims to bolster regional trade opportunities, September 14, 2000. (2) ECO strives to improve transportation and communication networks, November 1, 2000. (3) Economic cooperation organization presses energy initiative, December 5, 2000. (Available at www.eurasianet.org.)

Aghion, P., and M. Schankerman. 1999. Competition, entry and the social returns to infrastructure in transition economies. *Economics of Transition* 7(1):79–101.

Akbarzadeh, S. 1996. Why did nationalism fail in Tajikistan? *Europe–Asia Studies* 48(7): 1,105–29.

Akimov, A. 2001. Reforming the financial system: the case of Uzbekistan. CASE Studies and Analyses, No. 234. Working Paper, Warsaw Centrum Analiz Spolaczno-Ekonomicznych.

Akiner, S. 2001. *Tajikistan: Disintegration or Reconciliation*. London: The Royal Institute of International Affairs.

——. 2005. Violence in Andijan, 13 May 2005. *Central Asia–Caucasus Institute Silk Road Paper*. Washington, DC: The Johns Hopkins University-SAIS.

Alexeev, M., and J. Leitzel. 2001. Income distribution and price controls: targeting a social safety net during economic transition. *European Economic Review* 45:1,647–63.

Anderson, K., and C. Becker. 1999. Post-Soviet pension systems, retirement and elderly poverty: findings from the Kyrgyz Republic. *MOCT-MOST: Economic Policy in Transitional Economies* 9(4):459–78.

Anderson, K., and R. Pomfret. 2000. Living standards during transition to a market economy: the Kyrgyz Republic in 1993 and 1996. *Journal of Comparative Economics* 26(3):502–23.

——. 2001. Development of small and medium enterprises in the Kyrgyz Republic, 1993–1997. In *Enterprise in Transition* (ed. Faculty of Economics, University of Split, Croatia), pp. 400–401. (Summary in hard copy, full text on accompanying CD-ROM.)

——. 2002. Relative living standards in new market economies: evidence from Central Asian household surveys. *Journal of Comparative Economics* 30(4):683–708.

——. 2003. *Creating a Market Economy: Evidence from Household Surveys in Central Asia*. Cheltenham, U.K.: Edward Elgar.

——. 2005. Spatial inequality and development in Central Asia. In *Spatial Disparities in Human Development: Perspectives from Asia* (ed. R. Kanbur, A. Venables, and G. Wan). Tokyo: United Nations University Press.

Åslund, A. 2001. The myth of output collapse after communism. Carnegie Endowment Working Paper Series, #18.

Atkinson, A., and A. Brandolini. 2001. Promise and pitfalls in the use of "secondary" datasets: income inequality in OECD countries as a case study. *Journal of Economic Literature* 39(3):771–99.

Atkinson, A., and J. Micklewright. 1992. *Economic Transformation in Eastern Europe and the Distribution of Income*. Cambridge University Press.

Atkinson, G., and K. Hamilton. 2003. Savings, growth and the resource curse hypothesis. *World Development* 31(11):1,793–1,807.

Auty, R. 2001. *Resource Abundance and Economic Development*. Oxford University Press.

Babetskaia-Kukharchuk, O., and M. Maurel. 2004. Russia's accession to the WTO: what potential for trade increase? *Journal of Comparative Economics* 32:680–99.

Babetski, J., and M. Maurel. 2002. Unemployment, poverty, and reallocation of the labour force in the Kyrgyz Republic. Unpublished paper, The World Bank, Washington, DC.

Babetskii, I., A. Kolev, and M. Maurel. 2003. Kyrgyz labour market in the late 1990s: the challenge of formal job creation. *Comparative Economic Studies* 45(4):493–519.

Bacchetta, M., and Z. Drabek. 2002. Effects of WTO accession on policy-making in sovereign states: preliminary lessons from the recent experience of transition countries. WTO Working Paper DERD-2002-02, World Trade Organization, Geneva.

Baffes, J. 2004. Cotton: market setting, trade policies, and issues. Policy Research Working Paper 3218, The World Bank, Washington, DC.

Bailey, M. 1991. Mismeasurement of economic growth. International Center for Economic Growth Occasional Paper, No. 23, ICS Press, San Francisco, CA.

Bauer, A., N. Boschmann, and D. Green. 1997a. *Women and Gender Relations in Kazakstan: The Social Cost*. Manila: Asian Development Bank.

Bauer, A., D. Green, and K. Kuehnast. 1997b. *Women and Gender Relations: The Kyrgyz Republic in Transition*. Manila: Asian Development Bank.

Bauer, A., N. Boschmann, D. Green, and K. Kuehnast. 1998. *A Generation at Risk: Children in the Central Asian Republics of Kazakstan and Kyrgyzstan*. Manila: Asian Development Bank.

Becker, C., E. Musabek, A.-G. Seitenova, and D. Urzhumova. 2005. The migration response to economic shock: lessons from Kazakhstan. *Journal of Comparative Economics* 33:107–32.

Belopolsky, A., and M. Talwani. 2001. Geological basins and oil and gas reserves of the Greater Caspian Region. In *Energy in the Caspian Region: Present and Future* (ed. Y. Kalyuzhnova, A. Myers Jaffe, D. Lynch, and R. Sickles), pp. 13–33. London: Palgrave Macmillan.

Bergson, A. 1961. *The Real National Income of Soviet Russia since 1928*. Cambridge, MA: Harvard University Press.

Bhattasali, D., L. Shantong, and W. Martin (eds). 2004. *China and the WTO: Accession, Policy Reform and Poverty Reduction Strategies*. Washington, DC: The World Bank.

Biddison, J. M. 2002. The study on water and energy nexus in Central Asia. ADB Report ADM/01–576, RSC No. C10732, Asian Development Bank, Manila.

Blanchard, O. 1997. *The Economics of Post-Communist Transition*. Oxford: Clarendon Press.

Bloch, P. C., and K. Rasmussen. 1998. Land reform in Kyrgyzstan. In *Land Reform in the Former Soviet Union and Eastern Europe* (ed. S. K. Wegren), pp. 111–35. London: Routledge.

Bloem, A., P. Cotterell, and T. Gigantes. 1998. National accounts in the transition countries: balancing the biases. *Review of Income and Wealth* 44(1):1–24.

Bohr, A. 1998. *Uzbekistan: Politics and Foreign Policy*. London/Washington, DC: The Royal Institute of International Affairs/The Brookings Institution.

Brainerd, E. 1998. Winners and losers in Russia's economic transition. *American Economic Review* 88(5):1,094–1,115.

Brooks, D., and M. Thant. 1998. *Social Sector Issues in Transitional Economies of Asia*. Oxford University Press (for the Asian Development Bank).

Buchanan, J., and Y. Yoon. 2000. Symmetric tragedies: commons and anticommons. *Journal of Law and Economics* 43 (April):1–13.

Buckley, C. 1998. Rural/urban differentials in demographic processes: the Central Asian states. *Population Research and Policy Review* 17:71–89.

Buckley, R., and E. Gurenko. 1997. Housing and income distribution in Russia: Zhivago's legacy. *World Bank Research Observer* 12(1):19–32.

Bulir, A. 1998. The price incentive to smuggle and the cocoa supply in Ghana, 1950–96. IMF Working Paper 98/88, International Monetary Fund, Washington, DC.

Campos, N. 2004. What does WTO membership kindle in transition economies? An empirical investigation. *Journal of Economic Integration* 19(2):395–415.

Cangiano, M., C. Cottarelli, and L. Cubeddu. 1998. Pension developments and reforms in transition economies. IMF Working Paper WP/980/151, International Monetary Fund, Washington, DC.

Center for Preventive Action. 1999. *Calming the Ferghana Valley: Development and Dialogue in the Heart of Central Asia*. Preventive Action Reports, Volume 4. New York: The Century Foundation Press.

Chan-Lau, J. 2004. Pension funds and emerging markets. IMF Working Paper WP/04/181, International Monetary Fund, Washington, DC.

Chase, R. 1998. Markets for communist human capital: returns to education and experience in the Czech Republic and Slovakia. *Industrial and Labor Relations Review* 51(3):401–23.

Collins, K. Forthcoming. *The Logic of Clan Politics: Regime Transformation in Central Asia*. Cambridge University Press.

Connolly, M., and S. Vatnick. 1994. Uzbekistan: trade reform in a cotton based economy. In *Trade in the New Independent States* (ed. C. Michalopoulos and D. Tarr). Washington, DC: The World Bank.

Cord, L., R. Lopez, M. Huppi, and O. Melo. 2004. Growth and rural poverty in the CIS-7 countries: case studies of Georgia, the Kyrgyz Republic, and Moldova. In *The Low-Income Countries of the Commonwealth of Independent States: Progress and Challenges in Transition* (ed. C. Shiells and S. Sattar), pp. 171–202. Washington, DC: International Monetary Fund).

Coudouel, A., and S. Marnie. 1999. From universal to targeted social assistance: an assessment of the Uzbek experience. *MOCT-MOST: Economic Policy in Transitional Economies* 9(4):443–58.

Dalmazzo, A., and G. de Blasio. 2003. Resources and incentives to reform. *IMF Staff Papers* 50(2):250–73.

de Broeck, M., and V. Koen. 2000. The great contractions in Russia and the other countries of the former Soviet Union: a view from the supply side. IMF Working Paper WP/00/32, International Monetary Fund, Washington, DC.

de Broeck, M., and K. Kostial. 1998. Output decline in transition: the case of Kazakhstan. IMF Working Paper WP/98/45, International Monetary Fund, Washington, DC.

de Castello Branca, M. 1998. Pension reform in the Baltics, Russia and other countries of the former Soviet Union. IMF Working Paper WP/98/11, International Monetary Fund, Washington, DC.

Deaton, A. 2001. Counting the world's poor: problems and possible solutions. *World Bank Research Observer* 16(2):125–47.

Devlin, J., and M. Lewin. 2004. Managing oil booms and busts in developing countries. Draft chapter for *Managing Volatility and Crises: A Practitioner's Guide*. Washington, DC: The World Bank.

Dieter, H. 1996. Regional integration in Central Asia: current economic position and prospects. *Central Asian Survey* 15(3/4):369–86.

Djankov, S., and C. Freund. 2000. Disintegration and trade flows: evidence from the former Soviet Union. World Bank Working Paper WP 2378, The World Bank, Washington, DC (June).

——. 2002a. Trade flows in the former Soviet Union, 1987 to 1996. *Journal of Comparative Economics* 30(1):76–90.

——. 2002b. New borders: evidence from the former Soviet Union. *Weltwirtschaftliches Archiv* 138:493–508.

Downs, E. S. 2004. The Chinese energy security debate. *China Quarterly* 177:21–41.

Dudwick, N., E. Gomart, A. Marc, and K. Kuehnast (eds). 2003. *When Things Fall Apart: Qualitative Studies of Poverty in the Former Soviet Union*. Washington, DC: The World Bank.

Dukenbaev, A. 2004. Politics and public policy in post-Soviet Central Asia: the case of higher education reform in Kyrgyzstan. *Central Eurasian Studies Review* 3(2):16–18.

Eilat, Y., and C. Zinnes. 2002. The shadow economy in transition countries: friend or foe? A policy perspective. *World Development* 30(7):1,233–54.

Elborgh-Woytek, K. 2003. Of openness and distance: trade developments in the commonwealth of independent states, 1993–2002. IMF Working Paper WP/03/207, International Monetary Fund, Washington, DC.

Esentugelov, A. 2000. The Kazak regions in the transition process. *Kazakstan Economic Trends* 2000 (January–March):19–35.

Falkingham, J. 1999. Measuring household welfare: problems and pitfalls with household surveys in Central Asia. *MOCT-MOST: Economic Policy in Transitional Economies* 9(4):379–93.

——. 2000a. *Women in Tajikistan*. Manila: Asian Development Bank.

——. 2000b. From security to uncertainty: the impact of economic change on child welfare in Central Asia. Innocenti Working Paper 76, United Nations Children's Fund (UNICEF) Innocenti Research Centre, Florence.

——. 2000c. A profile of poverty in Tajikistan. CASE Paper 39, London School of Economics Centre for Analysis of Social Exclusion.

——. 2004. Inequality and poverty in the CIS-7 countries, 1989–2002. In *The Low-Income Countries of the Commonwealth of Independent States: Progress and Challenges in Transition* (ed. C. Shiells and S. Sattar), pp. 141–69. Washington, DC: International Monetary Fund.

Falkingham, J., J. Klugman, S. Marnie, and J. Micklewright (eds). 1997. *Household Welfare in Central Asia*. Basingstoke: Macmillan.

Feenstra, R. 1994. New product varieties and the measurement of international prices. *American Economic Review* 84(1):157–77.

Filer, R., and J. Hanousek. 2002. Data watch: research data from transition economies. *Journal of Economic Perspectives* 16(1):225–40.

Finkel, E., and H. Garcia. 1997. Rehabilitating the Kyrgyz Republic's power and district heating services. In *Social Assessments for Better Development: Case Studies in Russia and Central Asia* (ed. M. Cernia and A. Kudat), pp. 187–97. Washington, DC: The World Bank.

Fischer, S., and R. Sahay. 2000. The transition economies after ten years. IMF Working Paper WP/00/30, International Monetary Fund, Washington, DC.

Freinkman, L., E. Polyakov, and C. Revenco. 2004. Trade performance and regional integration of the CIS countries. World Bank Working Paper #38, Poverty Reduction and Economic Management Sector Unit, Europe and Central Asia Region, The World Bank, Washington, DC.

Freitag-Wirminghaus, R. 1998. Turkmenistan's place in Central Asia and the world. In *Post-Soviet Central Asia* (ed. T. Atabaki and J. O'Kane), pp. 157–76. London: Tauris Academic Studies.

Gelb, A. and associates. 1988. *Oil Windfalls: Blessing or Curse?* Oxford University Press.

Giovarelli, R. 1998. Land reform and farm reorganization in the Kyrgyz Republic. RDI Reports on Foreign Aid and Development #96, Rural Development Institute, Seattle, WA.

Gleason, G. 1997. *The New Central Asian States*. Boulder, CO: Westview Press.

——. 2001. Inter-state cooperation in Central Asia from the CIS to the Shanghai forum. *Europe–Asia Studies* 53(7):1,077–95.

——. 2003a. *Markets and Politics in Central Asia*. London: Routledge.

——. 2003b. The politics of structural reform in Uzbekistan. Paper presented at *The Central Eurasian Studies Society Annual Conference, Harvard University, October 3, 2003*. Unpublished.

Goletti, F., and P. Chabot. 2000. Food policy research for improving the reform of agricultural input and output markets in Central Asia. In *Food Policy Reforms in Central Asia* (ed. S. Babu and A. Tashmatov), pp. 45–69. Washington, DC: International Food Policy Research Institute. (Also 2000 *Food Policy* 25(6):661–79.)

Gray, C., J. Hellman, and R. Ryterman. 2004. *Anticorruption in Transition 2: Corruption in Enterprise–State Interactions in Europe and Central Asia 1999–2002*. Washington, DC: The World Bank.

Gray, J. 2000. Kazakhstan: a review of farm restructuring. World Bank Technical Paper No. 458, The World Bank, Washington, DC.

Griffin, K. (ed.). 1996. *Social Policy and Economic Transformation in Uzbekistan*. Geneva: International Labour Office.

Grosh, M., and P. Glewwe. 1998. Data watch: The World Bank's living standards measurement study household surveys. *Journal of Economic Perspectives* 12(1):187–96.

Gürgen, E., H. Snoek, J. Craig, J. McHugh, I. Izvorski, and R. van Rooden. 1999. Economic reforms in Kazakhstan, Kyrgyz Republic, Tajikistan, Turkmenistan, and Uzbekistan. Occasional Paper 183, International Monetary Fund, Washington, DC.

Gylfason, T. 2001. Natural resources, education, and economic development. *European Economic Review* 45:847–59.

Ham, J., J. Svejnar, and K. Terrell. 1999. Women's unemployment during transition: evidence from Czech and Slovak micro-data. *Economics of Transition* 7(1):47–78.

Havrylyshyn, O., and D. McGettigan. 1999. Privatization in transition countries: a sampling of the literature. IMF Working Paper 99/6, International Monetary Fund, Washington, DC.

Heleniak, T. 1997. Mass migration in post-Soviet space. *Transition* 8(5):15–17.

Hellman, J. 1998. Winners take all: the politics of partial reform in post-communist transitions. *World Politics* 50:203–34

Herman, M. 1999. Sustainable agricultural reform—the case of Uzbekistan. In *Central Asia 2010*, pp. 84–95. New York: United Nations Development Programme.

Hoff, K., and J. Stiglitz. 2004. After the big bang? Obstacles to the emergence of the rule of law in post-communist societies. *American Economic Review* 94(3):753–63.

Horsman, S. 2001. Water in Central Asia: regional cooperation or conflict? In *Central Asian Security: The New International Context* (ed. R. Allison and L. Jonson), pp. 69–94. London/Washington, DC: The Royal Institute of International Affairs/The Brookings Institution.

Howell, J. 1996a. Poverty and transition in Kyrgyzstan: how some households cope. *Central Asian Survey* 15(1):59–73.

——. 1996b. Coping with transition: insights from Kyrgyzstan. *Third World Quarterly* 17:53–68.

Hunt, J. 1998. The transition in East Germany: when is a ten point fall in the gender pay gap bad news? CEPR Discussion Paper Series in Transition Economies No. 1805, Centre for Economic Policy Research, London.

Hunter, S. 2000. The Afghan civil war: implications for Central Asian stability. In *Energy and Conflict in Central Asia and the Caucasus* (ed. R. Ebel and R. Menon), pp. 189–208. Lanham, MD: Rowman and Littlefield.

ICG. 2002. Central Asia: border disputes and conflict potential. ICG Asia Report No. 33, International Crisis Group, Osh and Brussels.

——. 2003. Uzbekistan's reform program: illusion or reality? ICG Asia Report No. 46, International Crisis Group, Osh and Brussels.

——. 2004a. The failure of reform in Uzbekistan: ways forward for the international community. ICG Asia Report No. 76, International Crisis Group, Osh and Brussels.

——. 2004b. Tajikistan's politics: confrontation or consolidation? ICG Asia Briefing, May 19, 2004, International Crisis Group, Brussels.

——. 2005. The curse of cotton: Central Asia's destructive monoculture. ICG Asia Report No. 93, International Crisis Group, Bishkek and Brussels.

Isham, J., M. Woolcock, L. Pritchett, and G. Busby. 2003. The varieties of resource experience: how natural resource export structures affect the political economy of economic growth. Middlebury College Economics Discussion Paper No. 03-08, Middlebury, VT.

Islamov, B. 2001. *The Central Asian States Ten Years After: How to Overcome Traps of Development, Transformation and Globalisation?* Tokyo: Maruzen.

Jensen, J., T. Rutherford, and D. Tarr. 2002. Economy-wide effects of Russia's accession to the WTO. Paper prepared for *SIDA-CEFIR Conference on Negotiating Russia's WTO Accession, Moscow, June 24–25, 2002*. Unpublished.

Jovanovic, B. 2001. Russian roller coaster: expenditure inequality and instability in Russia, 1994–98. *Review of Income and Wealth* 47(2):251–71.

Kalyuzhnova, Y. 1998. *The Kazakstani economy: independence and transition.* Basingstoke: Macmillan.

——. 2000. The economic transition in Kazakhstan and Uzbekistan. In *The Euro-Asian World: A period of Transition* (ed. Y. Kalyuzhnova and D. Lynch), pp. 164–87. Basingstoke: Macmillan.

——. 2003. Privatisation and structural reforms: case study Kazakhstan. In *Privatisation and Structural Change in Transition Economies* (ed. Y. Kalyuzhnova and W. Andreff), pp. 158–79. Basingstoke: Palgrave Macmillan.

Kalyuzhnova, Y., and M. Kaser. 2006. Prudential management of the hydrocarbon wealth in resource rich transition economies. *Post-Communist Economies*, in press.

Kalyuzhnova, Y., M. Vagliasindi, and M. Casson. 2003. Recent developments in the short-term employment in Kazakhstani firms. *Comparative Economic Studies* 45(4):466–92.

Kalyuzhnova, Y., J. Pemberton, and B. Mukhamediyev. 2004. Natural resources and economic growth in Kazakhstan. In *The Economic Prospects of the CIS—Sources of Long Term Growth since 1991* (ed. G. Ofer and R. Pomfret), pp. 249–67. Cheltenham, U.K.: Edward Elgar.

Kanbur, R. 2001. Economic policy, distribution and poverty: the nature of disagreements. *World Development* 29(6):1,083–94.

Kandiyoti, D. 1999. Poverty in transition: an ethnographic critique of household surveys in post-Soviet Central Asia. *Development and Change* 30(3):499–524.

Kaser, M. 1997. The Central Asian economies 1991–1996. In *Economic Survey of Europe in 1996–1997*, pp. 179–211. Geneva: United Nations Economic Commission for Europe.

Kennedy, D., S. Funkhauser, and M. Raiser. 2004. Low pressure, high tension: the energy–water nexus in the CIS-7 countries. In *The Low-Income Countries of the Commonwealth of Independent States: Progress and Challenges in Transition* (ed. C. Shiells and S. Sattar), pp. 283–306. Washington, DC: International Monetary Fund.

Khan, A. R. 1996. The transition to a market economy in agriculture. In *Social Policy and Economic Transformation in Uzbekistan* (ed. K. Griffin), pp. 65–92. Geneva: International Labour Organization.

Klugman, J. 1999. Financing and governance of education in Central Asia. *MOCT-MOST Economic Policy in Transitional Economies* 9(4):423–42.

Koen, V. 1995. Price measurement and mismeasurement in Central Asia. IMF Working Paper WP/95/82, International Monetary Fund, Washington, DC.

Kolstø, P. 2004. The price of stability: Kazakhstani control mechanisms under conditions of cultural and demographic bipolarity. In *Democracy and Pluralism in Muslim Eurasia* (ed. Y. Ro'i), pp. 165–85. London: Frank Cass.

Krueger, A., and J.-S. Pischke. 1995. A comparative analysis of East and West German labor markets: before and after unification. In *Differences and Changes in Wage Structure* (ed. R. Freeman and L. Katz). University of Chicago Press.

Krueger, A., M. Schiff, and A. Valdes. 1988. Agricultural incentives in developing countries: measuring the effect of sectoral and economywide policies. *World Bank Economic Review* 2(3):255–71.

Krueger, A., M. Schiff, and A. Valdes (eds). 1991–92. *The Political Economy of Agricultural Pricing Policies*, five volumes. Baltimore, MD: The Johns Hopkins University Press.

Lanjouw, P., and M. Ravallion. 1995. Poverty and household size. *Economic Journal* 105(433):1,415–34.

Lanjouw, P., B. Milanovic, and S. Paternostro. 1998. Poverty and economic transition: how do changes in economies of scale affect poverty rates of different households? Policy Research Working Paper WPS2009, The World Bank, Washington, DC.

Lerman, Z., and K. Brooks. 1998. Land reform in Turkmenistan. In *Land Reform in the Former Soviet Union and Eastern Europe* (ed. S. K. Wegren), pp. 162–85. London: Routledge.

——. 2001. Turkmenistan: an assessment of leasehold-based farm restructuring. World Bank Technical Paper No. 500, Europe and Central Asia Environmentally and Socially Sustainable Development Series, The World Bank, Washington, DC.

Lewis, R. (ed.). 1992. *Geographic Perspectives on Soviet Central Asia*. Routledge: London.

Lissovolik, B., and Y. Lissovolik. 2004. Russia and the WTO: the "gravity" of outsider status. IMF Working Paper WP/04/159, International Monetary Fund, Washington, DC.

Lubin, N. 1999a. Energy wealth, development, and stability in Turkmenistan. *NBR Analysis* 10(3):61–78. (Reprinted in Ebel, R., and R. Menon. 2000. *Energy and Conflict in Central Asia and the Caucasus*, pp. 107–21. Lanham, MD: Rowman and Littlefield.)

——. 1999b. *Calming the Ferghana Valley: Development and Dialogue in the Heart of Central Asia*. Preventive Action Reports, Volume 4. New York: The Century Foundation Press.

Luong, P. J. 2002. *Institutional Change and Political Continuity*. Cambridge University Press.

——. 2004a. Economic "decentralization" in Kazakhstan: causes and conseqences. In *The Transformation of Central Asia* (ed. P. J. Luong), pp. 182–210. Ithaca, NY: Cornell University Press.

——. 2004b. Political obstacles to economic reform in Uzbekistan, the Kyrgyz Republic, and Tajikistan: strategies for moving ahead. In *The Low-Income Countries of the Commonwealth of Independent States: Progress and Challenges in Transition* (ed. C. Shiells and S. Sattar), pp. 203–35. Washington, DC: International Monetary Fund.

Luong, P. J., and E. Weinthal. 2001. Prelude to the resource curse: explaining oil and gas development strategies in the Soviet successor states and beyond. *Comparative Political Studies* 34(4):367–99.

Marnie, S., and J. Micklewright. 1994. Poverty in pre-reform Uzbekistan: what do official data really reveal? *Review of Income and Wealth* 40:395–414.

Megoran, N., G. Raballand, and J. Bouyjou. 2005. Performance, representation, and the economics of border control in Uzbekistan. *Geopolitics* 10(4):712–40.

Melvin, N. 2004. Authoritarian pathways in Central Asia: a comparison of Kazakhstan, the Kyrgyz Republic and Uzbekistan. In *Democracy and Pluralism in Muslim Eurasia* (ed. Y. Ro'i), pp. 119–42. London: Frank Cass.

Meng, E., J. Longmire, and A. Moldashev. 2000. Kazakhstan's wheat system: priorities, constraints, and future prospects. *Food Policy* 25(6):701–17.

Mercer-Blackman, V., and A. Unigovskaya. 2000. Compliance with IMF program indicators and growth in transition economies. IMF Working Paper WP/00/47, International Monetary Fund, Washington, DC.

Michalopoulos, C. 2003. The integration of low income CIS members in the world trading system. Paper presented at *The Low Income Countries of the CIS: Progress and Challenges in Transition, Conference, Lucerne, Switzerland, January 20–22, 2003.* (Available at www.cis7.org.)

Milanovic, B. 1998. *Income, Inequality, and Poverty during the Transition from Planned to Market Economy*. Washington, DC: The World Bank.

Mogilevsky, R., and R. Hasanov. 2004. Economic growth in Kyrgyzstan. In *The Economic Prospects of the CIS—Sources of Long Term Growth since 1991* (ed. G. Ofer and R. Pomfret), pp. 224–48. Cheltenham, U.K.: Edward Elgar.

Mudahar, M. 1998. Kyrgyz Republic: strategy for rural growth and poverty alleviation. World Bank Discussion Paper No. 394, The World Bank, Washington, DC.

Nazarbayev, N. 1996. *Five Years of Independence*. Kazakhstan: Almaty.

Newell, A., and B. Reilly. 1996. The gender wage gap in Russia: some empirical evidence. *Labour Economics* 3(3):337–56.

———. 1999. Rates of return to educational qualifications in the transitional economies. *Education Economics* 7(1):67–84.

———. 2001. The gender pay gap in the transition from communism: some empirical evidence. *Economic Systems* 25(4):287–304.

Noorkiov, R., P. Orazem, A. Puur, and M. Vodopivec. 1997. How Estonia's economic transition affected employment and wages. Policy Research Working Paper 1837, Washington, DC, The World Bank.

Nursenkova, A. 2004. Kazakhstan has high hopes for agricultural reform. *Eurasianet Business and Economics*. (Available at www.eurasianet.org, posted January 29, 2004.)

Ochs, M. 1997. Turkmenistan: the quest for stability and control. In *Conflict, Cleavage, and Change in Central Asia and the Caucasus* (ed. K. Dawisha and B. Parrott), pp. 312–59. Cambridge University Press.

Ofer, G., and R. Pomfret (eds). 2004. *The Economic Prospects of the CIS—Sources of Long Term Growth since 1991*. Cheltenham, U.K.: Edward Elgar.

O'Hara, S., and T. Hannan. 1999. Irrigation and water management in Turkmenistan: past systems, present problems and future scenarios. *Europe–Asia Studies* 51(1):21–41.

Olcott, M. B. 1996a. *Central Asia's New States*. Washington, DC: United States Institute of Peace Press.

———. 1996b. Demographic upheavals in Central Asia. *Orbis* 40(4):537–55.

Olcott, M. B. 2002. *Kazakhstan: A Faint-Hearted Democracy*. Washington, DC: Carnegie Endowment for International Peace.

Orazem, P., and M. Vodopivec. 1995. Winners and losers in transition: returns to education, experience and gender in Slovenia. *World Bank Economic Review* 9(2):201–30.

Orenstein, M. 2000. How policies and institutions affect pension reform in three postcommunist countries. Policy Research Working Paper 2310, The World Bank, Washington, DC.

Paci, P. 2002. *Gender in Transition*. Washington, DC: The World Bank.

Papyrakis, E., and R. Gerlagh. 2004. The resource curse hypothesis and its transmission channels. *Journal of Comparative Economics* 32(1):181–93.

Pastor, G., and R. van Rooden. 2000. Turkmenistan—the burden of current agricultural policies. IMF Working Paper WP/00/98, International Monetary Fund, Washington, DC.

Pomfret, R. 1995. *The Economies of Central Asia*. Princeton University Press.

——. 1996. *Asian Economies in Transition*. Cheltenham, U.K.: Edward Elgar.

——. 1997a. *The Economics of Regional Trading Arrangements*. Oxford: Clarendon Press. (Paperback edition with new preface published by Oxford University Press in 2001.)

——. 1997b. *Development Economics*. London: Prentice Hall.

——. 1999a. Living standards in Central Asia. *MOCT-MOST Economic Policy in Transitional Economies* 9(4):395–421.

——. 1999b. *Central Asia Turns South? Trade Relations in Transition*. London/Washington, DC: The Royal Institute of International Affairs/The Brookings Institution.

——. 2000a. Transition and democracy in Mongolia. *Europe–Asia Studies* 52(1):149–60.

——. 2000b. Agrarian reform in Uzbekistan: why has the Chinese model failed to deliver? *Economic Development and Cultural Change* 48(2):269–84.

——. 2000c. The Uzbek model of economic development 1991–9. *Economics of Transition* 8(3):733–48.

——. 2001. Turkmenistan: from communism to nationalism by gradual economic reform. *MOCT-MOST Economic Policy in Transitional Economies* 11(2):155–66.

——. 2002a. State-directed diffusion of technology: the mechanization of cotton-harvesting in soviet Central Asia. *Journal of Economic History* 62(1):170–88.

——. 2002b. *Constructing a Market Economy: Diverse Paths from Central Planning in Asia and Europe*. Cheltenham, U.K.: Edward Elgar.

——. 2002c. The IMF and the ruble zone. *Comparative Economic Studies* 44(4):37–48.

——. 2003a. Trade and exchange rate policies in formerly centrally planned economies. *The World Economy* 26(4):585–612.

——. 2003b. Central Asia since 1991: the experience of the new independent states. OECD Development Centre Technical Paper 212, Organisation for Economic Co-operation and Development, Paris.

——. 2003c. Economic performance in Central Asia since 1991: macro and micro evidence. *Comparative Economic Studies* 45(4):442–65.

——. 2004. Structural reform in the CIS-7 countries. In *The Low-Income Countries of the Commonwealth of Independent States: Progress and Challenges in Transition* (ed. C. Shiells and S. Sattar), pp. 75–107. Washington, DC: International Monetary Fund.

——. 2005a. Development lessons for Central Asia. In *The Impact and Coherence of OECD Country Policies on Asian Developing Economies* (ed. K. Fukasaku, M. Kawai, M. G. Plummer, and A. Trzeciak-Duval). Paris: Organisation for Economic Co-operation and Development.

Pomfret, R. 2005b. Trade policies in Central Asia after EU enlargement and before Russian WTO accession: regionalism and integration into the world economy. *Economic Systems* 25(1):32–58.

———. 2005c. Resource abundance and long-run growth: when is oil a curse? The effects of oil discoveries on Kazakhstan's economy. Paper presented at *Canadian Network for Economic History Conference, Kingston, ON, April 15–17, 2005*.

———. 2005d. Sequencing trade and monetary integration: issues and application to Asia. *Journal of Asian Economics* 16(1):105–24.

———. 2005e. Uzbekistan: economic reform and economic performance, 1991–99. In *The Political Economy of Reform Failure* (ed. M. Lundahl), pp. 219–37. London: Routledge.

———. 2005f. Kazakhstan's economy since independence: does the oil boom offer a second chance for sustainable development? *Europe–Asia Studies* 57(6):859–76.

Pomfret, R., and K. Anderson. 1997. Uzbekistan: welfare impact of slow transition. United Nations University World Institute for Development Economics Research, Working Paper UNU/WIDER WP135, Helsinki.

———. 1999. Poverty in Kyrgyzstan. *Asia-Pacific Development Journal* 6(1):73–88.

———. 2001. Economic development strategies in Central Asia since 1991. *Asian Studies Review* 25(2):185–200.

Poulton, C., P. Gibbon, B. Hanyani-Mlambo, J. Kydd, W. Maro, M. N. Larsen, A. Osorio, D. Tschirley, and B. Zulu. 2004. Competition and coordination in liberalized African cotton market systems. *World Development* 32(3):519–36.

Raballand, G. 2003a. Determinants of the negative impact of being landlocked on trade: an empirical investigation through the Central Asian case. *Comparative Economic Studies* 45(4):520–36.

———. 2003b. L'intégration economique régionale en Asie Centrale: réussite ou chimère? Unpublished paper, ROSES—Maison des Sciences Économiques, Université Paris I (Panthéon-Sorbonne), France.

Raballand, G., and F. Esen. N.D. Transport of Caspian hydrocarbons: conciling economic and political considerations. Unpublished manuscript.

Rama, M., and K. Scott. 1999. Labor earnings in one-company towns: theory and evidence from Kazakhstan. *World Bank Economic Review* 11(1):185–209.

Ravallion, M. 2001. Measuring aggregate welfare in developing countries: how well do national accounts and surveys agree? World Bank Working Paper 2665, The World Bank, Washington, DC.

Redo, S. 2004. *Organized Crime and its Control in Central Asia*. Huntsville, TX: Office of International Criminal Justice.

Roberts, B. 1997. New evidence on household consumption, the shadow economy, and relative prices during transition to a market economy. Unpublished paper, University of Miami, Coral Gables, FL.

Rosenberg, C., and M. de Zeeuw. 2000. Welfare effects of Uzbekistan's foreign exchange regime. IMF Working Paper 00/61, International Monetary Fund, Washington, DC.

Roy, O. 2000. *The New Central Asia*. New York University Press.

Rumer, B., and S. Zhukov (eds). 1998. *Central Asia: The Challenges of Independence*. Armonk, NY: M. E. Sharpe.

Ruseckas, L. 1998. Energy and politics in Central Asia and the Caucasus. *Access Asia Review* 1(2):41–84.

Rutkowski, J. 1996. High skills pay off: the changing wage structure during economic transition in Poland. *Economics of Transition* 4(1):89–112.

Rutkowski, J. 2001. Earnings mobility during the transition: the case of Hungary, 1992–1997. *MOCT-MOST: Economic Policy in Transitional Economies* 11(1):69–89.

Rutland, P. 2003. Russia's response to U.S. regional influence. *NBR Analysis* 14(4):27–50.

Sabonis-Helf, T. 2005. Power, influence and stability: the united energy systems of Russia in the southern tier FSU. *Central Eurasian Studies Review* 4(1):24–29.

Sachs, J., and A. Warner. 1995. Natural resource abundance and economic growth. Harvard Institute of Economic Research Discussion Paper 517, Harvard University, Cambridge, MA.

Sagers, M. 1999. Turkmenistan's gas trade: the case of exports to Ukraine. *Post-Soviet Geography and Economics* 40(2):142–49.

Sakwa, R., and M. Webber. 1999. The Commonwealth of Independent States, 1991–1998: stagnation and survival. *Europe–Asia Studies* 51:379–415.

Sala-i-Martin, X., and A. Subramanian. 2003. Addressing the natural resource curse: an illustration from Nigeria. IMF Working Paper WP/03/139, International Monetary Fund, Washington, DC.

Schultz, T. W. 1975. The value of ability to deal with disequilibria. *Journal of Economic Literature* 13(3):827–46.

Sharma, K. 2004. Development challenges of a newly independent state: lessons from Tajikistan. Charles Sturt University Faculty of Commerce Working Paper No. 04/04, June.

Skagen, O. 1997. *Caspian Gas*. London/Washington, DC: The Royal Institute of International Affairs/The Brookings Institution.

Spechler, M. 1999. Uzbekistan: the silk road to nowhere? *Contemporary Economic Policy* 18(3):295–303.

———. 2000. Hunting the Central Asian tiger. *Comparative Economic Studies* 42(3):101–20.

———. 2003. Returning to convertibility in Uzbekistan? *The Journal of Policy Reform* 6(1):51–56.

Spechler, M., K. Bektemirov, S. Chepel', and F. Suvankulov. 2004. The Uzbek paradox: progress without neo-liberal reform. In *The Economic Prospects of the CIS—Sources of Long Term Growth since 1991* (ed. G. Ofer and R. Pomfret), pp. 177–97. Cheltenham, U.K.: Edward Elgar.

Suleimenov, M., and P. Oram. 2000. Trends in feed, livestock production, and rangelands during the transition period in three Central Asian countries. *Food Policy* 25(6):681–700.

Svejnar, J. 1999. Labor markets in the transitional Central and East European economies. In *Handbook of Labor Economics* (ed. O. Ashenfelter and D. Card), Volume 3, pp. 2,809–57. Amsterdam: Elsevier.

Swinnen, J. 2003. Eastern enlargement of the EU and its implications for agriculture and agricultural policies. *Food Economics* 1(1):5–11.

Tarr, D. 1994. How moving to world prices affects the terms of trade of 15 countries of the former Soviet Union. *Journal of Comparative Economics* 18(1):1–24.

Taube, G., and J. Zettelmeyer. 1998. Output decline and recovery in Uzbekistan: past performance and future prospects. IMF Working Paper WP/98/132, International Monetary Fund, Washington, DC.

Tornell, A., and P. Lane. 1999. The voracity effect. *American Economic Review* 89(1):22–46.

Theesfeld, I. 2004. Constraints on collective action in a transitional economy: the case of Bulgaria's irrigation sector. *World Development* 32(2):251–71.

Trend. 2003. *Impact of Membership of Azerbaijan into World Trade Organisation on the Lives of Poor People: Final Report*. Analytical-Information Agency "Trend" with support from Oxfam, Baku.

Trevisani, T. 2004. From Kolkhoz to Shirkat, from Shirkat to private farms: a view from Khorezm on Uzbekistan's ongoing land reform. Paper presented at *Symposium on Post-Soviet Transition in Central Asia, Sponsored by the Associazione per lo Studio in Italia dell'Asia centrale e del Caucaso, Cortona, Italy, April 23–24, 2004*. Unpublished.

Tumbarello, P. 2005. Regional integration and WTO accession: which is the right sequencing? An application to the CIS. IMF Working Paper, International Monetary Fund, Washington, DC (February).

Umarov, K., and A. Repkine. 2004. Tajikistan's growth performance: the first decade of transition. In *The Economic Prospects of the CIS—Sources of Long Term Growth since 1991* (ed. G. Ofer and R. Pomfret), pp. 198–223. Cheltenham, U.K.: Edward Elgar.

UNDP. 2005. *Central Asia Human Development Report: Bringing Down barriers: Regional Cooperation for Human Development and Human Security*. Bratislava: United Nations Development Programme.

Vecernik, J. 1995. Changing earnings distributions in the Czech Republic: survey evidence from 1988–1994. *Economics of Transition* 3(3):333–53.

Verme, P. 2001. *Transition, Recession and Labour Supply*. Aldershot, U.K.: Ashgate.

Webber, M. 1997. *CIS Integration Trends: Russia and the Former Soviet South*. London/Washington, DC: The Royal Institute of International Affairs/The Brookings Institution.

Weber, G. 2003. Russia's and Kazakhstan's agro-food sectors under liberalized agricultural trade: a case for national product differentiation. *Economic Systems* 27:391–413.

Wegren, S. K. (ed.). 1998. *Land Reform in the Former Soviet Union and Eastern Europe*. London: Routledge.

Weinthal, E. 2002. *State Making and Environmental Cooperation: Linking Domestic and International Politics in Central Asia*. Cambridge, MA: MIT Press.

Wen, M., and S. King. 2004. Push or pull? The relationship between development, trade and primary resource endowment. *Journal of Economic Behavior and Organization* 53:569–91.

Werner, M. 2001. Im Reich des grossen Führers: Turkmenistan—eine zentralasiatische Despotie. *Osteuropa* 51(2):127–34.

Whitlock, M. 2002. *Beyond the Oxus: The Central Asians*. London: John Murray.

Wiemer, C. 2000. PRC Trade with Central Asia. In *Regional Economic Cooperation in Central Asia* (TA No. 58181-REG). Manila: Asian Development Bank.

World Bank. 1992. Measuring the incomes of economies of the former Soviet Union. Policy Research Working Paper WPS 1057, The World Bank, Washington, DC.

———. 2000. Republic of Tajikistan: poverty assessment. World Bank Report No. 20285-TJ, The World Bank, Washington, DC.

———. 2002. *Irrigation in Central Asia: Where to Rehabilitate and Why*. Washington, DC: The World Bank.

———. 2004. Kyrgyz Republic: pubic expenditure review. World Bank Report No. 28123-KG, The World Bank, Washington, DC.

Wu, H.-L., and C.-H. Chen. 2004. The prospects for regional economic cooperation between China and the five Central Asian countries. *Europe–Asia Studies* 36(7):1,059–80.

Yudaeva, K. 2003. Impact of WTO accession on the Russian economy: a review of current findings. *Transition* 14(4–6):18–19.

Zettelmeyer, J. 1998. The Uzbek growth puzzle. IMF Working Paper WP/98/133, International Monetary Fund, Washington, DC.

Zhalimbetova, R., and G. Gleason. 2001. Bridges and fences: the Eurasian economic community and policy harmonization in Eurasia. Unpublished paper, University of New Mexico. (A shorter version, "Eurasian economic community comes into being," from June 20, 2001, is available at www.cacianalyst.org.)

Index